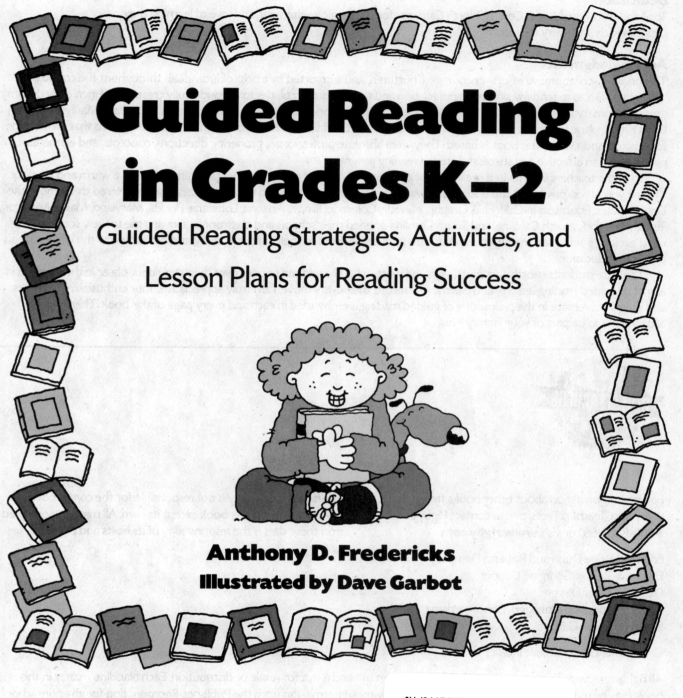

Guided Reading
in Grades K–2

Guided Reading Strategies, Activities, and
Lesson Plans for Reading Success

Anthony D. Fredericks
Illustrated by Dave Garbot

Rigby Best Teachers Press

An imprint of Rigby

Dedication

To all the teachers of Burke County, North Carolina—for the magic, excitement, and love of learning they create in each and every classroom!

Acknowledgments

This book is a collaborative effort—encouraged, nurtured, and supported by a host of individuals throughout the country.

I would like to extend my sincerest appreciation and thunderous accolades to a wonderfully creative and incredibly dynamic group of primary teachers at Valley View Elementary School in York, Pennsylvania. Lonna Ashton, Amy Hare, Marilyn Henning, Dana Kitting, Jane Piepmeier, and principal Tawn Ketterman provided a plethora of insights and contributions that formed the foundation upon which this book is based. They were absolute professionals, proffering directions, concepts, and elements necessary to an effective and successful guided reading program.

To all the teachers who invited me into their classrooms and their guided reading programs, I extend a warm and gracious "Thank you." I was privileged and honored to watch the excitement of guided reading in classrooms scattered throughout the United States. Educators in California, Oregon, Nevada, Colorado, Illinois, Arizona, Louisiana, Florida, Maryland, Maine, Michigan, Texas, New York, North Carolina, and South Carolina opened their schools and classrooms, allowing me to view some of the most exciting guided reading programs ever. I am forever indebted to their spirit, creativity, and dedication to the highest ideals of literacy education!

To all the students—north and south, east and west—who allowed me to peer over their shoulders, observe their actions in a host of guided reading lessons, and (seemingly) record their every move, I am truly appreciative. Your enthusiasm for books and your involvement in the philosophy of guided reading is embedded in each and every page of this book. Thank you for allowing me to be part of your literary lives.

For more information about other books from Rigby Best Teachers Press, please contact Rigby at 1-800-822-8661 or visit **www.rigby.com**

Editor's note: Rigby is not responsible for the content of any website listed in this book except its own. All material contained on these sites is the responsibility of its hosts and creators.

Editors: Justine Dunn and Roberta Dempsey
Executive Editor: Georgine Cooper
Designer: Biner Design
Design Production Manager: Tom Sjoerdsma
Illustrator: Dave Garbot

© 2003 Harcourt Achieve Inc.

4 5 6 7 8 9 10 11 085 12 11 10 09 08 07 06

Printed in the United States of America.

ISBN 0-7398-8060-8
Guided Reading in Grades K–2

Rigby is a trademark of Harcourt Achieve Inc.

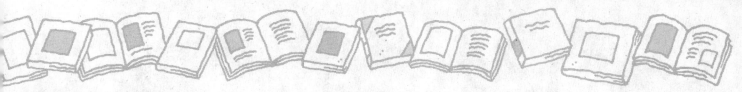

Preface

My teaching philosophy has been driven by the idea that teachers should act as facilitators of the learning process, rather than as rewarders. I believe the chief role of a competent teacher is to guide students to their own discoveries, providing them with the tools they need and the necessary instruction to use those tools, and then giving them the chance to investigate the joys and excitement of learning.

Nowhere is this truer than in the reading program. It is here that children begin to discover all the magic of language—the ways in which sounds become words, the ways in which they become personally involved in the plot and theme of a book, and the ways in which reading becomes a lifelong activity.

Guided Reading in Grades K–2 has been designed as an easy-to-use resource guide for the busy classroom teacher. The focus of this book is on developing invitational classrooms, those in which teachers invite students to become active participants in the reading process. The reading strategies, literacy centers, pre-reading ideas, assessment tools, lesson plans, leveled books, and activities included within these pages have all been implemented in a variety of primary classrooms. They have been embraced by teachers and administrators, and shared with students with remarkable success.

I sincerely hope that you and your students will discover the fun and excitement of guided reading within the pages of this book. May your classroom be filled with happiness, laughter, stories, and, most important, the love of learning!

Tony Fredericks

Contents

Introduction 6
A Comprehensive Literacy Program 6
   Reading Aloud to Children 7
   Shared Book Experience 7
   Guided Reading 7
   Individualized Reading 7
   Paired Reading 7
   Sustained Silent Reading 8
   Language Exploration 8
   Reading and Writing 8
Guided Reading in a Comprehensive
   Literacy Program 10
How to Use This Book 11

1 Guided Reading: A Closer Look 13
Looking at Guided Reading 13
When to Start Guided Reading 16

2 Pre-reading Development 17
Pre-reading Competencies 17
   Alphabetic Knowledge 17
   Concepts of Print 17
   Phonemic Awareness 18
Pre-reading Assessment 20
   Letter Identification 20
   Concepts of Print 24
   Phonemic Awareness
   Assessment 26
Pre-reading Activities 32

3 Guided Reading Lessons 45
Lesson Planning 45
Designing and Teaching a
   Guided Reading Lesson 50
A Sample Guided Reading Lesson 52

4 Literacy Stages 56
Reader Characteristics 56
Lesson Plans for Each Stage 60
Quick Reference Charts 65

5 Assessment: Running Records 70
Assessment Overview 70
Administering Running Records 71
Running Record Notations 74
   Substitution 76
   Omission 76
   Insertion 76
   Attempt 76
   Self-correction 76
   Repetition 77
   Skip and Return 77
   Asks for Help 77
   Told the Word 77
   Try Again 77
   Teacher Prompt 78
Scoring Running Records 79

6 Matching Books and Readers 82
Book Leveling Systems 82
Basal Readers and Guided Reading 84
Leveled Books 85
   Emergent Readers 85
   Early Readers 96
   Transitional Readers 116
   Fluent Readers 134

7 Dynamic Grouping 167
Grouping in Guided Reading 167
   Whole-class Guided Reading 167
   Small-group Guided Reading 168
Individualized Guided Reading 169
Alternate Grouping Strategies 170
Grouping Considerations 171

8 Strategies for Success — 173

Traditional vs. Transactional Teaching — 173
Strategies in Place — 175
Instructional Strategies — 179
   Universal Strategies — 179
   Specific Strategies — 182
More Strategies — 183
   Semantic Webbing — 183
   Student Motivated Active
    Reading Technique
    (S.M.A.R.T.) — 185
   Concept Cards — 185
   Mental Imagery — 186
   K-W-L — 189
   Possible Sentences — 189
   Directed Reading-Thinking
    Activity (DRTA) — 191
   MM & M (Metacognitive
    Modeling and Monitoring) — 192
   Answer First! — 193
   Cloze Technique — 195
   Story Map — 196
   What If — 196
   Story Frames — 197
Questions and Prompts — 202
   Questions — 202
    Process Questions — 203
    Prior Knowledge and
    Purpose-Setting Questions — 203
    Open-ended Questions — 204
    Metacognitive Questions — 205
   Prompts — 206
Strategy Planning Guides — 207

9 Literacy Centers — 212

The Importance of Literacy Centers
  to Guided Reading — 212
Suggested Literacy Centers — 216
   Listening Center — 216
   ABC/Spelling Center — 217

   Art Center — 218
   Writing Center — 219
   Reading Around the
    Room Center — 220
   Readers Theatre Center — 221
   Pocket Chart Center — 224
   Free Reading Center — 225
   Drama/Storytelling Center — 226
   Buddy Reading Center — 228
   Poetry Center — 229
   Big Book Center — 230
Literacy Centers and Multiple
  Intelligences — 232
Literacy Center Planning Materials — 234

10 Organizing and Managing Your Classroom — 240

Key Factors for Success — 240
The Basics of Classroom Layout — 241
Plans and Schedules for
  Guided Reading — 246
   Plans — 247
   Schedules — 249
Helpful Planning Forms — 252

11 Parent Involvement Activities — 256

The Importance of Parent Participation — 256
Letters — 257
Activity Calendars — 275

Appendix — 280

100 Must-Have Books for
  Guided Reading — 280
Concepts of Print Checklist — 283
Websites — 284
Additional Resources — 285
References — 286

About the Author — 288

Introduction

A Comprehensive Literacy Program

Stef Whittlesey's first-grade classroom was buzzing with activity. Some children were checking out books, others were sharing information and resources with one another. Some students were reading independently, while others were forming groups to pursue a particular task. A group of five students was working with Stef in a guided reading session. Stef's classroom was an assembly of reading activities that supported and stimulated literacy development in a variety of ways.

Stef's classroom was indeed an oasis of learning, language, and literature. An assortment of books lined every shelf of the room. A plethora of charts, diagrams, and graphic organizers hung from the ceiling and in every corner of the classroom. Words could be seen across the walls, cabinets, and storage bins that lined the back of the room.

> *...Students' future success in reading is dependent on their ability to become actively engaged in the process of reading...*

Stef has been a first-grade teacher for the last six years. Her classroom reveals a world that stimulates, encourages, and promotes reading through a diverse assembly of well-planned and well-articulated lessons. Stef has created a classroom that not only integrates reading into every subject area, but also celebrates the value of reading as a purposeful lifelong activity.

Stef knows that her students need solid instruction and dynamic strategies to become independent readers. She also knows that her students' future success in reading is dependent on their ability to become actively engaged in the processes of reading which moves them from teacher-directed instruction to student independence.

There is a growing legion of classroom teachers and university researchers who recognize the significance and importance of a comprehensive literacy program (Freppon & Dahl, 1998; Strickland, 1995; Weaver, 1998). A comprehensive literacy program is one in which the following elements are integrated into a well-coordinated literacy effort for all students:

1. Reading aloud to children
2. Shared book experience
3. Guided reading
4. Individualized reading
5. Paired reading
6. Sustained silent reading
7. Language exploration
8. Reading and writing

Reading Aloud to Children

At the heart of any classroom reading program are the daily opportunities for teachers to read aloud to their students. Reading aloud introduces children to quality literature in a pleasing and comfortable format. Reading aloud also models for students the strategies mature readers (teachers) use as well as the pleasure obtained from a variety of genres.

Shared Book Experience

The shared book experience involves the teacher and the entire class. It is a cooperative learning activity in which the teacher reads a favorite book and the students reread it independently. It offers students numerous opportunities to view reading as both a pleasurable and meaningful experience. Students have a variety of ways to respond to stories, including drama, arts and crafts, writing, puppetry, and so on.

Guided Reading

Guided reading involves a teacher and a small group of students who read a book together for a specific purpose. The selected book is geared for the approximate instructional level of the students and they are challenged to think about the reading material through specific reading strategies. The ultimate goal is to help students become independent readers.

Individualized Reading

Individualized reading emanates from guided reading. Each student is matched with an appropriate book and is invited to work at his or her own pace on material suited to individual needs. Careful monitoring of individual progress is essential to the success of this component of the overall reading program.

Paired Reading

Paired reading allows children the opportunity to work with a partner or buddy. Each pair of students can read the same book together and share appropriate reading strategies and/or interpretations. The individuals within a pair may be at the same instructional level or at different levels. This is a cooperative activity that encourages a free flow of ideas in a nonthreatening environment.

Sustained Silent Reading

Sustained silent reading is the time of day when everyone—including the teacher—simply reads for an extended period of time. Materials are selected by each individual according to personal interests or needs. The advantages are that the teacher can model appropriate reading behaviors and students have sufficient opportunities to utilize their developing reading abilities in meaningful self-selected texts.

Language Exploration

Language exploration encourages children to become involved in a wide range of literacy extensions related to a book. These extensions may include discussions, writing, art, music, drama, cross-curricular, and other hands-on, minds-on activities that promote and elaborate the ideas in text. Integration of the language arts (reading, writing, speaking, and listening) is encouraged and stimulated.

Reading and Writing

Reading and writing are natural partners. As children listen and respond to a wide variety of literature, they are provided with models of efficient writing. These models serve as springboards for the writing that students can do in the classroom as a logical and natural extension of book-related activities. There is convincing evidence that students who read and listen to a wide variety of high-quality children's literature are able to write stories rich in language and are able to use a variety of linguistic structures (Fredericks, et al., 1997).

A Comprehensive Literacy Program, Grades K–2

Component	Value to Students
Reading Aloud	• Exposes children to a wide range of literature • Assists children in matching oral and written language • Helps develop knowledge of text structure • Develops a sense of story • Models enjoyment of reading • Demonstrates fluent reading • Enhances vocabulary development (oral and written)
Shared Book Experience	• Provides opportunities for active participation in the reading process • Offers a social context and support structure for reading • Helps students learn about story structure • Develops and enhances students' predictive abilities • Helps students establish purposes for reading
Guided Reading	• Students can read from a variety of texts and a variety of genres • Students engage in strategic reading practices • Enhances the development of metacognitive abilities • Promotes predictive abilities • Provides a match between reading ability and text difficulty • Provides a structure for developing and increasing reading proficiency
Individualized Reading	• Encourages students to use reading strategies independently • Provides time to utilize developing reading abilities in productive work • Enhances fluency • Promotes and enhances confidence, attitudes, and self-concept
Paired Reading	• Assists in the development of communication skills • Promotes self-confidence and assurance • Stimulates the development of reading as a social activity • Provides an intermediary step leading toward the development of independent reading skills • Teaches students how to predict, evaluate, and confirm
Sustained Silent Reading	• Provides students with a realistic opportunity to utilize reading strategies independently • Gives students sustained opportunities to read for interest and pleasure • Helps students engage in self-selection activities that build confidence and assurance • Allows students to "try" newly learned reading strategies in a variety of genres
Language Exploration	• Helps students understand the universality of reading across all subject areas • Gives students an opportunity to develop an understanding of reading as a creative and expressive means of learning • Integrates the curriculum • Portrays reading as an active process of learning
Reading and Writing	• Enhances reading strategies through purposeful writing activities • Gives children an opportunity to appreciate the concept of integrated language arts • Strengthens and enhances fluency • Taps, expands, and recognizes students' background knowledge • Stimulates vocabulary growth and development

Guided Reading in a Comprehensive Literacy Program

Acomprehensive literacy program is one in which students are provided with direct instruction, a support structure, and opportunities to utilize reading strategies in meaningful text. They are encouraged, supported, and sustained in many literacy activities. Margaret Mooney (1990) defines this process as reading *to*, reading *with*, and reading *by* students.

Reading To: Children are provided with regular opportunities to listen to a reading expert (the teacher) read from a variety of texts and books. Typically referred to as "read-aloud" time, this is the time when children hear language in use by practiced and accomplished models.

Reading With: Children are gathered into small, homogeneous groups for direct reading instruction. This is the time when reading strategies are introduced to children as well as opportunities to apply those strategies in appropriate reading materials. This is typically when guided reading takes place.

Reading By: Children have opportunities to utilize their reading strategies in independent activities. Students can select their own reading materials, work at literacy centers, and engage in activities such as Drop Everything and Read (D.E.A.R.) or Sustained Silent Reading (S.S.R.).

The following chart illustrates these components of a balanced reading program:

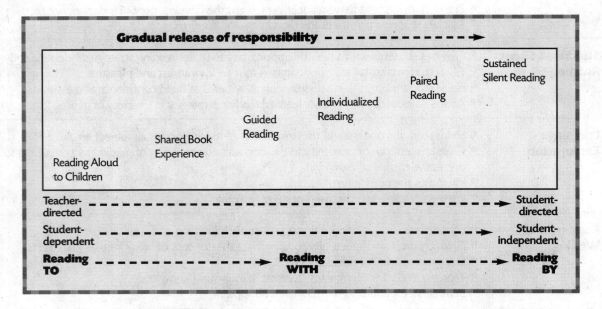

Gradual release of responsibility - - - - - - - - - - - →

Reading Aloud to Children — Shared Book Experience — Guided Reading — Individualized Reading — Paired Reading — Sustained Silent Reading

Teacher-directed - - - - - - - - - - - → Student-directed

Student-dependent - - - - - - - - - - - → Student-independent

Reading TO - - - - - - - → **Reading WITH** - - - - - - - → **Reading BY**

How to Use This Book

The success of your guided reading program will revolve around regular, systematic, and sustained strategies naturally incorporated into a balanced reading program. As mentioned earlier, guided reading instruction should be one element in your overall literacy program. The strategies, activities, and lesson plans in this book are designed to offer you endless possibilities and opportunities for engaging students in the dynamics of reading. Here are some ideas to consider:

• Guided reading should be a regular and daily occurrence. Plan sufficient time each day for students (in small groups) to participate in selected guided reading activities.

• Guided reading is one element in the overall reading program. Plan sufficient time for the other components, too—shared reading, reading aloud, individualized reading, paired reading, and sustained silent reading.

• Administer running records throughout your guided reading program. This will provide you with data that is valuable in establishing guided reading groups as well as information on the progress of individual students throughout the year.

Assessment is fully integrated throughout the entire guided reading program.

• Be aware of students' changing instructional needs throughout the year. Provide strategies appropriate to each individual's level of development.

• Remember that groupings are flexible. As students learn new strategies and work with increasingly more difficult texts, the groups are adjusted accordingly. Students may move through any number of *ad hoc* groups throughout the year. The emphasis is not on the permanency of the groups, but the instructional practices that will allow students to move forward in their reading growth and development.

> **G**uided Reading can be used with all types of literature and within all types of reading programs.

• Guided reading can be used with all types of literature and within all types of reading programs. One of its greatest advantages is that it is easily adaptable to any type of reading curriculum or school/district philosophy.

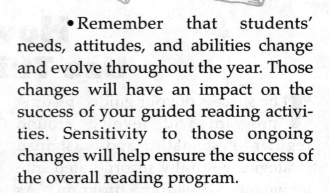

• Feel free to experiment with the guided reading strategies in this book. There is no single strategy that should be used with any single book. Any piece of literature can be coupled with one or more strategies to enhance the teaching of reading.

• Keep in mind that the ideas throughout this book can be viewed as generic in nature. They have been designed as applicable to a wide range of literature and a wide range of teaching/learning situations.

• Remember that students' needs, attitudes, and abilities change and evolve throughout the year. Those changes will have an impact on the success of your guided reading activities. Sensitivity to those ongoing changes will help ensure the success of the overall reading program.

• The key to success with guided reading is flexibility—flexibility in designing your lessons, selecting appropriate literature, grouping students, choosing reading strategies, and in integrating guided reading into your overall instructional plans.

All of the activities, strategies, and lesson plans in this book have been classroom-tested and kid-approved. All are designed to offer you and your students some wonderful adventures and exciting discoveries. Make these ideas a regular part of your overall reading program, modify them according to the specific needs of students in your classroom, and add to them using ideas and suggestions that naturally occur in any dynamic reading curriculum.

Guided Reading: A Closer Look

Looking at Guided Reading

Guided reading is the heart and soul of the reading program! It is the time to teach students the strategies used by accomplished readers and to involve students in the dynamics of quality literature. It is a time for opening up new worlds of literary discovery, investigation, and exploration.

Fountas and Pinnell (1996) define guided reading as "a context in which a teacher supports each reader's development of effective strategies for processing novel texts at increasingly challenging levels of difficulty." They further clarify guided reading as follows:

- It gives children the opportunity to develop as individual readers while participating in a socially supported activity.

- It gives teachers the opportunity to observe individuals as they process new texts.

- It gives individual readers the opportunity to develop reading strategies so that they can read increasingly difficult texts independently.

- It gives children enjoyable, successful experiences in reading for meaning.

- It develops the abilities needed for independent reading.

- It helps children learn how to introduce texts to themselves.

The implication of this definition is that teachers guide students (via appropriate reading strategies) through increasingly more difficult reading material in order to achieve higher levels of comprehension and greater independence in reading. One of the major differences between guided reading and more traditional forms of reading instruction is that guided reading is conducted within small, flexible, and ever-changing groups. Traditional reading instruction is a whole-class

> *Fountas and Pinnell (1996) define guided reading as "a context in which a teacher supports each reader's development of effective strategies for processing novel texts at increasingly challenging levels of difficulty."*

activity directed by the teacher, or is performed within semipermanent groups determined by scores on a standardized reading test.

Schulman and Payne (2000) define guided reading as "a structured, practical way of matching reading instruction to the diverse individual readers in the classroom. "Their definition supports that of Fountas and Pinnell and adds the following elements:

> *Schulman and Payne (2000) define guided reading as "a structured, practical way of matching reading instruction to the diverse individual readers in the classroom."*

• Respects the belief that every child is capable of learning to read.

• Recognizes that children learn to read at varying rates of development.

• Provides opportunities to tailor direct instruction to each child's specific reading needs.

• Provides a format in which the teacher guides students to think about the reading process.

• Provides a format in which the teacher guides students to think about various reading strategies they need to use to make sense of the text.

• Offers a context in which instruction is guided by careful assessment and observation of each student's reading.

The key to Schulman and Payne's definition is that guided reading provides a logical and natural support structure that enhances success and helps children along the road to independent reading. Students are provided with multiple opportunities to become active problem-solvers through the guidance and modeling of the teacher.

Regie Routman (1991) says that guided reading is the time when "we meet with students to think critically about a book." Guided reading is a collaborative effort between a teacher and a small group of students in which strategies are taught and ideas are discussed in a mutually supportive atmosphere. The term *guided* is critical, since teachers are responsible for *guiding* students to higher levels of comprehension and appreciation as opposed to *directing* students as is customary in more traditional models of reading instruction.

The success of guided reading is predicated on the following concepts:

• Groups are small and flexible.

Typically, a guided reading group will consist of 4–6 students and the teacher. Group members form a circle of desks or may sit on the floor in a circular pattern in order to facilitate interaction and discussion.

• Members of a group have similar reading abilities.

Members of a guided reading group share a similar level of reading competence. This level has been determined by informal reading tests (see "Assessment: Running Records" on page 70).

• Groups are dynamic.

Groups are formed for indefinite periods of time. A group may convene for a few days or several weeks. A group may collectively read one book, or a selection of books, all at the same level.

• Each student within a group has an individual copy of a book.

Multiple copies of each book are necessary. Class sets of selected literature ensure that each member of a group has his or her own copy to read.

• Reading strategies are taught in context.

Students are provided with opportunities to engage in meaningful interactions with text via selected reading strategies that have universal application in a host of reading materials.

• Evaluation is continuous.

Through the use of observations, one-on-one interviews, and running records, teachers will know whether students are using effective reading strategies in a variety of materials. End-of-the-year standardized testing is of less importance than continual informal evaluation with individual students.

• Cooperation is emphasized; competition is de-emphasized.

Students work collaboratively to support each other in a variety of interactive tasks and activities.

The following chart briefly outlines what happens during a guided reading session.

The Teacher:	• Works with a small group of students
	• Briefly introduces a new text to the group
	• Activates background knowledge
	• Encourages predictions
	• Presents an appropriate reading strategy or reinforces a previously shared strategy
	• Interacts with individual students
	• Monitors students' progress
	• Discusses the text with students after reading
	• Provides application opportunities
The Students:	• Listen as the teacher introduces a new text
	• Link background knowledge with textual knowledge
	• Utilize appropriate reading strategies
	• Employ a reading strategy with the text
	• Discuss the text, after reading, with the teacher and other students in the group
	• Read related reading materials during or after school
	• Participate in on-the-spot learning activities

When to Start Guided Reading

For guided reading to be effective, it must be predicated on several factors that will ensure its success, especially for primary-level students. The following concepts must be in place before guided reading can begin. Students must:

- Have an initial understanding of the alphabet

- Know that reading makes sense

- Have a reading vocabulary of a few high-frequency words

- Understand the left-to-right progression of reading

- Be able to match (point to) the written equivalent of spoken words

- Be able to write a few words

- Be able to match some words that appear in different contexts

- Be able to obtain some information from illustrations

- Have an initial understanding of letter/sound relationships

The next unit will provide you with important pre-reading skills that form the foundation for a strong guided reading program.

Pre-reading Development

Pre-reading Competencies

Students need a solid background and a strong understanding of pre-reading skills before they can read and comprehend written language. Students' future success in a guided reading program is dependent on their ability to master essential pre-reading skills. The strategies that form the foundation of a guided reading program are dependent upon students' abilities and skills in three pre-reading areas: alphabetic knowledge, concepts of print, and phonemic awareness.

Alphabetic Knowledge

Alphabetic knowledge is an awareness that words are constructed from units known as letters. It is important for children to know that there is consistency in the symbols we use to read and write words. There are twenty-six letters we can use to create larger units known as words. Eventually, children begin to understand that word units can be combined into other sequences and patterns known as sentences.

Children must be able to recognize the shape of individual letters (e.g., the shape of a *p*), the differences between letter shapes (a *p* looks considerably different than an *m*), and even some of the similarities between selected letters (a *p* can be confused with a *q*). This type of visual information is important as a precursor to phonemic awareness development as well as future phonics instruction.

Concepts of Print

Concepts of print refers to how a book "works." Children must have knowledge of the organizational structure of a book, its components, and the way in which it is designed. Young readers need to understand the separate parts of a book (front, middle, and back), the progression of a story in the book (from front to back), directionality cues (top to bottom, left to right), the arrangement of letters into words, and the meaning of punctuation and other details about printed materials.

This skill provides children with an awareness of how every piece of written material operates. For teachers, it is a way of knowing what children know about reading before they can actually read. Much of children's concepts about print comes from home experience (e.g., parents who have read to their children on a regular basis). Children who have adequate concepts about print are ready to move into the preliminary stages of guided reading.

Phonemic Awareness

The ability to hear and manipulate sounds is referred to as *phonemic awareness*. Children need to hear the sounds of language and understand the relationship that phonemes play in word formation. Hearing the sounds of words is completely independent of knowing the meaning of those words. It is also important for children to identify the sequence of sounds within a word. Phonemic awareness instruction provides children with opportunities to experience spoken language before they start to learn written language.

By combining sounds, subtracting sounds, and rearranging sounds, we can create elements known as words. It is these words that help us communicate. For young children, the path to communication begins with the ability to hear the sounds in words, the various positions of those sounds within words, and an understanding of the role of those sounds within a word. Phonemic awareness comprises oral language skills that precede a child's transition into written language. These are illustrated in the chart on the next page.

Pre-reading Competencies

Alphabetic Knowledge	Concepts of Print	Phonemic Awareness
• There are twenty-six letters in the alphabet.	• Books have a front and a back.	• There are word patterns that are similar (rhyming) and there are similar sounds at the beginning of words (alliteration).
• Alphabetic letters are arranged in a specific sequence (A, B, C, D . . .).	• Reading begins at the front of a book.	
• Each letter has a name.	• Letters in words are read from left to right.	• Words can be divided into more than one sound and the sounds in a word occur in a particular sequence (beginning sound + ending sound).
• Letters can be uppercase.	• Words can be long or short.	
• Letters can be lowercase.	• Words on a page are read from left to right.	
• A letter may have one or more sounds.	• Words on a page are read from top to bottom.	• Each sound within a word has a specific and logical position within that word (beginning, middle, and end).
• A group of letters makes a word.	• There are spaces between individual words on a page.	• Sounds in a word (phonemes) can be separated.
• The sounds of letters can be heard in words.	• Words appear in groups or clusters known as sentences.	• The sounds in a word can be manipulated, rearranged, resequenced, and reconfigured.

Pre-reading Assessment

Determining students' pre-reading skills should be an integral part of the overall assessment program (see Unit 5). Knowledge of individual student abilities will assist you in the development of a well-rounded instructional program that is both responsive to the needs of students and attentive to their ongoing reading growth and development.

The following assessment tools provide you with important data on each student's pre-reading skill development. Kindergarten and first-grade teachers are encouraged to use these tools throughout the year as an integral part of their overall assessment program. Second-grade teachers may find these tools appropriate, particularly for those students who are encountering challenges or demonstrating other reading deficiencies in the guided reading program.

Letter Identification

The instrument on page 23 can be used to determine each child's awareness of and knowledge about the letters of the alphabet. It can be administered in an individual setting and should not take more than five minutes to complete. It is appropriate for use with kindergarten and first-grade students as well as students in second grade who may indicate some difficulties in beginning reading abilities.

I. Administer the assessment in a quiet location in the classroom.

2. Provide the child with the alphabet chart. Point to each capital letter and ask the child to tell you the name of the letter ("Here is a letter. Can you tell me the name of this letter?").

3. If the child has difficulty, consider using the following sequence of queries:

   a. "Can you tell me the name of this letter?"

   b. "What sound does it make?"

   c. "Can you tell me a word that begins with this letter (or sound)?"

4. Record each correct response on the Alphabet Record Sheet (page 22).

5. Next, invite the child to point to each small letter and to tell you the name of that letter (suggested prompt, "Here is a letter that is sometimes used in a word. Can you tell me the name of the letter?")

6. If the child has difficulty, consider using the following sequence of queries:

   a. "Can you tell me the name of this letter?"

   b. "What sound does it make?"

   c. "Can you tell me a word that begins with this letter (or sound)?"

7. Record observational notes in the appropriate column (especially for those letters/sounds/words that are challenging for the student). Also make notes on any incorrect responses. This can help to identify reversals.

8. Add up the total number of correct responses (both upper and lowercase) and record the results in the appropriate boxes.

Alphabet Record Sheet

Name: _____

Date: _____

✓ = correct response   ✗ = incorrect response   **Total Score:** _____ /52

	letter	sound	word		letter	sound	word	comments
K				k				
E				e				
H				h				
G				g				
L				l				
C				c				
V				v				
O				o				
F				f				
M				m				
D				d				
A				a				
W				w				
P				p				
Q				q				
J				j				
I				i				
S				s				
U				u				
T				t				
Z				z				
B				b				
Y				y				
R				r				
X				x				
N				n				

Total Correct: _____   **Total Correct:** _____

Alphabet Chart

K	E	H	G	L	C	V
O	F	M	D	A	W	P
Q	J	I	S	U	T	Z
B	Y	R	X	N		

k	e	h	g	l	c	v
o	f	m	d	a	w	p
q	j	i	s	u	t	z
b	y	r	x	n		

Concepts of Print

The assessment instrument on the following page can be used to help you determine a child's familiarity with the concepts of print. This tool will be especially useful for children in the emergent stage of reading development. It will help you gauge their knowledge of reading before they actually begin reading. Just as important, it is a useful device that provides important information about students' readiness for guided reading instruction. To use the instrument, follow these directions:

1. This assessment is to be administered individually to each child. It will take approximately seven to ten minutes.

2. Obtain a book (from the earliest or beginning levels) and place it on the table in front of the child. Tell the child that you will be asking him or her to do some things with that book while you take notes.

3. Follow the oral directions on the accompanying record sheet for each of the individual concepts. If the child responds correctly, mark that in the appropriate space. If the child responds incorrectly, record a brief note in the comment section.

4. It may not be necessary to assess every child in the class. Some students may have sufficient knowledge about book concepts that will preclude them from taking this test.

5. You may discover that a child has a sufficient background of concepts that do not require administering the entire test. You may need to end the test early for those students who demonstrate requisite competencies. By the same token, you may discover one or more children who cannot complete the test because of several deficiencies. Be sure to indicate these observations in the comment section of the form.

Notes:

• This test does not require any reading skills and can be used with any book. It is designed to assess a student's concepts of print, *not* his or her ability to read the print. These concepts need to be in place before reading or reading instruction can begin.

• The sequence of concepts outlined in the record sheet is a suggested progression for the assessment process. If a child does not understand a specific direction or is having unusual difficulty with the concept, you may wish to return to one or more of the concepts for re-testing at the conclusion of the test. The emphasis should be on determining a student's competencies with regard to concepts of print, rather than to assess all of his or her deficiencies.

Concepts of Print Record Sheet

Name: _____   **Date:** _____

Teacher: _____

Book Title: _____

Guided Reading Level: _____

Reading Recovery® Level: _____   **Total Score:** _____ /21

Concept	Directions	Correct	Comment(s)
1. Front of book	(Place book upside down and backwards.) "Please point to the front of the book."		
2. Back of book	"Please point to the back of the book."		
3. Top of book	"Please point to the top of the book."		
4. Bottom of book	"Please point to the bottom of the book."		
5. Title	"Please show me the title of the book."		
6. Author	"Please show me who wrote the book."		
7. Where to Begin Reading	"Please show me where you would start reading this book."		
8. Page	(Point to an isolated page.) "What is this called?"		
9. Letter Recognition	(Point to three or four individual letters.) "What are these called?"		
10. Word Recognition	(Point to three or four isolated words.) "What are these?"		
11. Direction	"Please show me which way (direction [left–right]) people read a book."		
12. Sweep	"Please show me what happens when people get to the end of this line."		
13. Illustration/Picture	(Point to an illustration.) "Please tell me what this is."		
14. Left page first (before right)	"Point to the first page in this book."		
15. Word Order	"Point to the first word you would read on this page."		
16. Word Order	"Point to the next word on this page."		
17. Word Order	"Point to the last word on this page."		
18. Capitalization	(Point to capital letter.) "Why is this different from this?" (Point to small letter.)		
19. Punctuation	(Point to a period.) "What is this?"		
20. Punctuation	(Point to a question mark.) "What is this?"		
21. Word Spacing	(Point to space between two words.) "Why is there a space here?"		

Phonemic Awareness Assessment

The following assessment is designed to help you determine the appropriate stage of phonemic awareness development for individual students in your classroom. It is not designed as a group or class test.

1. The assessment is to be administered in an oral format, one child at a time. The administration will take approximately ten minutes per child and an entire class can usually be assessed in less than one week.

2. It may not be appropriate or necessary to assess every child in the class. Some will have sufficient phonemic awareness skills that will preclude them from this assessment.

3. It is not necessary to go through the entire test with every child. Some children will indicate early stages of phonemic awareness development (e.g., rhyming), but will become frustrated when attempting later stages (e.g., sound positions). Teacher judgment in stopping the testing process at an appropriate point is always preferable to forcing a child to go through a complete assessment procedure.

Phonemic Awareness Assessment

Student Name: _____

Date: _____

Test Administrator: _____

Stage One: Rhyming and Alliteration

Rhyming Identification

Read each pair of words orally. Circle each pair the child correctly identifies.
"Here are two words that rhyme: ball–fall. Here are two words that don't rhyme: ball–bat.
I will read two words to you. Tell me if the two words rhyme."

bed–red	crack–pink	pill–grill	tuck–tack
boat–float	nose–close	mail–rake	bank–rice

Rhyming Utility

Read each word orally. Write the word the child supplies on the appropriate space.
"I will read a word to you. Tell me another word that rhymes with the first word.
Here's an example: meet–feet."

nail_____	sick_____	bug_____
bake_____	map_____	cot_____

Alliteration Identification

Read each set of words orally. Circle each set the child correctly identifies.
"I will read three words to you. Tell me if the three words all begin with the same sound.
Here's an example of three words that all begin with the same sound: nose, nail, nice."

set, sail, soar	rub, frog, rack	pen, pat, poke
bun, best, ton	hole, hair, help	gate, goat, goose

Alliteration Utility

Read each pair of words orally. Write the word the child supplies on the appropriate space.
"I will read two words to you. Tell me one more word that has the same beginning sound as the first two words. Here's an example: bank, boy, boat."

meet, mail, _____	coat, cap, _____
fog, fast, _____	date, deer, _____
nice, nail, _____	tape, tail, _____

Possible Score: 26 **Student's Score:** _____

Stage Two: Word Parts

Onsets

Say each sound orally. Write the word the child says next to the sound.
"I will make the sound of a letter. Tell me a word that begins with that sound.
Here's an example: /d/, dive."

/s/ _____   /t/ _____   /b/ _____
/m/ _____   /j/ _____   /k/ _____

Rimes

Say each sound orally. Write the word the child says next to the sound.
"I will make a sound. Tell me a word that ends with that sound. Here's an example: /ad/, dad."

/ed/ _____   /op/ _____   /ing/ _____
/ake/ _____   /ell/ _____   /id/ _____

Syllabication

Say each two-syllable word slowly. Circle each word the child correctly blends.
"I'll say a word very slowly. I'll say it in two parts. Put the two parts together and tell me what the word is. Here's an example: birth . . . day, birthday."

base . . . ball   fun . . . ny   pop . . . corn
mop . . . ping   sun . . . set   can . . . dy

Phoneme Blending

For each word, say the individual phonemes slowly. Circle each word in which the child correctly blends the phonemes.
"I will say some sounds very slowly. Put the sounds together and tell me the word you hear.
Here's an example: /b/ /o/ /t/, boat."

/i/ /t/   /p/ /e/ /n/   /f/ /r/ /o/ /g/
/s/ /o/   /j/ /um/ /p/   /s/ /t/ /o/ /p/

> **Possible Score: 24   Student's Score:** _____

Stage Three: Sound Positions

Beginning Sounds

Read each word orally to the child. Circle the words the child correctly identifies.
"Tell me the sound you hear at the beginning of each word I say to you. Here's an example: five, /f/."

say	pail	dice
jump	old	chain

Middle Sounds

Read each word orally to the child. Circle the words the child correctly identifies.
"Tell me the sound you hear in the middle of each word I say to you. Here's an example: chain, /a/."

green	big	yes
ride	mouse	rack

Ending Sounds

Read each word orally to the child. Circle the words the child correctly identifies.
"Tell me the sound you hear at the end of each word I say to you. Here's an example: pain, /n/."

top	ride	flat
duck	skill	plum

Possible Score: 18   Student's Score: _____

Stage Four: Sound Separation

Phoneme Counting

Say each word for the child. Circle the words the child correctly identifies.
"I will say a word. For each word, tell me how many sounds you hear. Here's an example: dig. There are three sounds, /d/ /i/ /g/."

hen (3)	cow (2)	but (3)
horse (3)	me (2)	this (3)

Phoneme Segmentation

Say each word for the child. Circle the words the child correctly identifies.
"I will say a word. Then I would like you to say the word back to me very slowly so I can hear each sound in the word. Here's an example: bell, /b/ /e/ /l/."

brown	eat	help
truck	pig	gum

Possible Score: 12   Student's Score: _____

Stage Five: Sound Manipulation

Sound Deletion

Say each sentence for the child. Circle the sentence the child correctly responds to.
"I will say a word. Then, I will ask you to say the same word, but to leave off a sound that I tell you. Here's an example: Say jet *without the /j/, /et/."*

Say *bird* without the /b/.
Say *sad* without the /s/.
Say *work* without the /w/.

Say *must* without the /t/.
Say *sleep* without the /p/.
Say *flag* without the /g/.

Say *ball* without the /a/.
Say *run* without the /u/.
Say *well* without the /e/.

Sound Substitution

Say each sentence for the child. Circle the sentence the child correctly responds to.
"I will say a word. Then, I will ask you to change something about the word and say it back to me. Here's an example: Take away the first sound in sell *and replace it with a /f/, fell."*

Take away the first sound in *hit* and replace it with a /b/.
Take away the first sound in *dog* and replace it with a /f/.
Take away the first sound in *best* and replace it with a /n/.

Take away the last sound in *bug* and replace it with a /s/.
Take away the last sound in *skin* and replace it with a /p/.
Take away the last sound in *rock* and replace it with a /b/.

Take away the middle sound in *cat* and replace it with a /u/.
Take away the middle sound in *bell* and replace it with a /i/.
Take away the middle sound in *tub* and replace it with a /a/.

Possible Score: 18   Student's Score: _____

Phonemic Awareness Assessment Scoring Rubric

Directions: To use the following rubric, add the total number of points for each of the five sections of the assessment. Put a check mark in one of the four boxes following the title of each section to indicate the child's score for that section. The column with the highest number of check marks indicates the student's overall level of competency in phonemic awareness.

Name		Date		
	Child is very competent	**Child is moderately competent**	**Child is minimally competent**	**Child is not competent**
Rhyming and Alliteration	24–26 points	20–23 points	15–19 points	0–14 points
Word Parts	22–24 points	18–21 points	13–17 points	0–12 points
Sound Positions	16–18 points	12–15 points	8–11 points	0–7 points
Sound Separation	10–12 points	7–9 points	5–6 points	0–4 points
Sound Manipulation	16–18 points	12–15 points	8–11 points	0–7 points

Pre-reading Activities

Primary teachers incorporate a variety of pre-reading activities into their reading curriculum. While these activities are not specifically guided reading activities, they do provide students with foundational skills for a successful guided reading program. Preschool, kindergarten, and first-grade teachers should consider utilizing a variety of pre-reading activities in order to help children become comfortable with the "instruments" and "tools" of reading.

Listed below is a collection of pre-reading activities. They can be easily incorporated into any beginning literacy program. Activities have been specifically designed to be non-book activities. You can introduce them to your students without necessarily attaching them to a specific book or story. These activities can be a daily classroom occurrence with about fifteen to twenty minutes per day sufficient for most children. Keep the emphasis on informality and playfulness and plan some time to share a random mix of selected activities every day.

▶**1** Share a single letter with your students (use the Alphabet Chart, page 23). Invite one or more students to lie on the floor to form the shape of the designated letter. For example, to form a *P*, one student can lie in a straight line and a second student can lie on the floor in a curved shape.

Hint: After students have formed a letter, obtain a stepladder and an instant camera. Stand on the ladder directly over the "human letter" and take a picture. Be sure to post the photos on a special bulletin board or in place of the letters typically found over the top of the classroom chalkboard. You may wish to provide a caption for each shot such as, "Thomas and Nora are the letter K." This is a quick and easy way for students to learn their letters.

▶**2** Alliterations are words that all "start the same." Introduce this concept to children by creating simple alliterative sentences using the names of children in the room. For example:

"Roberto rests."
"Danielle dances."
"Terry taps."

© 2003 Rigby

Invite the children to repeat each sentence after you. Ask them to listen for the sound at the beginning of each word in the sentence. What do they notice about the sounds at the beginning of all the words in each sentence?

After creating several two-word sentences, invent three-word sentences, each of which has the name of a child in the room. For example:

"Jacob jumps joyfully."
"Maria makes mudpies."
"Byron bounces basketballs."

Encourage children to repeat each sentence after you have said it aloud. Afterward, create some four-word alliterative sentences. For example:

"Laura loves licking lollipops."
"Willie's wearing western wear."
"Sally sips salty soup."

Hint: Say each sentence slowly so children can hear the beginning sound in each word. At the beginning or end of this activity, show the students the corresponding alphabet card or post the card in the front of the classroom throughout the activity.

▶ **3** Invite the children to stand up. Tell them that you will be asking them a question about a rhyming word, and ask them to listen carefully. After you have asked the question, they are to point to a designated body part (see the following table) that rhymes with the selected word. Here is the procedure:

- Select a word from one of the four groups below (for example: *see*).

- Create a question using the word (for example, "Do you know a word that rhymes with *see*?").

- Encourage students to point to the correct body part (for example, *knee*).

- Invite them to use the name of the body part in a sentence (for example, "That word is *knee*.").

- Repeat with other words.

Head	Hand	Knee	Feet
bed	sand	me	meet
dead	land	see	seat
red	stand	we	beat
led	brand	tree	greet
sled	band	free	sheet
fed	grand	tea	heat
shed	and	flea	sleet
sped	planned	bee	neat
wed	canned	fee	wheat
shred	gland	he	treat

▶ **4** Use the following incomplete rhymes with children. Invite children to suggest a word to fill in each blank.

Note: Kids love this activity because it fosters a sense of silliness and playfulness in the classroom.

Snake, snake
Eat a _____.

Bear, bear
Eat a _____.

Cat, cat
Eat a _____.

Mouse, mouse
Eat a _____.

Dog, dog
Eat a _____.

Fly, fly
Eat a _____.

Fish, fish
Eat a _____.

Goat, goat
Eat a _____.

▶ **5** Play a game of "I Spy" with the children. Begin the game by sitting with them in a large circle. Create a sentence with two rhyming words (for example, "I spy a mat and a cat." or "I spy a tree and a knee."). Then turn to the child sitting to your right and invite that individual to create his or her own "I Spy" sentence.

Hint: Begin the game by identifying an object that is within the children's field of vision (e.g., something in the classroom). For example, "I spy a coat and a float" or "I spy a door and a score." The second item does not need to be in the field of vision but should be a complementary rhyming word.

Variation: Use children's names for the "I Spy" sentences. For example, "I spy Paul and a stall." Or "I spy Isabel and a shell." The second word can be a nonsense word. This adds a note of silliness to the game.

▶ **6** Use the song "Old MacDonald Had a Farm" to help children learn about onsets and rimes. Select a one-syllable word. Write it on a large index card and post it on a bulletin board or chalkboard. Tell children you are going to show them how this word can be separated into two different parts. Insert the onset, rime, and complete word into the song and sing it for children. Afterward, invite children to sing along with you as you repeat the song. Here are two examples:

Pig
Old Macdonald had a *pig*
E–I–E–I–O
With a /p/ /p/ here
And an /ig/ /ig/ there

Here a /p/
There an /ig/
Everywhere a /pig/ /pig/
Old Macdonald had a *pig*
E–I–E–I–O

Cow

Old Macdonald had a *cow*
E–I–E–I–O
With a /k/ /k/ here
And an /ow/ /ow/ there
Here a /k/
There an /ow/
Everywhere a /cow/ /cow/
Old Macdonald had a *cow*
E–I–E–I–O

▶ **7** One way to help children learn and appreciate book concepts is to lead them in a talk-through of the book. For example: "I will pick up this book from my desk. Here is the top of the book (pointing). Here is the bottom of the book (pointing). Here is the front of the book (pointing). Here is the back of the book (pointing)."

Variations: Invite a student to stand beside you. Hold his or her hand and move the hand to the top, bottom, front, and back of the book as you do a talk-through of its different parts.

Invite one or two students to the front of the room. Ask them to pantomime the positions of a book (top, bottom, front, back) as you do a talk through.

▶ **8** Here's a fun and easy way to help children practice and understand the nature of blending sounds together. Tell the children that when you read a book or story to them you will s–t–r–e–t–c–h out selected words. Each time you stretch a word, stop and ask children to say the word that you have stretched.

You may wish to alert children ahead of time that a stretched word is about to be said. For example, just before you begin to say a stretched word, put your finger on your nose or tap the top of your head three times.

Here's an example from the book *Slugs* by Anthony D. Fredericks (Minneapolis, MN: Lerner Publications, 2000):

"If slugs go out in the s–u–n, they will dry up. Slugs hide f–r–o–m the sun in moist soil. They also hide under plants or under r–o–ck–s."

Hint: Select words with which the students are familiar or that are within their listening vocabularies. Also, don't stretch more than three words per paragraph. Doing so will seriously detract from their enjoyment of the story. You may wish to consider doing this activity on the third or fourth reading of a book.

▶**9** Tell children that you will talk to them as if you are a ghost. When you say a "ghost word," encourage children to tell you what the word is. For example: "I went into the haunted hhhooooooowwwwwssssss," or "There was a black ccccccaaaaaaatttttt in the yard."

After children are comfortable with ghost words, invite them to create their own ghost words to say to each other. Tell them that they can only include one ghost word in each sentence. Encourage individual children to say a sentence with a ghost word in it and ask the remainder of the class to say what the word was.

Hint: It's really fun to preface each ghost word with a frightened or scared expression on your face as a clue to children that you are about to say a ghost word.

▶**10** Place three chairs in the front of the room. Invite three children to each select a chair and sit down. Give each child a number (1, 2, 3). Tell the three children that you will say three different words, one for each number. The sound at the beginning of two of those words will be the same. The other word will be different. Ask two of the children to stand up if their sounds are the same. For example, if you said, "dog," "dare," and "song," then children 1 and 2 would stand up. If you said, "cat," "wing," and "cost," then children 1 and 3 would stand up.

Variation: Repeat this activity using three words, two of which have the same *ending* sound, one of which does not.

▶**11** Select a target sound for the day (such as /b/). Invite children to look through old magazines for pictures or illustrations of objects that begin with the target sound (boat, bed, bird, bell, bone). Encourage the children to paste all of the pictures onto a large sheet of oak-tag or construction paper to create an oversized collage.

After creating a daily collage, take time during the day to ask the children to say all the represented words on the collage. Note how all the words begin with the same sound. Plan time for students to create a collage each day, while focusing on words that all begin with the same sound.

Variation: After children have become familiar with the above activity, invite them to create daily collages, each of which focuses on a single sound at the *end* of selected words. Please note that this is a challenging activity for most children.

▶**12** Fasten three manila envelopes to a bulletin board. Write the number 2 on the first envelope, the number 3 on the second envelope, and the number 4 on the third envelope. Obtain some old newspapers and cut out a selection of words (large headlines work best). Select a variety of words that have two letters, three letters, or four letters. Divide children into groups and give each group a random assortment of words. Ask each group to place the words in the appropriate envelopes according to the number of letters in each word.

Variation: When students have achieved a level of confidence with this activity, you may wish to develop it into a relay race. Divide the class into three or four teams. Provide each team with a random assortment of two-, three-, or four-letter words. The first person in each team selects a word from his or her team pile, dashes to the front of the room, and places the word in its appropriate envelope. That person then runs back to his or her team and tags the next person in line to go and do the same thing.

▶**13** Play a variation of "Simon Says" with the children. Select several words from a favorite book. Tell the children that you will ask them a question that they must answer with a "Yes" or a "No," but only if "Simon Says."

Ask the children to form a straight line. Tell them that if they answer correctly—and only when "Simon Says"—then they get to come forward one step. If they answer incorrectly or answer correctly but without "Simon Says," then they must remain where they are. Here are some sample questions:

Beginning Sounds

- "Simon says the following words all have the same beginning sound: pan, pick, pill."

- "Simon says the following words all have the same beginning sound: sub, sink, fog."

- "The following words all have the same beginning sound: sap, sing, sun."

Middle Sounds

- "Simon says the following words all have the same middle sound: cub, fun, cut."

- "Simon says the following words all have the same middle sound: rot, hum, hot."

- "The following words all have the same middle sound: gate, rake, pail."

Ending Sounds

- "Simon says the following words all have the same ending sound: map, chip, peep."

- "Simon says the following words all have the same ending sound: coat, mad, rid."

- "The following words all have the same ending sound: jack, lake, brick."

▶ **14** Obtain several paper lunch bags. On the bottom of each bag, glue a picture of a familiar object. Turn the bag over and place it on your hand to create a puppet (the bottom of the bag becomes the top of the puppet's head). Draw an illustration of a face on the front of the bag. (By arranging your hand inside the bag, you can make the puppet have a "mouth" and "talk.")

After creating several of these (each with a different picture on top), distribute them to small groups of children, one puppet per group. Tell each group that the item pictured on the top of the puppet's head indicates what kinds of things the puppet can "eat." A puppet can only eat things that begin with the same sound as the picture on its head. If there is a picture of a car on the top of a puppet's head, it can only eat cards, coins, cups, and crayons, for example.

Invite each group to search through the room for items that begin with the same sound as the picture on the puppet's head. Give the groups five minutes to collect as many items as they can. When the time limit has expired, invite all the groups to arrange their items on a table. Encourage each group to name all the items and note how they all begin with the same sound.

Hint: You may wish to bring in several items from home to distribute around the classroom and add to those that children would normally find in the room.

Variation: Invite selected children to take puppets home. Encourage them to look around their homes for items that the puppet would "eat." Ask each child to bring in the identified items (with parental permission) to share with the class.

▶ **15** Cut out forty or fifty pictures from old magazines and paste each one on a 5-x-8-inch index card. Punch holes and thread yarn through each one to make a necklace. Randomly distribute the cards to the class and ask each child to name the item on her or his card. After each child has named the item, the child may wear his or her necklace. Now ask the children to travel around the room, locating other individuals who also have an item that begins with the same sound as the item on his or her card. Invite all the children with the same beginning sound to gather together in one spot in the classroom. Call on a group and ask them to say all their picture words.

Continue the game by collecting all the cards, mixing them up, and redistributing them to every child.

Hint: After children have assembled in groups, ask which group had the most number of individuals and which group had the least number of individuals. If appropriate, you may wish to chart or graph these results on the chalkboard.

Variation: Invite children to focus on the ending sounds of the pictured items.

▶ **16** Obtain three 5-x-8-inch index cards. Using a thick black marker, write the following words individually on the index cards: FIRST, MIDDLE, and END. Punch two holes in the top of each card and thread yarn through to make a necklace. Invite three children to stand in the front of the room. Place a card over the head of each child and stand them in order: FIRST, MIDDLE, and END.

Select a series of one-syllable words. Tell the children that you will say one of the words and ask them about certain sounds in each word. For example:

> The target word is *boat*.
>
> "Karen (who has the FIRST card around her neck), what was the first sound you heard in the word *boat*?"
>
> "Angel (who has the MIDDLE card around her neck), what was the middle sound you heard in the word *boat*?"
>
> "Kenny (who has the END card around his neck), what was the end sound you heard in the word *boat*?"

Hint: Be careful how you select the children for this activity. Make sure that the selected children are comfortable with positional words.

Variation: Divide the class into three groups of children. Arrange the children in three lines. On each of three desks, place one of the cards as described above. Invite children in the first line to step up, one at a time, to the FIRST desk; those in the second line to step up to the MIDDLE desk; and those in the third line to step to the END desk. Say a target word and invite each of the three children at the desks to identify the first, middle, and ending sounds. If a child identifies the appropriate sound correctly, he or she gets a point for his or her team. The first team to reach ten points (or twenty points) is the winner.

▶ **17** Obtain an old suitcase or backpack. Collect approximately thirty or forty small objects that can be paired together by beginning sounds (e.g., sock + soap, cap + cup, pin + penny, dime + dollar). Lay all the items on a table and invite the children to gather around the table.

Tell children that you are going on a trip, but you are only allowed to take items in pairs. The names of items in a pair must begin with the same sound. Ask the children to assist you in selecting the appropriate pairs. Go around the table and ask each child to name two items with the same beginning sound. If the child names a correct pair, ask him or her to place the two items into the suitcase or backpack.

Hint:: Later, you can use this as a literacy center activity.

Variations: Invite children to identify *three* items, each with the same initial sound, to be placed into the suitcase. Invite children to collect pairs of items to be placed into the suitcase, but the names of each item in a pair must *end* with the same sound.

▶**18** Provide each child with a paper cup. Place ten edible items into each cup (raisins, candies, peanut halves), but be aware of any food allergies your students may have. Be sure to have a cup for yourself.

Tell the children that you are going to count words by taking a counter out of the cup and putting it on your table for each word you say in a sentence. Explain that you will say a sentence in the normal way and then say it again, pausing after each word to take a counter out of your cup and place it on the table. Demonstrate with the following:

"I run."

"I" (Take a counter out of your cup and place it down on the table.) "run." (Take a counter out of your cup and place it down on the table.)

Invite children to copy your actions as you repeat the previous sentence.

Now say a three-word sentence and repeat the sequence above. Follow with a four-word sentence and a five-word sentence, each time modeling the sentence and then inviting students to copy your actions.

Note: After children complete this activity, they can eat their counters. Be aware of any food allergies in your classroom.

▶**19** After children are comfortable with the previous activity, create original sentences, each of which includes the name of a child in the class. Start with sentences that are relatively short ("Maria laughs."). After you say the sentence, invite the children to repeat it after you. Say the sentence again, this time encouraging children to place a counter on their table for each word they hear in the sentence. (Place them left to right, if possible.)

Do two- or three-word sentences, each with a child's name embedded in the sentence. Make the sentences longer, one word at a time. Again, include a child's name in each sentence. For example:

"Carmen runs." (two words, two counters)

"Harold is sick." (three words, three counters)

"Michael lives next door." (four words, four counters)

"Ming has a new bike." (five words, five counters)

Depending on the ability level(s) of the children in your classroom, it is a good idea to use sentences of no more than five words each.

Variation: After you say several five-word sentences, create sentences with progressively fewer words in them (four words, three words, etc.). End with two-word sentences.

▶**20** Teach children the song below to the tune of "Happy Birthday." Each time you and the children sing the song, select a new target word for the last word in the third line. These target words can come from a nursery rhyme, a children's book, or other teacher resources.

Beginning Sound
Celebrate this fine word,
Celebrate this fine word,
Celebrate this word _____,
What's the first sound you heard?

Ending Sound
Celebrate this fine word,
Celebrate this fine word,
Celebrate this word _____,
What's the last sound you heard?

▶**21** Obtain three wooden clothespins. Using a thick black marker, write the number 1 on one clothespin, the number 2 on another, and the number 3 on the last.

Select several three-letter / three-phoneme words (see list). Write each word on a large index card in block letters. Select one card and show it to the children while saying the word aloud. Repeat the word slowly and clip an appropriately numbered clothespin to the top of the card over each phoneme / letter. Clip the 1 clothespin to the top of the card over the first phoneme; the 2 clothespin to the top of the card over the middle phoneme; and the 3 clothespin to the top of the card over the ending phoneme.

This activity provides children with visual reinforcement on the location and placement of individual sounds in a word. Here are a few three-letter / three-phoneme words to get you started:

bat	cup	pin
dad	bag	rag
ham	cap	cat
bed	hen	jet
pig	dog	cot

Variation: As students become familiar with this activity, move them into three-phoneme/four-letter, four-phoneme/four-letter, and four-phoneme/five-letter words.

Hint: Once you move from pictures to words, select the target words carefully, since silent letters or unusual sound/letter representations may confuse some children (for example: ph = /f/ in *phone*; gh = /f/ in *cough*).

▶ **22** Tell children that you are going to play a game with each of their names. Instead of saying each child's name in its normal manner, you will address each child by extending and expanding the first sound in her or his name. For example:

"S–s–s–s–s–s–arah will be our lunch counter today."

"Will you please take this note to the office M–m–m–m–m–m–iguel?"

"I really like the way A–a–a–a–a–a–a–ndrew is sitting in his chair."

Hint: You may be able to use this activity with the ending sounds of some of the children's names. For example: "Did everyone see what Mark–k–k–k–k–k–k brought in today?"

Variation: Use this activity when talking about other individuals in the school—the secretary, the principal, the librarian, the custodian, and so on.

▶ **23** Ask all of the children to stand up. Tell them that you will say some words, one at a time. Instruct them to place both hands on the side of their heads when they hear the first sound in each word, place both hands on the sides of their waists when they hear the middle sound in each word, and put their hands on their feet when they hear the ending sound in each word. (This activity requires the use of three-phoneme words only.) Here are some examples:

cake: /k/ (hands on head); /a/ (hands on waist); /k/ (hands on toes)

tub: /t/ (hands on head); /u/ (hands on waist); /b/ (hands on toes)

▶ **24** Tell the children that you are going to create some rhyming riddles for them. You will say a word and they are to think of a word that rhymes with your word and begins with an identified sound. For example:

You: I'm thinking of a word that rhymes with bag and starts with /w/.
Children: wag

You: I'm thinking of a word that rhymes with hen and starts with /m/.
Children: men

Hint: This is a great transition activity that can be done two minutes before recess, just before lunch, or while in line waiting for dismissal.

▶ **25** Sing to the tune of "The Itsy Bitsy Spider" and invite the children to sing along with you. Create some new words by substituting the initial sound with a new sound. Here is an example:

The *mitsy mitsy* spider
Climbed up the water spout.
Down came the rain
And washed the spider out.
Out came the sun
And dried up all the rain,
And the *mitsy mitsy* spider
Climbed up the spout again.

Variation: Invite the children to suggest other familiar tunes in which selected words can have their initial sounds replaced with other sounds. For example:

Tappy tirthday to tou
Tappy tirthday to tou
Tappy tirthday to tou-tou
Tappy tirthday to tou.

▶ **26** Write initial consonant sounds on several index cards, one sound per card. Place all the cards into a paper lunch bag. At the beginning of the day, invite one child to reach into the bag and select one card. Identify the sound for the children and then tell them that during the course of the day, you will say each of their names using the identified sound as the beginning sound for each name. For example:

/m/   Barry becomes Marry
Sandra becomes Mandra
José becomes Mosé
Carla becomes Marla

Ask children to use their "new names" throughout the day (a few gentle reminders about the target sound may be necessary).

Variation: Invite the children to select a favorite nursery rhyme. Share the nursery rhyme as a class. Then modify as many words as possible by substituting the sound of the day in place of initial letters. Read the revised nursery rhyme for the class.

Guided Reading Lessons

Lesson Planning

Your success with guided reading will depend upon the opportunities you provide students for actively engaging in the dynamics of text. While the following format provides you with a working outline for the necessary elements of a guided reading lesson, it is important to note that there is a great deal of flexibility in this design. You can modify this plan in line with the structure of your own classroom or reading program. For example, the time limits are only suggestions. Feel free to modify them according to your schedule of activities.

This sequence of processes and procedures is designed to help students become competent and independent readers. It is a model that can be easily changed as the needs and abilities of class members change.

The following five elements should be included in a guided reading lesson:

1. Setting the Stage includes all the pre-lesson activities you need to do prior to actual instruction.

2. Book Orientation includes those activities that introduce children to a book, provide them with a comprehension lesson, and prepare them for independent reading.

3. Independent Reading is the stage in which students read on their own and in which you intervene (as necessary) with appropriate prompts.

4. Responding and Rereading is an opportunity for students to reread a book from beginning to end utilizing appropriate strategies.

5. Assessment is an optional (but important) stage in guided reading. It is not necessary to include assessment as part of every lesson, but you need to be aware of the times when selected students need to be assessed to determine their correct placement in appropriate reading materials.

The chart on page 47 offers several suggestions for these five elements. This does not mean that you need to do all activities for every guided reading lesson. For example, you will not need to use running records for every student. Rather, the key to successful guided reading lessons is your degree of flexibility and readiness in meeting and addressing individual student needs.

On pages 48–49 you will find a Guided Reading Lesson Planner. It has been designed to offer you a flexible document that will help you design appropriate lessons for any guided reading group. Please feel free to modify and adapt this plan in accordance with the dynamics of your own philosophy and classroom organization.

Note: The actual guided reading lesson (as depicted in the chart on page 47) is approximately thirty to forty-five minutes long. This time frame encompasses the Book Orientation, Independent Reading, and Responding and Rereading elements of a guided reading lesson as described above. The Setting the Stage component takes place before the actual instructional time with a guided reading lesson, and the Assessment occurs immediately after the lesson.

Component	Strategies and Activities	Suggested Time Frame
Setting the Stage	• Select four to six students. • Select an appropriate book and give each student a copy. • Familiarize yourself with the text and anticipate challenging words or language structures. • Consider and select appropriate strategies and determine how to model them. • Think through reasons for grouping students and determine who to observe. • Determine any assessment needs. • Demonstrate excitement for the text.	4–5 minutes
Book Orientation	• Introduce the book and help the students set a purpose for reading. • Read and discuss the title and talk about the illustrations. • Do a "walk" through the book. • Call attention to text features. • Link the book to a similar story. • Guide a picture discussion. • Activate background knowledge. • Invite students to make appropriate predictions. • Introduce the appropriate reading strategy and discuss it with students. • Introduce and discuss key vocabulary in context. • Consider some of the following: Use some book language. Remind students about print concepts. Point out "tricky" parts. Talk about some previous strategies and connect them to the text. Identify punctuation.	10–15 minutes
Independent Reading	• Each child reads independently at his or her own pace. • Students can "track" print with finger(s). • Assist students (as necessary) with problem-solving and provide reinforcement. • Confirm good reader strategies and prompt when needed. • Observe student behavior and take notes. • Ask appropriate questions ("How did you know?").	15–20 minutes
Responding and Rereading	• Return to text with students. • Conduct a group reading conference. • Review and clarify the reading strategy. • Provide whole-group closure activities. • Encourage retellings and rereadings. • Discuss the connection of the strategies (introduced in "Book Orientation"). • Pose open-ended questions. • Ask the students to complete an extending book project or activity. • Allow students to visit literacy centers (as chosen independently or assigned).	5–10 minutes
Assessment (as necessary)	• Review observations and make necessary notes. • Maintain running records as needed. • Determine future reading needs (same stage or movement to new stage). • Involve students in self-evaluative processes, as necessary.	5–10 minutes

Guided Reading Lesson Planner

I. Setting the Stage

Students:

1. _____   4. _____

2. _____   5. _____

3. _____   6. _____

Circle one: Emergent   Early Reader   Transitional   Fluent

Book Title: _____   Level: _____

Strategy: _____

Challenging words: _____

2. Book Orientation

Book Introduction (title, illustrations, walk through, text features):

Background knowledge to activate:

Previews:

Predictions:

Word work and/or visual/graphophonics:

Guided Reading Lesson Planner

3. Independent Reading—Observational Notes

1.	2.	3.	4.	5.	6.
Behavior:	Behavior:	Behavior:	Behavior:	Behavior:	Behavior:
Prompts:	Prompts:	Prompts:	Prompts:	Prompts:	Prompts:

4. Responding and Rereading

Reinforcement needed (may need to be completed after teaching first three stages above):

Comprehension check:

Literacy Centers (circle):

Listening	ABC/Spelling	Art	Writing
Reading Around the Room	Readers Theatre	Pocket Chart	Free Reading
Drama/Storytelling	Buddy Reading	Poetry	Big Books

5. Assessment—Running Record (circle):   1 2 3 4 5 6

Other:

Designing and Teaching a Guided Reading Lesson

1. Based upon your ongoing and continuous assessment, select a group of students for a guided reading group. Write their names on the Guided Reading Lesson Planner on pages 48–49. Select a book that closely matches the instructional level of the group and record it on the planner.

2. Identify an appropriate reading strategy (in accordance with the book and the students' instructional level) and record it. Note any challenging words to introduce to the students beforehand.

3. Introduce the book to the students and orient them to its major features using some of the strategies and activities listed on page 47.

4. Ask questions that will assist the students in activating the necessary background knowledge related to the text (e.g., "How is the cover of this book similar to the ant colony we saw on the playground last month?").

5. Teach the strategy in the context of the book.

6. Provide students with appropriate previews. Consider the following:

a. Point out any necessary concepts of print.

b. Share some of the language of the book and point out any difficult language, vocabulary, or phonics needs.

c. Share significant words, phrases, or sentences and ask students to watch for them.

d. Encourage students to think about previously taught strategies and how they might apply to the new text.

e. Relate the book to others by the same author or illustrator, and/or in the same genre.

f. Point out any challenging or unusual punctuation.

7. Determine the predictions appropriate to the text and/or illustrations.

8. Focus on any necessary vocabulary or phonics skills.

9. Have students read the text independently. After students read on their own, determine the need for any reinforcement.

10. Record observational notes for each student.

11. Intervene only when necessary. Make interventions short and guided by prompts that help students focus on the strategy being taught.

12. Check for comprehension with open- or closed-ended questions.

13. Provide appropriate praise and encouragement for integrating strategies into the reading routine.

14. Assign students to literacy centers that provide related extending activities.

15. Determine the need for taking running records or other assessments.

16. Regroup as necessary (for future work). Consider grouping or regrouping based on reading levels as well as the need for specific reading strategies.

Please keep in mind that this sequence of planning and teaching activities is one way of designing your own lessons. Obviously, you will not want to include everything suggested above for your lessons—nor should you. This design provides you with a number of options, which are dependent upon the nature of the text, a guided reading group's instructional needs, and the resources you have available. You can modify and adapt these suggestions in keeping with your unique classroom situation and the evolving reading abilities of your students. As you become more comfortable in designing your own guided reading lessons, you will adjust this outline to your own teaching style and philosophy.

A Sample Guided Reading Lesson

Jerome Hawcock is a second-grade teacher in San Diego, California. He has been a classroom teacher for thirteen years. He says, "Second grade is undoubtedly my favorite grade. The kids are eager and ready to learn and the incredible variety of literature available for this level is staggering. The options for guided reading instruction help me design a reading program that is truly 'kid-oriented'."

Jerome is working with a group of students and is introducing them to several examples of nonfiction literature. He wants his students to experience the wide variety of books available in this genre and the numerous ways in which this literature can serve as springboards for learning experiences outside the classroom. This particular group of students consists of Andrea, Carlo, Dominic, Marti, and Serge. As a result of his ongoing assessment program, Jerome has assigned these students to the fluent stage in his guided reading program.

Jerome selects the book *In One Tidepool: Crabs, Snails, and Salty Tails* by Anthony D. Fredericks (Nevada City, CA: Dawn Publications, 2002). He wants his students to see how the author has blended both fiction and nonfiction into a text. Following is a transcription of some of the guided reading events that took place over a period of two days.

Jerome: I'd like to share a new book with you today. It's called *In One Tidepool*, and it's a combination of fiction and nonfiction.

Serge: The cover looks like it's a story about a girl and some of the things she finds inside a tidepool.

Dominic: Yeah, look at that really cool starfish on the cover. I've never seen one with all those colors.

Marti: I did once, when my grandmother took me and my sister to the aquarium.

Jerome: It seems like this book is stimulating some interest and discussion. However, before you read it, I'd like to point out some of the words that I would like you to pay attention to.

(Each student has his or her own paperback copy of the book and follows along as Jerome points out some pre-selected words.)

Jerome: Here are the words I want you to watch for: *clumps, barnacles, rugged, anemones, knobby,* and *realm.*

Andrea: I've heard of the word *barnacles* before. My brother and I go down to Point Loma all the time, and we've seen lots of barnacles on the rocks there. You have to be careful 'cause if you were to slip and fall, they could scratch you with their sharp shells.

Jerome: O.K., guys, now I want you to quickly browse through the book. As you do, I want you to think about anything you have done or anything else you have read that might be similar to this book. Look at all the illustrations, and when you're done, I'm going to ask you to make a prediction about the story.

(Students do a personal "walk-through" of the book.)

Jerome: O.K., what did you notice?

Carlo: This book reminded me of the time when that scientist came to school to show us all those neat fish and crabs and other stuff. I remember when Mr. Corwin, the principal, put that octopus on his arm and then had a hard time getting it off.

Dominic: Yeah, I've been to a couple of tidepools near La Jolla, but I don't think I've seen all the kinds of animals I saw in this book.

Serge: I read some ocean books before and some of them talked about different kinds of ocean animals. I remember reading about starfish and crabs, but I don't ever remember seeing anything about sponges. I thought that sponges were something you got at the grocery store.

Jerome: O.K., let's see if we can make a prediction about this book. What do you think it will be about?

Marti: I think it will be about a girl who goes to the beach and finds all kinds of different animals.

Carlo: I think it will be about some really weird creatures that live in a tidepool.

Andrea: I think we'll read about some fish and crabs and starfish and other tiny things at the beach.

Jerome: Those are all good predictions.

(Jerome writes all the predictions on a large sheet of newsprint. Students will be able to return to those predictions at the conclusion of the guided reading lesson.)

Jerome: Now I would like everyone to take out their Reading Journals and turn to a blank page. Remember when we did the K-W-L strategy last week with the book *Shark Lady*?

Carlo: Yeah!

Jerome: Well, we're going to use that strategy again with *In One Tidepool*. I'd like everyone to draw three columns on a blank page. Put the letter *K* at the top of the first column, the letter *W* at the top of the second column, and the letter *L* at the top of the third column.

Marti: I know, *K* stands for "What I know," *W* stands for "What I want to know," and *L* stands for "What I learned."

Jerome: That's right!

(The students create a K-W-L chart in their journals.)

Jerome: Now, when you read the book I'd like you to fill in each of the columns. Before you begin, I want you to think about what you may already know about tidepools and write that information in the first column on your charts.

(The students take a few minutes to record their prior knowledge about tidepools.)

Jerome: I want each of you to read the book. Watch for the words I told you about and also notice the rhyming pattern that the author uses to share his information with the reader. You also might want to pay attention to how the illustrations are matched with the words. Think about how this may be similar or different from the illustrations you've seen in other nonfiction books.

(The students begin reading the book. As they read, Jerome carefully monitors their progress and assists with prompts as necessary. He keeps his interventions short and quick and helps students attend to their K-W-L charts. He also records anecdotal comments about each student on his guided reading lesson planner. He notes that Serge seems to be handling the material particularly well and decides to do a running record on him after the lesson to see if he is ready for the next level. After students complete the reading, he follows up with a posted list of open-ended questions. Students work together to respond to the questions in their journals. They also check each other's K-W-L charts for completeness. Afterward, Jerome assigns the group to the Readers Theatre literacy center, where they will have an opportunity to share a readers theatre script of the book that Jerome has written and designed.)

Note: There is a great deal of flexibility in a guided reading lesson. Jerome has previously introduced his students to the K-W-L reading strategy, and he is now providing them with a guided reading text that will allow them to use this strategy in a meaningful way. The success of this lesson is largely due to a certain degree of independence Jerome is giving his students, as well as the opportunity to use a strategy in a planned and systematic way.

The guided reading lesson plan described in this unit is an outline, not a formula. It is respective of the developing nature of the children and the specific needs of your individual classroom.

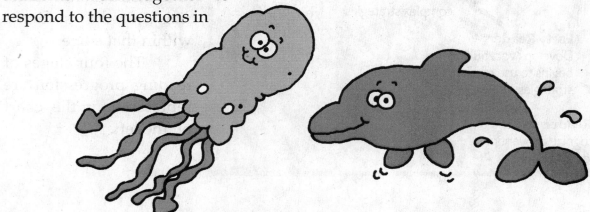

Literacy Stages

Reader Characteristics

Most authors and many teachers divide readers into four very broad categories or stages of reading development. It is understood that these stages are not grade-related; the lowest levels do not always appear in the lower grades, just as the higher stages are not predominate in the higher grades. The stages represent four levels or gradients that can appear in any primary-level (grades K–2) classroom.

Also implicit in these stages is the fact that children can move between the stages (preferably upward) as they acquire reading strategies and reading competence. The focus is more on what individual students can do, rather than assigning an arbitrary number or designation to an entire classroom full of students. One of the primary goals of the guided reading program is to determine where the student is and take him or her to increasingly higher levels of reading. By placing students into flexible stages, you can begin to address their instructional needs and tailor your instruction and instructional materials to the students within that stage.

The four stages of reading progression are represented in the chart on the left.

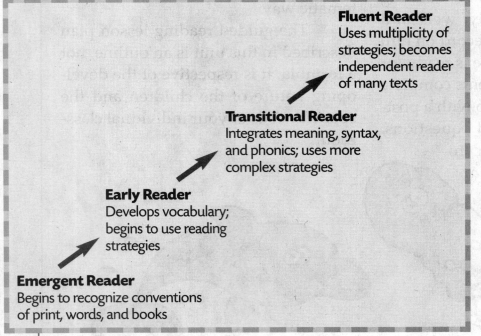

Fluent Reader
Uses multiplicity of strategies; becomes independent reader of many texts

Transitional Reader
Integrates meaning, syntax, and phonics; uses more complex strategies

Early Reader
Develops vocabulary; begins to use reading strategies

Emergent Reader
Begins to recognize conventions of print, words, and books

It could be inferred from the chart that emergent readers are those in the beginning stages of reading acquisition, while fluent readers are those who are able to use a wealth of reading skills in reading on their own. You will not have only emergent readers in your kindergarten classroom, just as you wouldn't have only fluent readers in your second-grade classroom. Each classroom is as unique as the students who occupy it. All classrooms will have students who are in all four stages of literacy development. The challenge, of course, is providing for the varied needs of all students within a program that is both structured and meaningful.

While it is easy to assign students to a stage or to a group, it is important to remember that reading is more than just an amalgam of cognitive skills. It also embodies a variety of social, psychological, and affective factors as well. Students' interest in reading, support from the home environment, prior exposure to literacy activities, emotionality, and ability to interact in a social environment will also affect their success in learning to read.

Charts that outline the characteristics for each of the four stages of readers appear on pages 58–59. Please keep in mind that these lists are not

exclusive to each stage. There are components and elements that "cross over" between stages and some that are universal to all stages. For example, alphabetic recognition is a necessary element in each stage. It is more appropriately emphasized in the emergent reader stage since a great deal of instructional time is devoted to those concepts at this level of reading development. However, the most important reading competencies are clearly *emphasized* at each stage.

Emergent Reader Characteristics

Approximate Grade Range: Preschool to early Grade 1

- Understands that print has a message
- Can recognize some high-frequency words
- Understands concept of directionality (top to bottom, left to right, and return sweep)
- Can locate some known words
- Uses illustrations to predict meaning
- Knows the difference between a letter and a word
- Can identify some beginning and ending sounds in words
- May invent text
- Begins to use pattern and repetition of text to read
- Is able to use prior experiences and background knowledge to gain meaning
- Is beginning to make connections between oral language and written language
- Can match voice to print with one-to-one word matching

Early Reader Characteristics

Approximate Grade Range: Kindergarten to late Grade 1

- Recognizes many high-frequency words
- Uses illustrations to confirm meaning
- Has good control of early reading strategies (letter/sound matching, locating unknown words)
- Beginning to gain more information from print than from illustrations
- Can figure out simple words using meaning, syntax, and phonics
- Begins to recognize regular spelling patterns
- Engages in some self-correction
- Can read using more than one source of information
- Is becoming more skilled at monitoring and cross-checking
- Is gaining control of reading strategies
- Can recognize and use beginning, middle, and ending letters/sounds to decode unfamiliar words
- Can read familiar texts with phrasing and fluency
- Can use prior knowledge to predict meaning
- Can retell a story in their own words
- Begins to attend to punctuation while reading
- Occasionally uses story language in writing and oral language activities

Transitional Reader Characteristics

Approximate Grade Range: Kindergarten to late Grade 2

- Has full control of early reading strategies
- Recognizes an increasing number of words
- Uses all sources of information quickly and easily
- Can integrate the use of cues
- Uses a variety of ways to figure out unfamiliar words
- Can detect and correct errors during silent reading
- Has developed a large core of sight vocabulary words
- Is able to read independent-level text with expression and proper phrasing
- Consistently monitors reading for understanding
- Relies very little on illustrations to read text
- Reads longer, more complex text
- Can adjust reading pace to the purposes for reading
- Can summarize texts read
- Is beginning to use inferencing abilities
- Can use semantic mapping strategies to make connections
- Is able to revisit text to support ideas and conclusions
- Reads from a variety of genres
- Is more aware of story and text structures
- Can synthesize and interpret what is read

Fluent Reader Characteristics

Approximate Grade Range: Late Grade 1 to Early Grade 3

- Uses all sources of information quickly and easily
- Can solve problems independently
- Is able to identify most words independently
- Can detect and correct errors, often silently
- Reads with phrasing and fluency
- Is able to read chapter books with comprehension
- Reads and understands more challenging vocabulary
- Reads a wide range of texts for different purposes
- Monitors reading for understanding
- Continues to learn from reading
- Reads a variety of genres independently
- Is able to revisit text to support ideas
- Reads much longer, more complex texts
- Is able to make connections to several different types of books
- Often emulates authors in their own writing
- Can synthesize and interpret what is read

Lesson Plans for Each Stage

Pages 61–64 show sample lesson plans for each of the four stages of literacy development. Using the lesson plan format introduced in Unit 3, you will be able to see how selected books can be used to teach important con-cepts and strategies at each appropriate stage of reading development. (For an explanation of the letters that designate guided reading levels, see the chart in Unit 6, page 83.)

sheep- jeep
grunt - front
yelp- help

Emergent Reader Level

Brown Bear, Brown Bear, What Do You See? by Bill Martin, Jr.
(Guided Reading Level: C)

Component	Strategies and Activities	Instruction
Setting the Stage	• Select four to six students for a guided reading group. • Select an appropriate book. • Give each student a copy of the book. • Familiarize yourself with the text and anticipate challenging words or language structures. • Consider and select appropriate strategies. • Think through reasons for grouping students and determine who to observe. • Determine how to model strategies. • Determine any assessment needs. • Demonstrate excitement for the text.	*Brown Bear, Brown Bear, What Do You See?* is appropriate for helping emergent readers track print, make predictions, and observe text patterns.

Book Orientation	• Introduce the book and help the students set a purpose for reading.
	• Read and discuss the title and talk about the illustrations.
	• Do a "walk" through the book.
	• Call attention to text features.
	• Link the book to a similar story.
	• Guide a picture discussion.
	• Activate background knowledge.
	• Invite students to make appropriate predictions.
	• Introduce the appropriate reading strategy and discuss with students.
	• Introduce and discuss key vocabulary in context.
	• Consider some of the following:
	  Use some book language.
	  Remind students about print concepts.
	  Point out "tricky" parts.
	  Talk about some previous strategies and connect them to the text.
	  Identify punctuation.
		Introduce the book by asking students to look at the pictures and recall what they have read in a previous lesson. Students suggest several animals that they remember, as well as colors associated with those animals. Begin reading pages 5-7 aloud and ask students to think about what they hear. Students recall some related colors and animals. Ask students to make predictions about other animal/color matches. Read page 8 and ask students to predict what will be on page 9. Continue this activity throughout the book, and ask students to predict the end of the story.

Independent Reading	• Each child reads independently at his or her own pace. • Students can "track" print with finger(s). • Assist students (as necessary) with problem-solving and provide reinforcement. • Confirm good reader strategies and prompt when needed. • Observe student behavior and take notes. • Ask appropriate questions ("How did you know?").	Provide each student with his or her own copy of the book and invite him or her to read in a quiet voice. Monitor student progress and prompt when necessary.
Responding and Rereading	• Return to text with students. • Conduct group reading conference. • Review and clarify reading strategy. • Provide whole-group closure activities. • Encourage retellings and rereadings. • Discuss the connection of the strategies (introduced in "Book Orientation"). • Pose open-ended questions. • Ask the students to complete extending book projects or activities. • Allow students to visit literacy centers (as chosen independently or assigned).	After students have finished the book, talk about the language pattern of the book, and picture cues. Ask students to retell their favorite part and discuss the similarities between them. Ask students to read a favorite page. Students can create animal/color matches for a class book. Invite students to select other books written by this author and look at them in the free reading center.
Assessment (as necessary)	• Review observations and make necessary notes. • Maintain running records as needed. • Determine future reading needs (same stage or movement to new stage). • Involve students in self-evaluative processes, as necessary.	Administer running records to see if the students are ready for more challenging material.

Early Reader Level

Sheep in a Jeep by Nancy Shaw
(Guided Reading Level: G)

Component	Strategies and Activities	Instruction
Setting the Stage	• Select four to six students for a guided reading group. • Select an appropriate book. • Give each student a copy of the book. • Familiarize yourself with the text and anticipate challenging words or language structures. • Consider and select appropriate strategies. • Think through reasons for grouping students and determine who to observe. • Determine how to model strategies. • Determine any assessment needs. • Demonstrate excitement for the text.	Create an environment in which print can be seen from every corner. *Sheep in a Jeep* is an appropriate book for early readers because it assists them in building a core of high-frequency words, and cross-checking to figure out others.

Book Orientation	• Introduce the book and help the students set a purpose for reading.
	• Read and discuss the title and talk about the illustrations.
	• Do a "walk" through the book.
	• Call attention to text features.
	• Link the book to a similar story.
	• Guide a picture discussion.
	• Activate background knowledge.
	• Invite students to make appropriate predictions.
	• Introduce the appropriate reading strategy and discuss with students.
	• Introduce and discuss key vocabulary in context.
	• Consider some of the following:
	  Use some book language.
	  Remind students about print concepts.
	  Point out "tricky" parts.
	  Talk about some previous strategies and connect them to the text.
	  Identify punctuation.
		Remind students of other books they have read about sheep, and discuss some of the similarities. Identify the simple sentence patterns in these books, and predict whether this author will follow a similar pattern. Ask students to look at the sentence on page 9 ("Sheep in a jeep on a hill that's steep.") and locate the word *steep*. Point out the rhyming word, *jeep*, noting the spelling pattern. Do the same with *shove, gooey,* and *steer*. Ask students to look for selected spelling patterns, and involve them in related phonemic awareness activities.

Independent Reading	• Each child reads independently at his or her own pace. • Students can "track" print with finger(s). • Assist students (as necessary) with problem-solving and provide reinforcement. • Confirm good reader strategies and prompt when needed. • Observe student behavior and take notes. • Ask appropriate questions ("How did you know?").	Give all students a copy of the book to read quietly on their own, reminding them to track the print with their finger. Encourage them to use rhyming skills to figure out unknown words. Monitor student progress and prompt when necessary.
Responding and Rereading	• Return to text with students. • Conduct group reading conference. • Review and clarify reading strategy. • Provide whole-group closure activities. • Encourage retellings and rereadings. • Discuss the connection of the strategies (introduced in "Book Orientation"). • Pose open-ended questions. • Ask the students to complete extending book project or activity. • Allow students to visit literacy centers (as chosen independently or assigned).	Post a large sheet of paper nearby and record students' suggestions for rhyming words from the book. Reread the book and ask them to listen for the word pairs on the list. Write each word pair on a note card and distribute them to the students. Throughout the day, ask students to share their word pairs with the class. Students can listen to recordings of other books about sheep in the listening center.
Assessment (as necessary)	• Review observations and make necessary notes. • Maintain running records as needed. • Determine future reading needs (same stage or movement to new stage). • Involve students in self-evaluative processes, as necessary.	Administer running records to see if the students are able to attend to syntax clues while reading.

Transitional Reader Level

Leo the Late Bloomer by Robert Kraus
(Guided Reading Level: I)

Component	Strategies and Activities	Instruction
Setting the Stage	• Select four to six students for a guided reading group. • Select an appropriate book. • Give each student a copy of the book. • Familiarize yourself with the text. • Consider and select appropriate strategies. • Think through reasons for grouping students and determine who to observe. • Determine how to model strategies. • Determine any assessment needs. • Demonstrate excitement for the text.	*Leo the Late Bloomer* is a book that can help transitional readers identify the many dimensions of a character in a book.
Book Orientation	• Introduce the book and help the students set a purpose for reading. • Read and discuss the title and talk about the illustrations. • Do a "walk" through the book. • Call attention to text features. • Link the book to a similar story. • Guide a picture discussion. • Activate background knowledge. • Invite students to make appropriate predictions. • Introduce the appropriate reading strategy and discuss with students. • Introduce and discuss key vocabulary in context. • Consider some of the following: 　Use some book language. 　Remind students about print concepts. 　Point out "tricky" parts. 　Talk about some previous strategies and connect them to the text. 　Identify punctuation.	Introduce the book to the students by inviting them to look at the cover and identify Leo. Discuss what the students might know about Leo based solely on the cover illustration. Construct a character map on the chalkboard with Leo's name in the center circle, and various lines radiating from the circle. Tell students that they will be using word and picture cues to help "flesh out" the main character. Read the first four pages of text, stopping after each one to record students' suggestions on the board. Prompt each suggestion by asking students to verify each word with an illustration.
Independent Reading	• Each child reads independently at his or her own pace. • Students can "track" print with finger(s). • Assist students (as necessary) with problem-solving and provide reinforcement. • Confirm good reader strategies and prompt when needed. • Observe student behavior and take notes. • Ask appropriate questions ("How did you know?").	Ask the students to continue reading, beginning with "He was a sloppy eater." Encourage them to suggest other character traits, which will be recorded on the board. For each trait, ask, "How do you know?"
Responding and Rereading	• Return to text with students. • Conduct group reading conference. • Review and clarify reading strategy. • Provide whole-group closure activities. • Encourage retellings and rereadings. • Discuss the connection of the strategies (introduced in "Book Orientation"). • Pose open-ended questions. • Ask the students to complete extending book project or activity. • Allow students to visit literacy centers (as chosen independently or assigned).	When the students have finished reading, ask them to look at the character map. Talk about Leo's many characteristics. Conclude with the students that most characters have multiple features.
Assessment (as necessary)	• Review observations and make necessary notes. • Maintain running records as needed. • Determine future reading needs (same stage or movement to new stage). • Involve students in self-evaluative processes, as necessary.	Administer running records to see if the students are ready for more challenging material.

Fluent Reader Level

Elephants for Kids by Anthony D. Fredericks

(Guided Reading Level: M)

Component	Strategies and Activities	Instruction
Setting the Stage	• Select four to six students for a guided reading group. • Select an appropriate book. • Give each student a copy of the book. • Familiarize yourself with the text. • Consider and select appropriate strategies. • Think through reasons for grouping students and determine who to observe. • Determine how to model strategies. • Determine any assessment needs. • Demonstrate excitement for the text.	*Elephants for Kids* is an appropriate book for students at the fluent reader level. This book can help them to begin to understand the relationships that exist between background knowledge and textual knowledge.
Book Orientation	• Introduce the book and help the students set a purpose for reading. • Read and discuss the title and talk about the illustrations. • Do a "walk" through the book. • Call attention to text features. • Link the book to a similar story. • Guide a picture discussion. • Activate background knowledge. • Invite students to make appropriate predictions. • Introduce the appropriate reading strategy and discuss with students. • Introduce and discuss key vocabulary in context. • Consider some of the following: 　Use some book language. 　Remind students about print concepts. 　Point out "tricky" parts. 　Talk about some previous strategies and connect them to the text. 　Identify punctuation.	Introduce the book to the students by asking them to think about what they already know about elephants. Record their background information on a K-W-L chart. Encourage the students to think about some questions to which they would like to find the answers while reading the book. Record these on the chart as well. Ask students to flip through the book, looking at the photographs. Based on what they see, ask students what kinds of information they think they will find in this book. Record their predictions on the chart. Ask the students to read the book silently and to look for answers to their questions.
Independent Reading	• Each child reads independently at his or her own pace. • Students can "track" print with finger(s). • Assist students (as necessary) with problem-solving and provide reinforcement. • Confirm good reader strategies and prompt when needed. • Observe student behavior and take notes. • Ask appropriate questions ("How did you know?").	Each student reads his or her own copy of the book silently. Prompt when necessary.
Responding and Rereading	• Return to text with students. • Conduct group reading conference. • Review and clarify reading strategy. • Provide whole-group closure activities. • Encourage retellings and rereadings. • Discuss the connection of the strategies (introduced in "Book Orientation"). • Pose open-ended questions. • Ask the students to complete extending book project or activity. • Allow students to visit literacy centers (as chosen independently or assigned).	Ask students to share what they learned from reading this book. Record this information on the K-W-L chart. Invite students to go back to the book to locate information about any unanswered questions. Allow students to go into the writing center to develop their own book about elephants.
Assessment (as necessary)	• Review observations and make necessary notes. • Maintain running records as needed. • Determine future reading needs (same stage or movement to new stage). • Involve students in self-evaluative processes, as necessary.	Administer running records if needed to see if the students are ready for more challenging material. Provide more nonfiction material for the students.

Quick Reference Charts

The four literacy stages are summarized in the following charts. In each one you are provided with general characteristics of readers at that stage, text features typically found in books appropriate for readers at that level, instructional demonstrations, and some suggested trade books and leveled books from commercial publishers that are appropriate for children at that level.

You can duplicate these charts, paste them on sheets of oaktag or cardboard, laminate them, and keep them as a reminder and guide for the various levels that may be present in your classroom. The Reader Characteristics and Instructional Demonstrations sections can be used as reference guides for the construction of specific lessons for specific groups of students.

Emergent Readers

Reader Characteristics

- Is aware of directions (left, right, top, bottom)
- Knows that there is a match between oral and written language
- Can identify known words
- Can identify some unknown words
- Is able to use picture clues
- Knows what a letter is
- Knows what a word is
- Is able to use some letter sounds
- Is aware that print carries a message
- Has some sight vocabulary
- Is aware of patterns in text
- Recognizes some high-frequency words
- May rely on others to read new text

Text Features

- Consistent placement of text on a page
- Font and spacing between words is consistent and regular
- Match between illustrations and text
- Illustrations carry most of the content
- Uses natural language
- Taps into background knowledge of readers
- Textual language is similar to reader's oral language
- Predictable text
- Simple story line
- Some repetition of sentence pattern
- One or two lines of text on a single page

Instructional Demonstrations

- Tracking print
- Making predictions using illustrations/pictures
- Observing patterns in text
- Paying attention to initial grapho-phonemic cues in words
- Paying attention to terminal grapho-phonemic cues in words

Suggested Trade Books

Brown Bear, Brown Bear, What Do You See? by Bill Martin, Jr.
Buzz Said the Bee by Wendy Lewison
Cat on the Mat by Brian Wildsmith
The Cat Who Loved Red by Lynn Salem and Josie Stewart
The Chick and the Duckling by Mirra Ginsburg
Have You Seen My Duckling? by Nancy Tafuri
I Went Walking by Sue Williams
Lunch at the Zoo by Wendy Blaxland and Christina Brimage
Making a Memory by Margaret Ballinger
Not Enough Water by Shane Armstrong and Susan Hartley
What Has Stripes? by Margaret Ballinger

Suggested Leveled Books

A Bear Lived in a Cave (Sundance)
Animal Habitats (Sundance)
Clever Little Bird (Storyteller)
Dad's Shirt (Dominie Press)
Father Goes Fishing (Rigby)
Freddie the Frog (Rigby)
The Ghost (Wright Group)
How Many Pets? (Mondo)
I Like (Rigby)
I See (Mondo)
Is This a Monster? (Mondo)
James Is Hiding (Rigby)
Jolly Roger, the Pirate (Rigby)
Little Pig (Wright Group)
Little Red Hen (Wright Group)
There's a Mouse in the House (Mondo)
The Three Goats (Storyteller)
What Animals Eat (Sundance)
Who Lives in the Sea? (Mondo)
Winter (Storyteller)

Notes

Early Readers

Reader Characteristics

- Is aware of early reading techniques, such as directionality and letter/sound matching
- Obtains information from text
- Is in beginning stages of self-correction
- Can read some familiar text
- May read word by word
- Is aware of punctuation
- Can discuss textual information
- Uses beginning, middle, and ending sounds in words
- Has an increased familiarity with and use of sight words
- Beginning to use reading strategies independently
- Self-monitoring behaviors
- Self-correcting behaviors
- Reads text with some phrasing
- Reads text with some fluency
- Begins to read with expression
- Predicts and cross-checks

Text Features

- Illustrations provide moderate support
- Sentences are longer and more complex
- More text on a page
- Text placement may vary
- Wide variety of genres
- More characters in a story
- Text is chunked into phrases
- Spacing between words and lines is consistent
- Book language is more reflective of students' oral language

Instructional Demonstrations

- Self-correction
- Using all three cueing systems
- Problem-solving new words
- Chunking words into phrases
- Maintaining fluency
- Detecting and correcting errors
- Making predictions
- Spelling patterns
- Checking multiple sources of information
- Using high-frequency words
- Reading with phrasing
- Self-monitoring

Suggested Trade Books

Across the Stream by Mirra Ginsberg
Are You My Mommy? by Carla Dijs
Boats by Ann Rockwell
The Foot Book by Dr. Seuss
Happy Egg by Robert Kraus
Harry Takes a Bath by Harriet Ziefert
Is This You? by Ruth Krauss
Norma Jean, Jumping Bean by Joanna Cole
Nose Book by Al Perkins
The School by John Burningham
Sheep in a Jeep by Nancy Shaw
Small Pig by Arnold Lobel
Wheels on the Bus by Harriet Ziefert
Where Can It Be? by Ann Jonas

Suggested Leveled Books

Around My School (Rigby)
Bossy Bettina (Rigby)
Come for a Swim (Wright Group)
Cows in the Garden (Rigby)
Deep in the Woods (Dominie Press)
Dreams (Wright Group)
Fishing (Wright Group)
Fizz and Sputter (Wright Group)
Floppy the Hero (Oxford)
Jessie's Flower (Rigby)
The Jumble Sale (Oxford)
Sally's Red Bucket (Rigby)
Skating on Thin Ice (Troll)
T-Shirts (Richard C. Owen)
Terrible Twos (Rigby)
Three Muddy Monkeys (Wright Group)

Notes

Transitional Readers

Reader Characteristics	Text Features	Instructional Demonstrations
• Selects new text with limited support • Begins reading independently • Gathers important information about a story based on the teacher's introduction • Becomes comfortable in making predictions • Can detect and self-correct some miscues • Is able to read in longer phrases	• Introduction of chapter books • Plot is easily sequenced by reader • Book concepts (table of contents, index, glossary) are introduced • Narration and dialogue are balanced • Familiar characters	• Making predictions • "Skip it and go on" • Retelling important story parts • Reading longer sections of text • Showing awareness of structural cues • Engaging in active discussions • Phrasing and fluency • Independent reading • Growing storehouse of sight words • Following plot line • Using story maps • Graphic organizers • Character traits

Suggested Trade Books	Suggested Leveled Books	Notes
Alligators All Around by Maurice Sendak *Are You My Mother?* by Philip D. Eastman *The Awful Mess* by Ann Rockwell *Bear Shadow* by Frank Asch *The Best Older Sister* by Sook Nyul Choi *Building a House* by Byron Barton *Danny and the Dinosaur* by Syd Hoff *Fish Face* by Patricia Reilly Giff *Goodnight Moon* by Margaret Wise Brown *Green Eggs and Ham* by Dr. Seuss *If I Had an Alligator* by Mercer Mayer *Leo the Late Bloomer* by Robert Kraus *Little Bear* by Else H. Minarik *My Best Friend* by Pat Hutchins *Peter's Chair* by Ezra Jack Keats *The Quilt* by Ann Jonas *Spot's Birthday* by Eric Hill *The Three Bears* by Paul Galdone *We Are Best Friends* by Aliki	*Ben's Tooth* (Rigby) *Cow Up a Tree* (Rigby) *Dinosaurs* (Wright Group) *Gregor the Grumblesome Giant* (Rigby) *Invisible* (Rigby) *Just This Once* (Wright Group) *Let Me In* (Wright Group) *Monster* (Rigby) *Mr. Wumple's Travels* (Rigby) *Old Grizzly* (Wright Group) *Rosie at the Zoo* (Richard C. Owen) *Slugs and Snails* (Wright Group) *The Three Little Pigs* (Dominie Press) *Victor and the Martian* (Oxford)	

Fluent Readers

Reader Characteristics

- Has control over reading process
- Is able to tap into background knowledge independently
- Has confidence in integrating all three cueing systems
- Is able to read from many genres
- Uses a variety of reading strategies independently
- Is able to read silently without prompts
- Is able to predict several story events
- Begins to adjust rate to level of difficulty

Text Features

- Longer texts
- More complex language structures
- All genres of literature can be accessed
- Most meaning comes from text, rather than from illustrations
- Stories may have multiple interpretations
- More emphasis on nonfiction topics

Instructional Demonstrations

- Using K-W-L charts
- Reading charts, graphs, maps, and other visuals
- Understanding figurative language
- Writing book summaries
- Making predictions
- Problem-solving new words
- Maintaining fluency
- Determining author objectivity
- Previewing
- Recalling significant story events
- Monitoring reading
- Building sight words
- Synthesizing information

Suggested Trade Books

Amelia Bedelia (series) by Peggy Parish
Arthur's Loose Tooth by Lillian Hoban
Beans on the Roof by Betsy Byars
Beany and the Magic Crystal by Susan Wojciechowski
Blueberries for Sal by Robert McCloskey
Bunnicula by James Howe
Busybody Nora by Joanna Hurwitz
Cam Jansen (series) by David Alder
Clifford the Big Red Dog by Norman Bridwell
Corn Is Maize by Aliki
Dinosaurs Days by Joyce Milton
Elephants for Kids by Anthony D. Fredericks
Frog and Toad Together by Arnold Lobel
If You Lived in Colonial Times by Ann McGovern
Katy and the Big Snow by Virginia Lee Burton
Madeline by Ludwig Bemelmans
Nate the Great and the Fishy Prize by Marjorie Sharmat
No Jumping on the Bed! by Ted Arnold
The Stories Julian Tells by Ann Cameron

Suggested Leveled Books

Animal Reports (Sundance)
Arguments (Rigby)
The Best Birthday Present (Rigby)
Day in Town (Wright Group)
Dinosaurs on the Motorway (Wright Group)
He Who Listens (Rigby)
Honey Bees (Steck-Vaughn)
Magic All Around (Rigby)
Maui and the Sun (Richard C. Owen)
Nature's Celebration (Rigby)
Pookie and Joe (Rigby)
The Totara Tree (Wright Group)
Triceratops on the Farm (Wright Group)
What's Inside? (Wright Group)

Notes

Assessment: Running Records

Assessment Overview

To be effective, assessment must be a continuous process. It must provide teachers with data that can be used to enhance learning opportunities. Assessment is more than the traditional pen-and-paper tests of yesterday; it is more a process of reaction, reflection, and redirection. It is more than the simple administration of a test and the recording of scores. Assessment is a combination of factors and forces that should have a positive impact on children's literacy growth and development.

> *Assessment ... is more a process of reaction, reflection, and redirection.*

Following are some of the purposes of assessment as it relates to guided reading.

• Assessment is a cooperative activity between teachers and students. It is not something done *to* students, but rather an activity done *with* students.

• Assessment provides opportunities for students to assume a sense of responsibility for their own learning. When actively engaged in the assessment process, students become less teacher-dependent and more independent.

• Assessment respects the child and preserves and enhances his or her self-esteem.

• Assessment should be used to improve instruction and gauge progress; it does not simply assign numerical scores to reading achievement.

• Assessment provides opportunities for teachers and students to work toward common curricular goals, both short-term and long-term.

Effective assessment is integrated into all aspects of a guided reading program, providing both teachers and students with data useful in gauging progress and determining the effectiveness of materials and procedures. It is important to consider assessment as a positive feature of guided reading.

Administering Running Records

Running records (Clay, 1993) are a necessary and important tool for gauging a student's progress in reading. They provide information on a student's use of sources of information while engaged in the act of reading. This enables you to determine a student's reading progress and the appropriateness of reading materials for the various stages of progress.

There are several advantages of running records:

I. Running records can be used with any and all types of reading materials—fiction and nonfiction; narrative and expository; and all the genres of children's literature.

2. Running records provide valuable insights into the strategies children use while reading, and the need to reinforce some strategies while reteaching and introducing others.

3. Preparation time for using running records is minimal. All you will need is a book and a blank sheet of paper or a recording sheet (see page 81).

4. Running records can be taken frequently to assess student progress. They are grounded in the books and literature with which children are most familiar.

5. Running records can be used with either new or familiar material. While it is often preferable to use unfamiliar material, you may elect to use material that a student has used previously so that he or she becomes used to the processes and procedures of this assessment method.

6. Running records provide you with valuable information on the pattern of errors exhibited by any single child. As you might expect, children may make a random error or two when reading (particularly when reading aloud). Running records, however, enable you to detect a pattern of errors—a pattern that will have implications for a child's mastery and comprehension of that material—unlike a random error.

7. Running records allow you to collect multiple samples of a student's progress. Because there is no advance preparation necessary (in terms of materials, time, or supplies), a running record can be administered at any time. Multiple administrations of this assessment practice will provide you with more data about a student's progress than a single test.

It is important to review the three basic sources of information students use to understand text. Here is a sample piece of text:

I like to go to the beach with my family.

Source of Information	Definition	Miscue	Explanation
Meaning (M)	Students are able to understand what they read. It makes sense in terms of the events of the story as well as in terms of one's background knowledge.	"I laugh to go to the beach with my family."	The student is using a word that looks similar to *like* but does not make sense with the rest of the sentence.
Language Structure (S)	Students are able to make a match between what they read and the patterns of language to which they have been exposed. We frequently ask, "Does that sound right?"	"I likely to go to the beach with my family."	The student is not using conventional language patterns (*likely* for *like*) or the usual structure of language.
Visual/Graphophonic (V)	Students are able to make a match between the sounds of words and their written representations.	"I like to go to the shore with my family."	The student has used a word that makes sense in the sentence, but has neglected to use the proper visual information to decode the word.

Here are some things to keep in mind when administering a running record:

1. Plan for approximately five to ten minutes (depending on the complexity of the text and the student's level of proficiency) to administer a running record.

2. Select a quiet area of the room away from any distractions.

3. Select a student for whom you would like to administer a running record. (You will want to do this with all students in your room on a consistently rotating basis.)

4. Provide the student with a copy of a book that is at his or her approximate instructional level.

5. Have copies of the Running Record form (see page 81) available.

6. Sit next to the child so you can see the material as she or he reads it.

7. Introduce the child to the procedure: "I would like to have you read this book out loud for me. As you read, I will be taking some notes on this piece of paper. I may need to ask you a few questions, too. Please go ahead and begin."

8. Mark every response the student makes on the Running Record form as described in the next section.

9. Wait until the student has finished reading (or rereading) and has left the area before analyzing the results.

Reading Stage	Suggested Frequency of Running Record(s)
Emergent Reader	Every fourteen to twenty-one days
Early Reader	Every four to five weeks
Transitional Reader	Every four to five weeks
Fluent Reader	Every two months

Running Record Notations

There are several notational conventions to keep in mind as you take a running record of an individual student.

- Notate each word in a text.

- It is not necessary to record or write down the text.

- Indicate each word read correctly with a check mark (✓).

- Record the check marks in the same way they are arranged on the page. For example, if there were four words on a line of text and the student read each of those words correctly, you would record four check marks (✓ ✓ ✓ ✓).

- For each new line of text, begin a new line of check marks.

- Record the page number for each line of text so that you can refer back to it later, if necessary.

- If there is an error, record what the child says above the line and what the text says below the line.

Below is an example of three lines of text from the book *Zebras* by Anthony D. Fredericks (Minneapolis, MN: Lerner, 2001; Level: Fluent) and how a student would accurately read them.

The chart on the following page provides you with conventional notations to use while taking a running record. You are encouraged to duplicate this page, laminate it and have it available nearby while administering a running record to a student—particularly as you begin using this assessment technique.

Page	Text	Running Record
14	Stripes help zebras find each other in a herd.	✓ ✓ ✓ ✓ ✓ ✓ ✓ ✓ ✓
14	This helps the herd stay together.	✓ ✓ ✓ ✓ ✓ ✓
14	Zebras take good care of each other.	✓ ✓ ✓ ✓ ✓ ✓ ✓

Notations to Use in Recording
a Child's Oral Reading

Accurate Reading	No error	$\dfrac{\text{child}}{\text{text}}$	✔
Substitution	One error	$\dfrac{\text{child}}{\text{text}}$	$\dfrac{\text{bad}}{\text{bald}}$
Omission	One error	$\dfrac{\text{child}}{\text{text}}$	$\dfrac{—}{\text{for}}$
Insertion	One error	$\dfrac{\text{child}}{\text{text}}$	$\dfrac{\wedge\text{over}}{—}$
Attempt	One error	$\dfrac{\text{child}}{\text{text}}$	$\dfrac{\text{ti– i– me}}{\text{time}}$
Self-correction	No error	$\dfrac{\text{child}}{\text{text}}$	$\dfrac{\text{dorp }^{\text{SC}}}{\text{drop}}$
Repetition	No error	$\dfrac{\text{child}}{\text{text}}$	$\dfrac{✔R}{\text{carry}}$
Skip and return	No error	$\dfrac{\text{child}}{\text{text}}$	$\dfrac{^{\text{SK}}}{\text{several}}$
Asks for help	One error	$\dfrac{\text{child}}{\text{text}}$	$\dfrac{^{\text{A}}}{\text{pairs}}$
Told the word	One error	$\dfrac{\text{child}}{\text{text}}$	$\dfrac{}{\text{famous }^{\text{T}}}$
Try again	One error	$\dfrac{\text{child}}{\text{text}}$	$\left[\dfrac{\text{funny how}}{\text{farmer's hat}}\right]^{\text{TA}}$
Teacher prompt	One error	$\dfrac{\text{child}}{\text{text}}$	$\dfrac{\text{rock }^{\text{TP}}}{\text{rain}}$

Following is a list of the different types of reading behaviors students may demonstrate while engaged in oral reading:

Note: The text samples are from *Under One Rock: Bugs, Slugs and Other Ughs* by Anthony D. Fredericks (Nevada City, CA: Dawn Publications, 2001; Level: Fluent).

Substitution

A Substitution occurs when a child reads a word that is different from that in the text. Record the textual word and record the word the child says above the line.

CHILD: ✓   ✓ ✓   farm
_____
TEXT: Here is a field.

Record only one error, no matter how many times the child reads the word incorrectly.

Omission

An Omission occurs when a child omits a word from the text. Omissions are recorded with a dash (—).

CHILD: ✓   ✓   —   ✓
_____
TEXT: He lifted the rock.

Insertion

When a child inserts a word that does not appear in the text, he or she has made an Insertion. Record it by writing the spoken word over the line in the sentence where the insertion occured.

CHILD   ✓   ✓   ✓ ˄big ✓
_____
TEXT   This is the   rock.

Attempt

A child has made an Attempt when he or she tried to read the word, but was unsuccessful. Record it by writing the actual attempt above the line.

CHILD: ✓   ✓   ✓   raw…
_____
TEXT: He lifted the rock.

Each Attempt at the same word is counted only as one error. If the child later self-corrects, it does not count as an error.

Self-correction

A child Self-corrects when he or she substitutes a word for one in the text and then makes a correction. Record it with the letters SC.

CHILD: ✓   ✓   ✓   happy sc ✓
_____
TEXT: There are one hundred ants.

Self-corrections are important signals that the child is monitoring his or her reading. They are not counted as errors.

Repetition

This occurs when a child repeats a word or a group of words. If a student repeats more than once, it can be recorded as R2, R3, etc.

CHILD: ✓   ✓R   ✓   ✓   ✓

TEXT: The   big   rock   is   gray.

Repetitions are not counted as errors.

Skip and Return

This occurs when a child tries to read a word but is unsuccessful. He or she may continue to read some more and then figure out the word from the context of the material. He or she may come back and read the word correctly. Skip and Return is a form of self-correction.

CHILD: ✓   ✓   ✓   SK

TEXT: This   is   the   spider.

A Skip and Return is not counted as an error.

Asks for Help

This occurs when a child struggles with a word and then asks for assistance. Record this with a capital A.

CHILD: ✓   ✓   ✓   A   ✓

TEXT: This   is   the   shiny   beetle.

This is counted as a single error.

Told the Word

At times it may be necessary to tell a child what a specific word is so that he or she can maintain the flow of the story. Some students may hesitate over a single word and thus lose the intent of the story. You may need to supply that word for him or her. This error is designated by a capital T.

CHILD: ✓   ✓   ✓   ✓   —   ✓

TEXT: They   live   in   a   dark T   place.

This is counted as a single error (even if the child must be told the same word several times).

Try Again

Sometimes it may be necessary to invite a student to attempt a word or part of a sentence one or more times. This is particularly true if the rest of the story depends on reading a preceding section correctly. You may decide to have a student go back and attempt a previous word, phrase, or section again. Record this by placing brackets around the section to be attempted again and by writing TA.

CHILD: ✓   │funny clowns│ TA ✓

TEXT: Some   │field crickets│   sing.

A Try Again is recorded as a single error (no matter how many words there are in the attempt).

Teacher Prompt

Occasionally, it may be necessary for you to prompt a student to use one or more sources of information to read a word. If a child makes an attempt, but is unable to self-correct, then it may be necessary to prompt him or her to look at the meaning (M) ("Did that make sense?"), the language structure (S) ("Does that sound right?"), or visual/graphophonic (V) elements ("Does it look right?"). Record this error by using a TP immediately after the student word.

CHILD:	✓	home TP	✓	✓
TEXT:	The	house	was	big.

A Teacher Prompt is counted as a single error.

When taking running records, intervene as little as possible. You want to get an accurate picture of the child's overall reading ability. There may be times, however, that it is necessary to assist a child so that the entire meaning or reading of a text is not lost. This is a judgment call and will depend on your knowledge of the students in your class, their individual rates of progression, and the stages of reading they are in or are ready for. This is a subjective judgment that you will need to make.

It's important to keep in mind that your expertise in conducting running records will come with time and practice. The more you use them, the more comfortable you will be in assessing the reading progress of your students. It is equally important that you invite students into this process. Help them see that running records are a normal and natural part of the overall reading program. They need to know that this assessment tool is not designed to determine how much they don't know, but rather how much they have progressed within the guided reading program. To that end, you are invited to share the results of these assessments with your students and engage them wholeheartedly in monitoring their own reading progress. Engaging students in open-ended discussions about the results of a running record and inviting their input will ensure the successful implementation of these tools as valid and valuable gauges of reading performance.

Scoring Running Records

To score a running record, there are two factors that are essential to a proper interpretation: error rate and self-corrections. The error rate is the number of errors a student makes while reading a piece of text. Self-corrections are the number of self-corrections a child makes (on his or her own) while reading. Knowing the error rate and the number of self-corrections will help you place students in the proper reading materials in addition to tracking their progress through those materials.

The error rate tells you the number of mistakes made per X number of words read. It can be easily computed by dividing the number of running words (the total number of words in a book) by the total number of errors. For example, if there are 127 running words in a book and a child makes 6 errors while reading that book, then the computation would be as follows;

$$\frac{RW}{E} = \frac{127}{6} = 21$$

RW	The exact number of *running words* in a reading selection or book
E	The number of *errors* a child makes while reading (from the beginning of the book to the end)
SC	The number of times a child *self-corrects* while reading a book or text

That means that this particular child made one error for every twenty-one words read (in your calculations rounded off to the nearest whole number). You may wish to express the error rate as a ratio—for example, 1:21.

Next, convert the error rate to an accuracy rate. The accuracy rate will help you determine the appropriateness of that particular level of reading material for instructional purposes. Using the example, we can convert the error rate to an accuracy rate with the following calculations:

$$\frac{(RW - E)}{E} \times 100 = \frac{(127 - 6)}{127} \times 100 = 95\%$$

You can now use the accuracy rate to determine the appropriateness of the reading material for that specific child. Use the following chart:

Easy/Independent Reading Level	95%–100%
Instructional Reading Level	90%–94%
Frustration/Difficult Reading Level	89% or below

For the child in the above example, he or she would find that material to be at his or her Easy/Independent Reading Level (95%).

The following page contains a simple conversion chart.

Accuracy Rate	Reading Level
99% 98% 97% 96% 95%	**Easy/Independent Reading Level** (Can be read independently)
94% 93% 92% 91% 90%	**Instructional Reading Level** (Guided reading level)
89% 88% 87% 86% 85%	**Frustration/Difficult Reading Level** (Can be used for read-alouds)

Self-correction Conversion Chart

Self-correction Rate	Interpretation
1:1 1:2 1:3 1:4	The child is self-monitoring his or her own reading.
1:5 1:6 1:7 1:8 1:9 1:10	Child needs instructional assistance with the material.

The self-correction rate provides you with valuable data on how often a child corrected errors while reading.

Using the sample student above (who made three self-corrections), the following calculations would be:

$$\frac{(E + SC)}{SC} = \frac{(6 + 3)}{3} = \frac{9}{3} = 3$$

In this particular example, the self-correction rate is 1:3—the child is correcting one out of every three errors. The following Self-correction Conversion Chart will help you interpret this piece of data.

Running records can provide information that is critical for placing students in appropriate reading materials, as well as assessing their progress through those materials. An analysis of students' errors will offer insights into the specific skills and/or strategies (see Unit 8) they may need as well as information about how well they're using the strategies you've taught them.

Running records provide an assessment of progress over time. You will be able to denote difficulties as well as successes and thus be better able to tailor your instruction (and the materials used) to the reading needs of individual students. You will be able to work alongside your students to help them through the stages of reading.

Running Record

Name: _____ **Date:** _____

Stage (circle one): Emergent Reader   Early Reader   Transitional Reader   Fluent Reader

Book Title: _____

Guided Reading Level: _____ **Reading Recovery® Level:** _____

(circle)

Page No.	Line	E (#)	SC (#)	Cues E	Cues SC
				M S V	M S V
				M S V	M S V
				M S V	M S V
				M S V	M S V
				M S V	M S V
				M S V	M S V
				M S V	M S V
				M S V	M S V
				M S V	M S V
				M S V	M S V
				M S V	M S V
				M S V	M S V
Totals:				

Accuracy Rate: Running Words = _____ = _____%

Errors

☐ Easy Reading Level (95%–100%)
☐ Instructional Reading Level (90%–94%)
☐ Frustration Reading Level (89% and below)

Self-correction Rate: _____

☐ Self-monitoring (1:1–1:4)
☐ Needs instructional assistance (1:5 and above)

Comments and Observations:

Matching Books and Readers

Book Leveling Systems

This book is designed to provide you with the specific tools you need to successfully implement and promote guided reading throughout your reading curriculum. One element that will have a significant impact on the success of your program is the match between books and students. By matching the reading ability of students with the reading level of books, you can help ensure that students are working with materials that are appropriate for their instructional needs. As students' reading abilities increase, you can match them with increasingly more challenging books.

Starting on page 85, you will find various lists of books that are appropriate for guided reading. These books have been selected from trade book lists and guided reading publisher sets. They have been assigned to one of the stages of reading development. For comparison purposes, you may wish to consult the chart on the following page, Book Leveling Systems, which provides comparative information on the leveling of these titles.

In determining the appropriate and proper placement of a book within a specific stage of reading development, several significant factors were considered. These included:

- The vocabulary level of the book

- The length of the book (number of words and number of pages)

- The number of illustrations in relation to the amount of text

- The level of difficulty of the concepts

- The format of a book (typography, text layout, etc.)

- The structure of language (sentence structure, repetition, natural language)

- The content of the book (relationship to background knowledge)

Although these books have been assigned to a specific list, it is important for you to consider students' personal factors when selecting the reading material for them. These include, but are not limited to:

- Interest level

- Background knowledge

- Motivation to learn from text

- Favorite authors and book characters

The consideration of these factors personalizes the matching of reader to material. This is done, not just in terms of grade-level designations, but also in terms of the needs, interests, and attitudes of individual readers in your classroom.

Consider these lists of books as evolving lists. You should feel free to add your own favorite titles to these lists on an ongoing basis. Work with other colleagues to add to these lists throughout the school year. Stay in touch with the school librarian as well as the children's department at your local public library for suggestions. Visit your local bookstore to stay up to date on the latest publications and most current literature. Attend seminars, workshops, and conferences on reading or children's literature to get ideas and suggestions on the availability and use of new titles.

The lists designate titles that are appropriate for students at specific ability levels to read in a guided reading program. That does not mean that they cannot be used in other arenas of the overall reading program. For example, you will discover titles appropriate for reading aloud as well as other titles

that students can self-select for sustained silent reading. The important thing to keep in mind is that you must expose students to a wide range of books across the entire reading curriculum. These lists can be appropriate starting points for the various dimensions of your reading program and individual students within your classroom.

Book Leveling Systems: A Comparison Chart

Guided Reading in Grades K–2	Grade Level	Traditional Basal Level	Guided Reading (Fountas & Pinnell, 1996)	Reading Recovery®
Emergent	K	Readiness	A	1
Reader	K, 1		B	2
	K, 1	PP1	C	3
				4
	1	PP2	D	5
				6
Early Reader	1	PP3	E	7
				8
	1	Primer	F	9
				10
	1		G	11
				12
Transitional	1	Grade 1	H	13
Reader				14
	1, 2		I	15
				16
				17
	2	Grade 2	J	18
				19
Fluent Reader	2		K	20
	2		L	
	2, 3		M	
	3	Grade 3	N	

Basal Readers and Guided Reading

One of the concerns teachers have when implementing a guided reading program is the availability of appropriate reading materials. Several commercial publishers have created and published extensive collections of leveled books for use in guided reading programs. Although the purchase of all these collections would be financially impossible, you can still have an effective guided reading program with minimal funds.

One answer may lie in your bookcase—the ever-present basal readers. These traditional textbooks are filled with a wide array of stories, tales, legends, narratives, and expository writing. Whereas basal readers of years past contained brief chunks of excerpted stories and formula writing, the basals of today are rich in complete works of children's literature in an array of genres.

For the clearest and most thorough description of how to use basal readers as a major component of your guided reading program, consult Fawson and Reutzel's article, "But I Only Have a Basal: Implementing Guided Reading in the Early Grades," in the September 2000 issue of *The Reading Teacher*. The article contains a complete listing of leveled stories within five major basal series in Grades K–2: those from Harcourt Brace, Silver Burdett Ginn, Houghton Mifflin, Scott Foresman, and Scholastic.

Leveled Books–Emergent Readers

Title	Fountas and Pinnell	Reading Recovery® Level	Words	Author	Publisher/Series
All Fall Down	C		72	Wildsmith, Brian	Oxford University Press
Animal Habitats	C	3	73	Sloan, Peter and Cheryl	Sundance/Little Red Readers
Animal Homes	B	2	48	Sloan, Peter and Cheryl	Sundance/Little Red Readers
Apples	C		45	Williams, Deborah	Kaeden Books
The Aquarium	C		18	Kloes, Carol	Kaeden Books
Astronaut	B		22	Hoenecke, Karen	Kaeden Books
At the Farm	C	2	52	Sloan, Peter and Cheryl	Sundance/Little Red Readers
At the Playground	C	4	86	Sloan, Peter and Cheryl	Sundance/Little Red Readers
At the Truckstop	C		25	Kloes, Carol	Kaeden Books
At the Wildlife Park	B	2	34	Sloan, Peter and Cheryl	Sundance/Little Red Readers
At the Zoo	C	3	73	Sloan, Peter and Cheryl	Sundance/Little Red Readers
At the Zoo	B	2	40	Randell, Beverly	Rigby/PM Starters
Baby Chimp	A	1	14		Wright Group/Twig
The Baby Owls	C	4	90	Randell, Beverly	Rigby/PM Extensions
Baby Says	C		26	Steptoe, John	William Morrow & Co.
Bags, Cans, Pots, and Pans	C	4	56		Modern Curriculum Press/ Ready Readers
The Bath	A	1	14		Modern Curriculum Press/ Ready Readers
The Bear	B	2	17		Dominie Press/ Carousel Earlybirds
Ben's Pets	C	3	30		Modern Curriculum Press/ Ready Readers
Big and Little	B	2	40		Dominie Press/ Carousel Earlybirds

Title	Fountas and Pinnell	Reading Recovery® Level	Words	Author	Publisher/Series
Big Things	A	2	33	Randell, Beverly	Rigby/PM Starters
The Bike	A	1	14		Wright Group/Twig
The Birthday Cake	A	1	22		Wright Group/Sunshine
Birthday Cakes	B	4	95		Sundance/AlphaKids
Birthday Candles	C	3	52		Dominie Press/Carousel Readers
Bo and Peter	C		45	Franco, Betsy	Scholastic
Boots	C		57	Schreiber, Anne, and Doughty, Arbo	Scholastic
Brown Bear, Brown Bear, What Do You See?	C		185	Martin, Bill Jr.	Henry Holt
Bubble Gum	B	2	21		Dominie Press/Carousel Readers
The Bumper Cars	C	4	94	Randell, Beverly	Rigby/PM Extensions
The Bus Ride	C	3	164		Celebration Press/Little Celebrations
Butterfly	B	3	39		Sundance/AlphaKids
Can I Have a Lick?	C	4	69		Dominie Press/Carousel Readers
Can You See Me?	A	1	34		Sundance/AlphaKids
The Car Ride	A	2	41	Sloan, Peter and Cheryl	Sundance/Little Red Readers
Cat and Dog	C	3	71		Creative Teaching Press/Learn to Read
Cat on the Mat	B	2	37	Wildsmith, Brian	Oxford University Press
Cats	C		45	Williams, Deborah	Kaeden Books
Chicken Soup	B		38	Fitros, Pamela	Kaeden Books
The Circus Train	A	1	48	Sloan, Peter and Cherly	Sundance/Little Red Readers
The Clown	B		29	Urmston, Kathleen, and Evans, Karen	Kaeden Books

Title	Fountas and Pinnell	Reading Recovery® Level	Words	Author	Publisher/Series
Colors in the City	B		61	Urmston, Kathleen and Evans, Karen	Kaeden Books
Copycat			54		Wright Group/Story Box
Dan the Flying Man	C	4	60		Wright Group/ Read Togethers
The Desert	C	3	34		Dominie Press/ Carousel Readers
Do You Want to Be My Friend?	A		8	Carle, Eric	The Penguin Group
Dog	A				Scholastic/ Guided Reading Program
Dogs	A	1	34		Sundance/AlphaKids
Don't Splash Me!	A	1	24	Randell, Beverly	Rigby/Windmill
Dressing Up	A	1	12	Avery, Dorothy	Rigby/PM Starters
The Farm	A	1	14		Modern Curriculum Press/Ready Readers
Flowers	A		27	Hoenecke, Karen	Kaeden Books
Flying and Floating	B	3	64	Sloan, Peter and Cheryl	Sundance/Little Red Readers
Four Ice Creams	C	4	61	Giles, Jenny	Rigby/PM Starters
The Fox on the Box	C		36	Gregorich, Barbara	School Zone
The Fox	C	4	24		Richard C. Owen/ Books for Young Learners
Fruit Salad	A	1	22		Sundance/AlphaKids
Ghost	A	1	26		Wright Group/Story Box
The Giant	A	1	20		Dominie Press/Joy Readers
Glasses	A	1	24		Sundance/AlphaKids
Going Shopping	B	5	105		Sundance/AlphaKids
Going to Grandpa's	C		37	Frankford, Marilyn	Kaeden Books
Grandpa's House	A	2	47		Sundance/AlphaKids
Halloween Mask for Monster	C			Mueller, Virginia	Whitman

Title	Fountas and Pinnell	Reading Recovery® Level	Words	Author	Publisher/Series
Hats	B		46	Williams, Deborah	Kaeden Books
Hats Around the World	B		59	Charlesworth, Liza	Scholastic
Have You Seen My Cat?	B	2	93	Carle, Eric	Scholastic
Have You Seen My Duckling?	B	2	28	Tafuri, Nancy	Greenwillow
Here's Skipper	B		28	Salem, Lynn, and Stewart, Josie	Seedling
Honk!	B	2	36	Smith, Sue	Mondo/Bookshop
How Many Fish?	B		30	Gossett, Rachel, and Ballinger, Margaret	Scholastic
How to Make Snack Mix	C		47	Oppenlander, Meredith	Kaeden Books
I Am	A				Scholastic/ Guided Reading Program
I Am Thankful	A	1	42		Dominie Press/ Carousel Earlybirds
I Can Draw	C	4	75		Dominie Press/ Carousel Earlybirds
I Can Make Music	B	2	41	Sloan, Peter and Cheryl	Sundance/Little Red Readers
I Can See	A				Scholastic/ Guided Reading Program
I Can Wash	C	4	66		Dominie Press/ Carousel Earlybirds
I Can Write, Can You?	B	2	30	Stewart, Josie, and Salem, Lynn	Seedling
I Can't Find My Roller Skates	B	5	73		Sundance/Alphakids
I Have a Watch!	C		60	Williams, Deborah	Kaeden Books
I Like	C	3	24	Butler, Andrea	Rigby/Literacy 2000
I Like	A				Scholastic/ Guided Reading Program
I Like Balloons	A	1	27		Dominie Press/ Reading Corners
I Like Shapes	B		21	Armstrong, Shane	Scholastic

Title	Fountas and Pinnell	Reading Recovery® Level	Words	Author	Publisher/Series
I Like to Count	C	3	40		Modern Curriculum Press/Ready Readers
I Like to Eat	A	1	41		Dominie Press/Reading Corners
I Like to Paint	A	1	29		Dominie Press/Reading Corners
I Like to Play	C	3	50		Dominie Press/Carousel Readers
I Love My Family	B	3	31		Wright Group/Sunshine
I Paint	A	2	22	Barker, Andrea	Rigby/Literacy Tree
I Read	A	1	38		Dominie Press/Reading Corners
I See	B	2	29		Mondo/Bookshop
I See Monkeys	C		39	Williams, Deborah	Kaeden Books
I Want a Pet	C		46	Gregorich, Barbara	School Zone
I Went Walking	C	4	105	Williams, Sue	Harcourt
I'm Brave	A	2	35		Sundance/AlphaKids
I'm Hungry	B		25	Fitros, Pamela	Kaeden Books
Ice Cream	A	1	41		Sundance/AlphaKids
In My Garden	C	3	36		Dominie Press/Carousel Readers
In the City	C		45	Pasternac, Susana	Scholastic
In the Forest	B				Scholastic/Guided Reading Program
In the Woods	B	2	48		Mondo/Bookshop
Is It Time?	C		52		Scholastic/Reading Discovery
Is It Time?	C		52	Campbell, J. G.	Scholastic
It's Football Time	C		24	Geddes, Diana	Kaeden Books
James Is Hiding	A	1	24	Randell, Beverly	Rigby/Windmill
Jolly Roger, the Pirate	D	6	138	Randell, Beverly	Rigby/PM Extensions
Leaves	C		29	Hoenecke, Karen	Kaeden Books

Title	Fountas and Pinnell	Reading Recovery® Level	Words	Author	Publisher/Series
Legs	A				Scholastic/ Guided Reading Program
Legs, Legs, Legs	A		15	Gossett, Rachel, and Ballinger, Margaret	Scholastic
Let's Move	B	2	29		Modern Curriculum Press/Ready Readers
The Library	C	3	33		Dominie Press/ Carousel Readers
Little Pig	C	4	63		Wright Group/Story Box
Little Red Hen	B	2	87		Wright Group/Windmill
Little Sister	C		40	Mitchell, Robin	Scholastic
Living and Non-Living	A	2	30		Sundance/AlphaKids
Lizard Loses His Tail	D	5	54	Randell, Beverly	Rigby/PM Story Books
Look at This	B	2	57		Dominie Press/ Carousel Earlybirds
Look What I Can Do	A		15	Aruego, Jose	Macmillan
Looking for Frog	B	5	185		Sundance/AlphaKids
Looking for Halloween	C		49	Urmston, Kathleen, and Evans, Karen	Kaeden Books
The Lost Mother	C	6	108		Sundance/AlphaKids
Lunch	A			Urmston, Kathleen, and Evans, Karen	Schloastic/ Guided Reading Program
Lunch at the Zoo	B		64		Scholastic/Reading Discovery
The Mailbox	B	3	46		Sundance/AlphaKids
Making Butter	B	4	106		Sundance/AlphaKids
Making Lunch	B	5	131		Sundance/AlphaKids
Making Mountains	B		35	Ballinger, Margaret, and Gossett, Rachel	Scholastic.
Marching Band	B		35	Urmston, Kathleen, and Evans, Karen	Kaeden Books
Me	A	1	24	Randell, Beverly	Rigby/PM Starters
Me (boy)	C		34	Tonon, Terry	Kaeden Books

Title	Fountas and Pinnell	Reading Recovery® Level	Words	Author	Publisher/Series
Me (girl)	C		34	Tonon, Terry	Kaeden Books
The Merry Go Round	C	4	66		Dominie Press/ Teacher's Choice
The Merry Go Round	C	3	84	Randell, Beverly	Rigby/PM Story Books
Mommy, Where Are You?	B		64	Ziefert, Harriet, and Boon, Emilie	Puffin Books
Monkeys	B		27	Canizares, Susan, and Chanko, P.	Scholastic
Monsters	B	3	93		Sundance/AlphaKids
Mother and Me	B		48	Spinelle, Nancy Louise	Kaeden Books
Moving	B	3	56	Sloan, Peter and Cheryl	Sundance/Little Red Readers
Mrs. Cook's Hats	C		31	Mader, Jan	Kaeden Books
Mrs. Wishy-Washy's Tub	B		38		Wright Group/Story Box
My Baby Sister	A	2	50		Sundance/ AlphaKids
My Book	A		17	Maris, Ron	Viking
My Cat Muffin	B		35	Gardner, Marjory	Scholastic
My Cats	A				Scholastic/ Guided Reading Program
My Circus Family	C	3	42	Lake, Mary Dixon	Mondo/Bookshop
My Class	A		14	Stewart, Josie, and Salem, Lynn	Seedling
My Day	C		51	Barney, Mike	Kaeden Books
My Dream	C		34	Wildsmith, Brian	Oxford University Press
My Home	B	2	56		Wright Group/Sunshine
My House	A	1	40		Dominie Press/ Carousel Earlybirds
My Kite	C		37	Williams, Deborah	Kaeden Books
My Little Brother	C	3	59		Wright Group/Windmill
My Little Dog	C	4	90	Cason, Sue	Rigby/PM Starters

Title	Fountas and Pinnell	Reading Recovery® Level	Words	Author	Publisher/Series
My Monster and Me	B	2	37		Modern Curriculum Press/Ready Readers
Now We Can Go	C			Jonas, Ann	Greenwillow
One for You, One for Me	C		27	Blaxland, Wendy	Scholastic
One Pig, Two Pigs	B	2	142		Peguis/Tiger Club
Our Dog Sam	C	5	56	Bacon, Ron	Rigby/Literacy Tree
Over the Bridge	B	3	50	Sloan, Peter and Cheryl	Sundance/Little Red Reader
The Party	B	3	61		Sundance/AlphaKids
Pat's Perfect Pizza	C	3	37		Modern Curriculum Press/Ready Readers
Pigs Peek	C	4	28		Richard C. Owen/Books for Young Learners
Places	C	4	88	Sloan, Peter and Cheryl	Sundance/Little Red Readers
Plants	B	5	122		Sundance/AlphaKids
Playhouse for Monster	C			Mueller, Virginia	Whitman
Playing	A	1	31		Sundance/AlphaKids
The Race	B	2	34	Randell, Beverly	Rigby/Windmill
Rain	B	4	140		Sundance/AlphaKids
Rain	C		56	Kalan, Robert	Greenwillow
Rainbow of My Own	C		268	Freeman, Don	The Penguin Group
Raindrops	C		66	Gay, Sandy	Scholastic
Roll Over!	C		201	Peek, Merle	Clarion
The Royal Family	A		17	Stewart, Josie, and Salem, Lynn	Seedling
Runaway Monkey	B		39	Stewart, Josie, and Salem, Lynn	Seedling
Sammy at the Farm	C	6	83	Urmston, Kathleen, and Evans, Karen	Kaeden Books

Title	Fountas and Pinnell	Reading Recovery® Level	Words	Author	Publisher/Series
Sandwiches	A	2	59		Sundance/AlphaKids
Scary Monster	C		19	Eifrig, Kate	Kaeden Books
Shapes	A		24	Urmston, Kathleen, and Evans, Karen	Kaeden Books
Shark in a Sack	C	4	65		Wright Group/Sunshine
Shopping	C	4	78	Sloan, Peter and Cheryl	Sundance/Little Red Readers
Sleeping Animals	C	6	193		Sundance/AlphaKids
Snow	B		33	Hoenecke, Karen	Kaeden Books
Spaceship	B		27	Hoenecke, Karen	Kaeden Books
Spots, Feathers and Curly Tails	C			Tafuri, Nancy	William Morrow & Co.
Springs	C	6	128		Sundance/AlphaKids
Story Time	C		32		Modern Curriculum Press/ Emergent/Set 2
Sunburn	B		48	Prokopchak, Ann	Kaeden Books
Swing, Swing, Swing	C		93	Tuchman, Gail	Scholastic
Tadpoles and Frogs	B	5	41		Sundance/AlphaKids
Taking Pictures	C	6	137		Sundance/AlphaKids
Terrific Shoes	C	3	19		Modern Curriculum Press/Ready Readers
That Fly	C	3	29		Modern Curriculum Press/Ready Readers
Things on Wheels	C	3	69	Sloan, Peter and Cheryl	Sundance/Little Red Readers
This Game	B	2	63		Dominie Press/ Carousel Early Birds
Tickling	B	4	74		Sundance/AlphaKids
Too Busy	B	3	50		Sundance/AlphaKids
Toot, Toot	C		47	Wildsmith, Brian	Oxford University Press
The Transportation Museum	C	4	79	Sloan, Peter and Cheryl	Sundance/Little Red Readers

Title	Fountas and Pinnell	Reading Recovery® Level	Words	Author	Publisher/Series
A Tree Fell Over the River	C	3	72	Sloan, Peter and Cheryl	Sundance/Little Red Readers
The Tree	C	6	94		Sundance/AlphaKids
A Trip to the Aquarium	C		18	Kloes, Carol	Kaeden Books
The Trolley Ride	C	4	87		Rigby/Tadpoles
The Truck Stop	C		25	Kloes, Carol	Kaeden Books
Twins	B	4	76		Sundance/AlphaKids
Two Points	B	2	40	Kennedy, Jane, and Eaton, Audrey	Seedling
Up in a Tree	C	4	47		Wright Group/Sunshine
Up Went the Goat	C		38	Gregorich, Barbara	School Zone
The Way I Go to School	B	2	53	Randell, Beverly	Rigby/PM Starters
We Go to School	B	2	27		Dominie Press/Carousel Earlybirds
We Like Fruit	A				Scholastic/Guided Reading Program
We Need Trees	C		33	Hoenecke, Karen	Kaeden Books
We Went to the Zoo	B	2	32	Sloan, Peter and Cheryl	Sundance/Little Red Readers
Weather	C		54	Chanko, P., and Morton, D.	Scholastic
We Like to Graph	C		48	Coulton, Mia	Kaeden Books
What a Tale!	C		38	Wildsmith, Brian	Oxford University Press
What Am I?	C		51	Williams, Deborah	Kaeden Books
What Comes Out at Night?	B	2	48	Sloan, Peter and Cheryl	Sundance/Little Red Readers
What Do Insects Do?	A		24	Canizares, Susan, and Chanko, P.	Scholastic
What Has Stripes?	C		28	Ballinger, Margaret	Scholastic
What Has Wheels?	A		28	Hoenecke, Karen	Kaeden Books

Title	Fountas and Pinnell	Reading Recovery® Level	Words	Author	Publisher/Series
What I Like at School	C	3	64	Sloan, Peter and Cheryl	Sundance/ Little Red Readers
What Is Green?	B	2	30		Dominie Press/ Carousel Readers
What's for Dinner?	B	3	38		Sundance/AlphaKids
What's for Dinner?	B		35	Hoenecke, Karen	Kaeden Books
What's for Lunch?	C		48	Carle, Eric	Scholastic
What's Inside?	C		47	Hoenecke, Karen	Kaeden Books
What's That Noise?	B	4	102		Sundance/AlphaKids
What's This, What's That?	A	2	35		Sundance/AlphaKids
When the Circus Comes to Town	A	2	40	Sloan, Peter and Cheryl	Sundance/Little Red Readers
Where Are the Car Keys?	B	2	36	Randell, Beverly	Rigby/Windmill
Where Are We?	B	2	72		Pioneer Valley/ Early Emergent/Set 1
Where Does the Teacher Sleep?	C		50	Gibson, Kathleen	Seedling
Where's the Baby?	C	6	138		Sundance/AlphaKids
Where's the Halloween Treat?	C		102	Ziefert, Harriet	The Penguin Group
Who Can?	B	2	35		Mondo/Bookshop
Who Lives In a Tree?	B		46		Scholastic/ Guided Reading Program
Who Lives in the Arctic?	B		48		Scholastic/ Guided Reading Program
Who Lives in the Sea?	B	2	69		Mondo/Bookshop
Who Made That?	C	3	31		Modern Curriculum Press/Ready Readers
Who Will Help?	B	2	20		Dominie Press/ Carousel Readers
Zippers	C	3	21		Richard C. Owen/ Books for Young Learners

Leveled Books–Early Readers

Title	Fountas and Pinnell	Reading Recovery® Level	Words	Author	Publisher/Series
1 Is for One	E	7–8	82	Wheatley, Nadia	Mondo/ Bookshop
All About You	G		250+	Anholt, Catherine and Laurence	Puffin
All by Myself	E		157	Mayer, Mercer	Golden
All Over the World	E		82	Jones, D.	Seedling
Alligator Shoes	G		122	Dorros, Arthur	Dutton
Amanda's Bear	G	12	154		Dominie Press/ Reading Corners
Amy Loves the Snow	F		127	Hoban, Julia	Harper/Collins
Amy Loves the Sun	F		122	Hoban, Julia	Harper/Collins
Amy Loves the Wind	F		116	Hoban, Julia	Harper/Collins
Animal Babies	E	8	114	Hamsa, Bobbie	Childrens Press/ Rookie Reader
Animal Shapes	D		14	Wildsmith, Brian	Oxford University Press
Animals at the Zoo	F	10	158	Greydanus, Rose	Troll/First Start
Apple Tree Apple Tree	G		340	Blocksma, Mary	Childrens Press
Are You My Mommy?	F		112	Dijs, Carla	Simon & Schuster
Are You There, Bear?	F			Maris, Ron	Viking Press
Art	E	12	238		Sundance/AlphaKids
The Artist	F	9	83	Podoshen, Lois	Richard C. Owen/ Books for Young Learners
Ask Nicely	F	10	110	Cartwright, Pauline	Rigby/ Literacy 2000
At the Park	D		37	Hoenecke, Karen	Kaeden Books
Awful Waffles	G		296	Williams, D. H.	Seedling
The Baby	E		60	Burningham, John	Crowell
Bandages	F		139	Moskowitz, Ellen	Kaeden Books
Baseball Fun	E		51	Geddes, Diana	Kaeden Books
A Bath for Patches	E	8	86		Dominie Press/ Carousel Readers

Title	Fountas and Pinnell	Reading Recovery® Level	Words	Author	Publisher/Series
Beaks and Feet	D	11	244	O'Neil, Sarah	Sundance/AlphaKids
Bears in the Night	D		108	Berenstain, Stan and Jan	Random House
Bears on Wheels	D		89	Berenstain, Stan and Jan	Random House
Beautiful Bugs	F		69	Fleming, Maria	Scholastic/ Guided Reading Program
Beep, Beep	F		51	Gregorich, Barbara	School Zone
Best Birthday Mole Ever Had	E	8–9	252		Modern Curriculum Press/ Ready Readers
Best Friends	E		31	Fitros, Pamela	Kaeden Books
Betsy the Babysitter	F	10	115	Crawford, T.	Troll/First Start
Big Bird's Copycat Day	F		232	Lerner, Sharon	Random House
The Big Box	G	11	183		Steck-Vaughn/New Way
Big Egg	E		103	Coxe, Molly	Random House
The Big Fat Worm	G		250+	Van Laan, Nancy	Knopf
Big Friend, Little Friend	E			Greenfield, Eloise	Houghton Mifflin
Big Red Fire Engine	G	12	158	Greydanus, Rose	Troll/First Start
Billy Goats Gruff	F		381	Hunia, Fran	Ladybird Books
The Bird Feeder	D		55	Coulton, Mia	Kaeden Books
The Birthday Bird	F	11	82	Podeshen, Lois	Richard C. Owen/ Books for Young Learners
A Birthday in the Woods	F		199	Salem, Lynn, and Stewart, Josie.	Seedling
Biscuit	G			Capucilli, Alyssa Satin	Harper Trophy
Biscuit Finds a Friend	G		114	Capucilli, Alyssa Satin	Harper Trophy
The Blanket	E		65	Burningham, John	Crowell
Blue Bug and the Bullies	D		18	Poulet, Virginia	Childrens Press
Blue Bug Goes to School	D		57	Poulet, Virginia	Childrens Press

Title	Fountas and Pinnell	Reading Recovery® Level	Words	Author	Publisher/Series
Blue Bug Goes to the Library	F			Poulet, Virginia	Childrens Press
Blue Bug's Book of Colors	E		49	Poulet, Virginia	Childrens Press
Blue Bug's Vegetable Garden	D		27	Poulet, Virginia	Childrens Press
BMX Billy	G	11	93	Beck, Jennifer	Rigby/Literacy 2000
Boats	G		84	Rockwell, Anne	EP Dutton
Boots and Shoes	E		68	Cooper, Anne	Kaeden Books
Boris Bad Enough	G			Kraus, Robert	Windmill Books
Boxes, Boxes, Boxes	E		63	Stewart, Josie, and Salem, Lynn	Seedling
Bread, Bread, Bread	F		95	Morris, Ann	Scott Foresman
Bruno's Birthday	E	8	32	Vaughan, Marcia	Rigby/Literacy 2000
A Bug, a Bear, and a Boy	F		250+	McPhail, David	Cartwheel Books
Bumpity, Bumpity, Bump	F		62	Parker, C.	Seedling
The Bus Stop	G			Hellen, Nancy	Orchard
Buzzzzz Said the Bee	G		62	Lewison, Wendy Cheyette	Scholastic/ Guided Reading Program
Calico Cat	F			Charles, Donald	Childrens Press
Calico Cat at School	G			Charles, Donald	Childrens Press
Calico Cat at the Zoo	F			Charles, Donald	Childrens Press
Calico Cat Meets Bookworm	G			Charles, Donald	Childrens Press
Calico Cat's Rainbow	E			Charles, Donald	Childrens Press
Camping	D		64	Hooker, Karen	Kaeden Books
Carla's Breakfast	G		225	Harper, Leslie	Kaeden Books
Carla's Ribbons	G		212	Harper, Leslie	Kaeden Books
The Carrot Seed	G	12	101	Krauss, Ruth	Harper Festival
Cars	F		72	Rockwell, Anne	Dutton
Cat and Dog	G			Minarik, Else H.	HarperCollins
Cat Chat	F	9	85		Modern Curriculum Press/ Ready Readers
Cat Goes Fiddle-I-Fee	F		333	Galdone, Paul	Houghton Mifflin

Title	Fountas and Pinnell	Reading Recovery® Level	Words	Author	Publisher/Series
The Cat That Broke the Rules	G	11	192		Modern Curriculum Press/ Ready Readers
Cat Traps	D		93	Coxe, Molly	Random House
The Cat Who Loved Red	D		63	Salem, Lynn, and Stewart, Josie	Seedling
Catch That Frog	E	8	131		Celebration Press/ Reading Unlimited
Cats and Kittens	F	9	51		Celebration Press/ Reading Unlimited
Cement Tent	G	12	358	Crawford, Thomas	Troll/First Start
The Changing Caterpillar	G	12	56	Shahan, Sherry	Richard C. Owen/ Books for Young Learners
The Chick and the Duckling	D		112	Ginsburg, Mirra	Aladdin Library
Chickens	D	8	23	Cox, Rhonda	Richard C. Owen/ Books for Young Learners
Chickens	G	12	105	Snowball, Diane	Mondo/ Bookshop
Choosing a Puppy	E	7	158	Giles, Jenny	Rigby/PM Extensions
City Sounds	G		142	Emberley, Rebecca	Little, Brown & Co.
City Sounds	G		142	Marzollo, Jean	Scholastic
A Coat Full of Bubbles	G	10	72	Shahan, Sherry	Richard C. Owen/ Books for Young Learners
Cock-a-Doodle Do	F			Brandenberg, Franz	Greenwillow
The Cold Day	F	9	80	Hunt, Roderick	Oxford University Press/ Oxford Reading Tree
Coo Coo Caroo	G	12	79	Mitchell, Marianne	Richard C. Owen/ Books for Young Learners
The Cooking Pot	F	10	132	Cowley, Joy	Wright Group/Sunshine
The Cow in the Garden			158		Steck-Vaughn/New Way
Cows in the Garden	E	8	163	Randell, Beverly	Rigby/PM Story Books
The Crazy Quilt	G	11	148	Avery, Kristin	Celebration Press/ Little Celebrations
Critter Race	G			Reese, Bob	Childrens Press

Title	Fountas and Pinnell	Reading Recovery® Level	Words	Author	Publisher/Series
Dad's Headache	F	10	86		Wright Group/Sunshine
A Dark, Dark Tale	F	10	115	Brown, Ruth	Penguin
The Day I Had to Play with My Sister	G		139	Bonsall, Crosby	HarperCollins
Dear Zoo	F	9	115	Campbell, Rod	Little Simon
Dee and Me	G	12	189		Modern Curriculum Press/ Ready Readers
Dinosaurs, Dinosaurs	G		96	Barton, Byron	Harper Festival
Dinosaurs Galore	D		34	Eaton, Audrey, and Kennedy, Jane	Seedling
Dive In!	F	9	133		Modern Curriculum Press/ Ready Readers
Dog and Cat	E		62	Fehlner, Paul	Childrens Press
Dog at School	F	10	94	Hardin, Suzanne	Richard C. Owen/ Books for Young Learners
The Dog	G			Burningham, John	Candlewick Press
Don't Panic	E	8	122		Wright Group/Book Bank
A Dozen Dogs	F		228	Ziefert, Harriet	Random House
Dragon Flies	G	11	53		Richard C. Owen/ Books for Young Learners
The Dragon Hunt	F	9	53	Steck-Vaughn	New Way
Dragon's Lunch	F	9	85		Modern Curriculum Press/ Ready Readers
Drawbridge	E	7	29	Latta, Richard	Richard C. Owen/ Books for Young Learners
Dreams	E	8	93		Wright Group/ Book Bank
Dressed Up Sammy	E		91	Urmston, Kathleen, and Evans, Karen	Kaeden Books
Each Peach Pear Plum	G	11	115	Ahlberg, Allan and Janet	Penguin
Ear Book	E			Perkins, Al	Random House
Elephant and Envelope	G		158	Gregorich, Barbara	School Zone

Title	Fountas and Pinnell	Reading Recovery® Level	Words	Author	Publisher/Series
Excuses, Excuses	E	8	104	Butler, Andrea	Rigby/Tadpoles
Family Soccer	D		55	Geddes, Diana	Kaeden Books
Farmer and the Skunk	E	8	127		Peguis/Tiger Club
Farmer Had a Pig	G	11	149		Peguis/Tiger Club
Farmer in the Dell	E			Parkinson, Kathy	Whitman
The Fat Cat Sat on the Mat	G		250+	Karlin, Nurit	Harper Trophy
Fire, Fire	E	8	164		Rigby/PM Story Books
Fishing	D	7	48	Yukish, Joe	Kaeden Books
Fishy Alphabet Story	F		126	Wylie, Joanne and David	Childrens Press
Five Little Monkeys	F	8	81		Mondo/Bookshop
Five Little Monkeys Jumping on the Bed	E	8	200	Christelow, Eileen	Houghton Mifflin
Five Silly Fisherman	E		250+	Edwards, Roberta	Random House
Flip Flop	G	11	70	Becker, Neesa	Richard C. Owen/ Books for Young Learners
Floating and Sinking	D	11	220		Sundance/AlphaKids
The Foot Book	E			Dr. Seuss	Random House
Footprints in the Snow	D			Benjamin, Cynthia	Cartwheel Books
Forgetful Fred	E	7	78	Butler, Andrea	Rigby/Tadpoles
The Four Getters and Arf	G	11	123		Celebration Press/ Little Celebrations
The Fox and the Crow	D	9	201	Resnick, Jane	C.R. Gibson Co.
Freddie's Spaghetti	F		205+	Doyle, R. H.	Random House
Free to Fly	E	8–9	96	Gibson, Kathleen	Seedling
Friend for Little White Rabbit	E	8	113	Randell, Beverly	Rigby/PM Story Books
Friendly Snowman	F	11	134	Gordon, Sharon	Troll/First Start
Friendly Snowman	F			Joyce, William	Scholastic
Friends	G	12	195		Celebration Press/ Reading Unlimited

Title	Fountas and Pinnell	Reading Recovery® Level	Words	Author	Publisher/Series
Frog's Lunch	F		89	Lillgard, Dee, and Zimmerman, J.	Scholastic
Fruit Salad	D		18	Hoenecke, Karen	Kaeden Books
Fun	D		45	Yannone, Deborah	Kaeden Books
Fun at the Amusement Park	G		176	Frankford, Marilyn	Kaeden Books
A Fun Place to Eat	E	7	90		Modern Curriculum Press/ Ready Readers
A Funny Man	E		244	Jensen, Patricia	Cartwheel Books
Fur	D			Mark, Jan	Harper & Row
Gecko's Story	F	12	61	Moeller, Kathleen Hardcastle	Richard C. Owen/ Books for Young Readers
The Giant Gingerbread Man	D	9	243		Sundance/AlphaKids
The Gingerbread Boy	F	10-11	137		Steck-Vaughn/New Way
Go, Dog, Go	E			Eastman, Philip D.	Random House
Goldilocks and the Three Bears	E			Hunia, Fran	Ladybird Books
Gone Fishing	G		180	Long, Erlene	Houghton Mifflin
The Good Catch!	E	6-7	191		Steck-Vaughn/New Way
Grandma and the Pirate	F			Lloyd, David	Crown
Grandmother	E	7	60	Cowley, Joy	Dominie Press/Joy Readers
Grandpa, Grandpa	G	11	122	Cowley, Joy	Wright Group/ Read-Togethers
Great Day	D	10	162		Sundance/AlphaKids
The Great Race	G		250+	McPhail, David	Cartwheel Books
The Greedy Gray Octopus			195	Buckley, Christel	Rigby/Tadpoles
Green Eyes	F	10	111	Semple, Cheryl	Rigby/Literacy 2000
Green Footprints	E	7	42	Kehoe, Connie	Rigby/Literacy 2000
Grocery Shopping	D		34	Yannone, Deborah	Kaeden Books
Grumpy Elephant	E	7	100	Cowley, Joy	Wright Group/Story Box
Guess What Kind of Ball	E		219	Urmston, Kathleen, and Evans, Karen	Kaeden Books

Title	Fountas and Pinnell	Reading Recovery® Level	Words	Author	Publisher/Series
Gum on the Drum	E		41	Gregorich, Barbara	School Zone
Hairy Bear	G	11	109	Cowley, Joy	Wright Group/ Read-Togethers
Hansel and Gretel	G		451	Hunia, Fran	Ladybird Books
Happy Birthday, Danny and the Dinosaur!	D		250+	Hoff, Syd	HarperTrophy
Happy Egg	E		210	Kraus, Robert	Scholastic
Harry Takes a Bath	F		132	Ziefert, Harriet	The Penguin Group
Have You Seen the Crocodile?	F		150	West, Colin	Harper & Row
Henry	E	8	77	Beveridge, Donna	Richard C. Owen/ Books for Young Learners
Henry's Busy Day	E			Campbell, Rod	The Penguin Group
Here Comes a Bus	F		171	Ziefert, Harriet	The Penguin Group
Herman the Helper Lends a Hand	F			Kraus, Robert	Windmill
Hockey Practice	G		134	Geddes, Diana	Kaeden Books
Home Sweet Home	E			Roffey, Maureen	Bodley
Hooray for Snail	F		102	Stadler, John	HarperCollins
How Do You Make a Bubble?	G		250+	Hooks, William H.	Bantam Doubleday Dell
How Far Will I Fly?	F		94		Scholastic/ Guided Reading Program
How Have I Grown?	G		235	Reid, Mary	Scholastic
How Have I Grown?	G		235		Scholastic/ Guided Reading Program
How Many Bugs in a Box?	D		126	Carter, David	Simon & Schuster
How the Chick Tricked the Fox	G	12	167		Modern Curriculum Press/ Ready Readers
How to Make a Card	G		69	Urmston, Kathleen, and Evans, Karen	Kaeden Books
Howie Has a Stomachache	E		100	Moore, J. R.	Seedling
Humpty Dumpty	D			Peppe, Rodney	Viking Press
A Hunt for Clues	G	12	157		Modern Curriculum Press/ Ready Readers

Title	Fountas and Pinnell	Reading Recovery® Level	Words	Author	Publisher/Series
Huzzard Buzzard	F			Reese, Bob	Childrens Press
I Got a Goldfish	E	8	92		Modern Curriculum Press/ Ready Readers
I Like Books	D			Browne, Anthony	Candlewick Press
I Love Camping	E	8	83		Dominie Press/ Carousel Readers
I Love Mud and Mud Loves Me	D		121	Stephens, Vicki	Scholastic
I Shop with My Daddy	G		131	Maccarone, Grace	Cartwheel Books
I Wish I Was Sick Too	G			Brandenburg, Franz	Mulberry Books
I'm a Caterpillar	G		169	Marzollo, Jean	Cartwheel Books
I'm Hungry	D		84	Tuer, Judy	Scholastic
I'm King of the Castle	F			Watanabe, Shigeo	Putnam
If I Were You	E		77	Wildsmith, Brian	Oxford University Press
In the Hen House	G		82	Oppenlander, Meredith	Kaeden Books
Inside, Outside, Upside Down	E			Berenstain, Stan and Jan	Random House
Is Anyone Home?	F		65	Maris, Ron	William Morrow & Co.
Is This You?	F		250+	Krauss, Ruth	Scholastic
The Island	D		24	Wildsmith, Brian	Oxford University Press
It Looked Like Spilt Milk	E		172	Shaw, Charles	Harper & Row
It's Game Day	D		65	Salem, Lynn, and Stewart, Josie	Seedling
Itchy, Itchy Chicken Pox	F		131	Maccarone, Grace	Scholastic/ Guided Reading Program
Jackie's New Friend	F		168	O'Connor, C. M.	Seedling
Jason's Bus Ride	G		117	Ziefert, Harriet	The Penguin Group
The Jigaree	E	7	128	Cowley, Joy	Wright Group/Story Box
Jim's Visit to Kim	G	12	149		Modern Curriculum Press/ Ready Readers
Jobs	E		112	Benger, Wendy	Kaeden Books

Title	Fountas and Pinnell	Reading Recovery® Level	Words	Author	Publisher/Series
Jog, Frog, Jog	F		72	Gregorich, Barbara	School Zone
Johnny Lion's Rubber Boots	F			Hurd, Edith Thacher	HarperCollins
Jungle Tiger Cat	G		120	Frankford, Marilyn	Kaeden Books
Just a Seed	E		74		Scholastic/ Guided Reading Program
Just a Seed	E		74	Blaxland, Wendy	Scholastic
Just Enough	G		107	Salem, Lynn, and Stewart, Josie	Seedling
Just for You	G		160	Mayer, Mercer	Donovan
Just Like Dad	D		44	Hiris, Monica	Kaeden Books
Just Like Daddy	F		93	Asch, Frank	Simon & Schuster
Just Like Grandpa	E	8	81	Semple, Cheryl	Rigby/Literacy Tree
Just Like Me	E	7	138		Childrens Press/ Rookie Reader
Just Like Us	E	7	55		Modern Curriculum Press/ Ready Readers
Katydids	E	7	20	Bishop, Nic	Richard C. Owen/ Books for Young Readers
The King's Surprise	D		54	Stewart, Josie, and Salem, Lynn	Seedling
Late for Soccer	F	11	185	Giles, Jenny	Rigby/PM Story Books
Late One Night	D		97	Mader, Jan	Kaeden Books
Let's Play Basketball	E		46	Geddes, Diana	Kaeden Books
The Lion and the Mouse	F	10	115		Steck-Vaughn/New Way
The Lion's Tail	F	10	147		Celebration Press/ Reading Unlimited
Little Bulldozer Helps Again	F	9	197	Smith, Annette	Rigby/PM Extensions
Little Monkey	D	11	315		Sundance/AlphaKids
Little Rabbit Is Sad	D		97	Williams, Deborah	Kaeden Books
Lollipop	G			Watson, Wendy	Crowell
Lost at the Fun Park	F	9	192	Smith, Annette	Rigby/PM Extensions

Title	Fountas and Pinnell	Reading Recovery® Level	Words	Author	Publisher/Series
A Lucky Day for Little Dinosaur	F	8	135	Price, Hugh	Rigby/PM Extensions
The Lucky Duck	E	7	73		Modern Curriculum Press/ Ready Readers
Lucky Goes to Dog School	E	7	127	Randell, Beverly	Rigby/PM Story Books
Lunch	F		156	Urmston, Kathleen, and Evans, Karen	Kaeden Books
Mai-Li's Surprise	F	7	61	Jackson, Marjorie	Richard C. Owen/ Books for Young Learners
Making a Memory	D		53	Ballinger, Margaret	Scholastic
Making Concrete	D	9	134		Sundance/AlphaKids
Marmalade's Nap	F		57	Wheeler, Cindy	Alfred A. Knopf
Marmalade's Snowy Day	F			Wheeler, Cindy	Alfred A. Knopf
Mary Wore Her Red Dress	D		170	Peek, Merle	Clarion
Meanies	F	8	158	Cowley, Joy	Wright Group/Story Box
Meet Mr. Cricket	E	8	86		Dominie Press/ Carousel Readers
Message on a Rocket	E	12	174		Econo Clad Books
Messages	F		79		Scholastic/ Guided Reading Program
Messy Mark	F	9	180	Peters, Sharon	Troll/First Start
Mike and Tony: Best Friends	G		171	Ziefert, Harriet	The Penguin Group
Mike's First Haircut	G	9	136	Gordon, Sharon	Troll/First Start
Mike's New Bike	F	9	183	Greydanus, Rose	Troll/First Start
Mine's the Best	G		104	Bonsall, Crosby	HarperCollins
Monkey See, Monkey Do	F		89	Gave, Marc	Scholastic
Monster and the Baby	D			Mueller, Virginia	Puffin Books
Monster Can't Sleep	D			Mueller, Virginia	Puffin Books
Monster Math Picnic	F		98	Maccarone, Grace	Cartwheel Books
Monster Math School Time	G		120	Maccarone, Grace	Cartwheel Books
More and More Clowns	D		249	Allen, R. V.	SRA/McGraw-Hill

Title	Fountas and Pinnell	Reading Recovery® Level	Words	Author	Publisher/Series
More or Less Fish Story	E			Wylie, Joanne and David	Childrens Press
More Spaghetti I Say	G		340	Gelman, Rita	Scholastic
Morris the Mouse	E		250+	Wiseman, Bernard	Harper Trophy
Mouse's Baby Blanket	D		68	Swerdlow Brown, Beverly	Seedling
Mr. Cricket Finds a Friend	G	11	134		Dominie Press/ Carousel Readers
Mr. Cricket Takes a Vacation	E	8	165		Dominie Press/ Carousel Readers
Mr. Cricket's New Home	F	10	121		Dominie Press/ Carousel Readers
Mr. Wolf Leaves Town	D	10	211		Sundance/AlphaKids
Mr. Wolf Tries Again	D	9	215		Sundance/AlphaKids
Mrs. Wishy-Washy	E	8	102	Cowley, Joy	Wright Group/Story Box
Mud	D			Lewison, Wendy	Random House
My Brother Wants to Be Like Me	D		62	Mader, Jan	Kaeden Books
My Brother, the Brat	E			Hall, Kirsten	Scholastic
My Bug Box	E	7	98		Mouse Works
My Dad's Truck	E		57	Costain, Meredith	Scholastic
My Dog	G		72	Taylor, Judy	Macmillan
My Dog's the Best	F		175	Calmenson, Stephanie	Scholastic
My Doll	E		86	Yukish, Joe	Kaeden Books
My Friend Goes Left	F		72	Gregorich, Barbara	School Zone
My Friends	G		152	Gomi, Taro	Scholastic
My Grandpa	F	9	75	Mitchell, Greg	Mondo/ Bookshop
My Kitchen	F			Rockwell, Harlow	William Morrow & Co.
My Lost Top	E	7	70		Modern Curriculum Press/ Ready Readers

Title	Fountas and Pinnell	Reading Recovery® Level	Words	Author	Publisher/Series
My Messy Room	D			Packard, Mary	Scholastic
My Native American School	F		86	Gould, Carol	Kaeden Books
My Pet	D		65	Salem, Lynn, and Stewart, Josie	Seedling
My Shadow	F	10	116	Hall, Lynn	Modern Curriculum Press/Ready Readers
My Tiger Cat	E		76	Frankford, Marilyn	Kaeden Books
Nana's Orchard	F		92	Gould, Carol	Kaeden Books
Never Be	D		73	Salem, Lynn, and Stewart, Josie	Seedling
New Gym Shoes	F		175	Yukish, Joe	Kaeden Books
The New House for Mole and Mouse	G		223	Ziefert, Harriet	The Penguin Group
New York City Buildings	F	12	59	Mace, Ann	Richard C. Owen/Books for Young Learners
Nickels and Pennies	E		53	Williams, Deborah	Kaeden Books
Nicky Upstairs and Down	G	12	179	Ziefert, Harriet	The Penguin Group
Night Walk	F	9	51	Kenny, Ann	Richard C. Owen/Books for Young Learners
Night Walk	E		47	Prokopchak, Ann	Kaeden Books
Nine Men Chase a Hen	G		74	Gregorich, Barbara	School Zone
No Dogs Allowed	F	10	73	Hardin, Suzanne	Richard C. Owen/Books for Young Learners
No Luck	F		120	Stewart, Josie, and Salem, Lynn	Seedling
No Mail for Mitchell	G		250+	Siracusa, Catherine	Random House
Noisy Breakfast	D			Blonder, Ellen	Scholastic
Nose Book	E			Perkins, Al	Random House
Not Enough Water	D		84	Armstrong, Shane, and Hartley, Sue	Scholastic
Not Me, Said the Monkey	E		118	West, Colin	Harper & Row

© 2003 Rigby

Title	Fountas and Pinnell	Reading Recovery® Level	Words	Author	Publisher/Series
Notes from Mom	F		99	Salem, Lynn, and Stewart, Josie	Seedling
Notes to Dad	F		114	Stewart, Josie, and Salem, Lynn	Seedling
Nothing in the Mailbox	F	9	73		Richard C. Owen/ Books for Young Learners
Oh a-Hunting We Will Go	E		346	Langstaff, John	Macmillan
Oh Dear	F			Campbell, Rod	Macmillan
Oh, Cats!	E		93	Buck, Nola	Harper Trophy
Oh, No, Sherman	E		66	Erickson, Betty	Seedling
Old MacDonald Had a Farm	D		505	Rounds, Glen	Holiday House
The Old Train	F	11	68		Richard C. Owen/ Books for Young Learners
On Top of Spaghetti	G	11	105		Celebration Press/ Little Celebrations
One Monday Morning	G		180	Shulevitz, Uri	Scribner
Oops!	D			Mayer, Mercer	The Penguin Group
Our Garage	F		80	Urmston, Kathleen, and Evans, Karen	Kaeden Books
Our House Had a Mouse	E		102	Worthington, Denise	Seedling
P. J. Funnybunny Camps Out	G		250+	Sadler, Marilyn	Random House
The Package	E		35	Bauer, Roger	Kaeden Books
Paco's Garden	G	12	120	Podoshen, Lois	Richard C. Owen/ Books for Young Learners
Papa's Spaghetti	G	12	248	Cowley, Joy	Rigby/Literacy 2000
Paper Bag Trail	E		67	Schreiber, Anne, and Doughty, Arbo	Scholastic
Pardon? Said the Giraffe	F		123	West, Colin	Harper & Row
Pat's New Puppy	E	7	88		Celebration Press/ Reading Unlimited

Title	Fountas and Pinnell	Reading Recovery® Level	Words	Author	Publisher/Series
Peanut Butter and Jelly	G		156	Wescott, Nadine B.	The Penguin Group
The Pet That I Want	E			Packard, Mary	Scholastic
Pete Little	G	12	222	Randell, Beverly	Rigby/PM Story Book
Pizza Party!	F			Maccarone, Grace	Scholastic
Play Ball, Sherman	F		88	Erickson, Betty	Seedling
Polly's Shop	E	7	130		Modern Curriculum Press/ Ready Readers
The Quarter Story	E		99	Williams, Deborah	Kaeden Books
Rainforest Plants	D	10	145		Sundance/AlphaKids
The Red Rose	E	7	127	Cowley, Joy	Wright Group/Story Box
Red Socks and Yellow Socks	G	12	155	Cowley, Joy	Wright Group/Sunshine
Roads and Bridge	D	11	253		Sundance/AlphaKids
Roll Over	F		220	Gerstein, Mordicai	Crown
Rose	F			Wheeler, Cindy	Alfred A. Knopf
Rosie's Walk	F	9	32	Hutchins, Pat	Scholastic
Rush, Rush, Rush	E	8	52		Modern Curriculum Press/ Ready Readers
Sally and the Sparrows	E	7	151	Giles, Jenny	Rigby/PM Extensions
Sally's Space Ship	E	7	87		Modern Curriculum Press/ Ready Readers
Sam's Ball	D		64	Lindgren, Barbro	William Morrow & Co.
Sam's Cookie	D		52	Lindgren, Barbro	William Morrow & Co.
Sam's Teddy Bear	D		60	Lindgren, Barbro	William Morrow & Co.
Sam's Wagon	D		83	Lindgren, Barbro	William Morrow & Co.
Sammy Gets a Ride	F	10	91	Evans, Karen, and Urmston, Kathleen	Kaeden Books
Sammy's Moving	F		166	Urmston, Kathleen, and Evans, Karen	Kaeden Books
Say Goodnight	G			Gregorich, Barbara	School Zone

Title	Fountas and Pinnell	Reading Recovery® Level	Words	Author	Publisher/Series
Say It, Sign It	G		169		Scholastic/ Guided Reading Program
School Bus	D		51	Crews, Donald	William Morrow & Co.
The School	E		27	Burningham, John	Crowell
A Sea Star	E	7	82		Modern Curriculum Press/ Ready Readers
Secret Soup	E	8	51	Hessell, Jenny	Rigby/Literacy Tree
Sheep in a Jeep	G		83	Shaw, Nancy	Houghton Mifflin
Shell Shopping	F	9	145		Modern Curriculum Press/ Ready Readers
SHHH	F		66	Henkes, Kevin	William Morrow & Co.
Shhhh!	G			Kline, Suzy	Whitman
Shoes	D	8	79	Beck, Jennifer	Wright Group/Book Bank
Shopping at the Mall	G		145	Urmston, Kathleen, and Evans, Karen	Kaeden Books
Shoveling Snow	F		109	Cummings, Pat	Scholastic
Sick in Bed	F	9	109		Sundance/Little Red Readers
Sid and Sam	D		120	Buck, Nola	HarperTrophy
Sing a Song	E	7	154		Wright Group/Story Box
Sleepy Dog	D		118	Ziefert, Harriet	Random House
Sly Fox and Red Hen	F		314	Hunia, Fran	Ladybird Books
A Small Baby Raccoon	G	11	104		Modern Curriculum Press/ Ready Readers
Snail Saves the Day	G			Stadler, John	HarperCollins
The Snow	G			Burningham, John	Crowell
Snowflakes	D		49	Urmston, Kathleen, and Evans, Karen	Kaeden Books
Snowy Gets a Wash	F	8	181	Randell, Beverly	Rigby/PM Extensions
Snuggle Up	F		125	Harrison, P, and Worthington, Denise	Seedling

Title	Fountas and Pinnell	Reading Recovery® Level	Words	Author	Publisher/Series
Soccer at the Park	F	8	131	Giles, Jenny	Rigby/PM Extensions
Soccer Game!	F		63	Maccarone, Grace	Scholastic
Socks Off!	D	10	178		Sundance/AlphaKids
Sooty	E	12	218		Sundance/AlphaKids
The Sparrows	F	11	60	Slaughter, Robert	Richard C. Owen/ Books for Young Learners
Spot's First Walk	G		63	Hill, Eric	Putnam
The Stallion's Call	E		77	Salem, Lynn, and Stewart, Josie	Seedling
Staying with Grandma Norma	F		168	Salem, Lynn, and Stewart, Josie	Seedling
Steve's Room	G	12	171		Modern Curriculum Press/ Ready Readers
A Stew for Igor's Mom	G	12	162		Modern Curriculum Press/ Ready Readers
Stop That Rabbit	G	12	168	Peters, Sharon	Troll/First Start
The Storm	G	11	75	Sawyer, Walter	Richard C. Owen/ Books for Young Learners
The Strongest Animal	F	7	58		Richard C. Owen/ Books for Young Learners
The Stubborn Goat	D	11	222		Sundance/AlphaKids
Stuck in the Muck	E		139	Spinelle, Nancy Louise	Kaeden Books
Sue Likes Blue	G		131	Gregorich, Barbara	School Zone
Summer at Cove Lake	G	11	288		Modern Curriculum Press/ Ready Readers
Sunshine, Moonshine	E		128	Armstrong, Jennifer	Random House
Super Pig's Adventure	E	8-9	133		Steck-Vaughn/New Way
Surprise for Mom	E		101	Urmston, Kathleen, and Evans, Karen	Kaeden Books
Susie Goes Shopping	F	10	194		Troll/First Start

Title	Fountas and Pinnell	Reading Recovery® Level	Words	Author	Publisher/Series
Swat It!	D		46	Bauer, Roger	Kaeden Books
Take a Bow, Jody	D		78	Eaton, Audrey, and Kennedy, Jane	Seedling
Taking Care of Rosie	E		61	Salem, Lynn, and Stewart, Josie	Seedling
Tarantula	D	11	140		Sundance/AlphaKids
Teasing Dad	F	9	158	Smith, Annette	Rigby/PM Extensions
Teddy Bear for Sale	G		152	Herman, Gail	Cartwheel Books
The Teeny Tiny Woman	F		250+	O'Connor, Jane	Random House
Ten Bears in My Bed	G		252	Mack, Stan	Pantheon
Ten Sleepy Sheep	G			Keller, Holly	Greenwillow
Thank You, Nicky!	F	10	119	Ziefert, Harriet	The Penguin Group
That Cat!	G	12	146		Modern Curriculum Press/ Ready Readers
That Pig Can't Do a Thing	F	10	83		Modern Curriculum Press/ Ready Readers
There Is a Town	D		116	Heiman, Gail	Random House
Things I Like	D			Browne, Anthony	Random House
The Three Billy Goats Gruff	E	8	123		MacMillan/McGraw
Three Cheers for Hippo	G		90	Stadler, John	HarperCollins
Three Kittens	G		116	Ginsburg, Mirra	Crown
Three Little Witches	G	12	189	Gordon, Sharon	Troll/First Start
Tiger Dave	G	12	33	Boucher, Carter	Richard C. Owen/ Books for Young Learners
Tiger Is a Scaredy Cat	F		220	Phillips, Joan	Random House
Time for a Bath	D		60	Mader, Jan	Kaeden Books
Tiny and the Big Wave	E		163	Smith, Annette	Rigby/PM Extensions
Titch	G	12	121	Hutchins, Pat	The Penguin Group
To the Beach	D		43	Urmston, Kathleen, and Evans, Karen	Kaeden Books

Title	Fountas and Pinnell	Reading Recovery® Level	Words	Author	Publisher/Series
Too Many Bones	G	12	125		Steck-Vaughn/New Way
Tornado	E		37	Spinelle, Nancy Louise	Kaeden Books
Traffic Jam	E		133	Harper, Leslie	Kaeden Books
Tricking Tracy	F	9	125	Donovan, Sue	Rigby/Tadpoles
The Trip	E	7	108		Modern Curriculum Press/ Ready Readers
TweedledeeDee Tumbleweed	G			Reese, Bob	Childrens Press
Two Crazy Pigs	D		250+	Nagel, Karen	Scholastic
Two Little Dogs	E	7	74	Melser, June	Wright Group/Story Box
Under My Sombrero	F	9	79	Schraff, Anne E.	Richard C. Owen/ Books for Young Learners
Use Your Beak!	F		106	Erickson, Betty	Seedling
Waiting for a Frog	G		124	Coats, Glenn	Kaeden Books
Wake Me in Spring	E		250+	Preller, James	Scholastic/ Guided Reading Program
Wake Up, Sun!	E		250+	Harrison, David	Random House
Wake Up, Wake Up!	D			Wildsmith, Brian and Rebecca	Scholastic
What a Dog!	F	9	134	Gordon, Sharon	Troll/First Start
What a Mess!	G	11	124		Steck-Vaughn/New Way
What a School	F		100	Salem, Lynn, and Stewart, Josie	Seedling
What Is That? Said the Cat	F		118	Maccarone, Grace	Scholastic
What Would the Zoo Do?	D		59	Salem, Lynn	Seedling
What's for Dinner?	E		112	Salem, Lynn, and Stewart, Josie	Seedling
Wheels	D		69	Cobb, Annie	Random House
When It Rains	F		106	Frankford, Marilyn	Kaeden Books
When We Are Big	E	7	123	Minkoff, Marilyn	Modern Curriculum Press/ Ready Readers

Title	Fountas and Pinnell	Reading Recovery® Level	Words	Author	Publisher/Series
When You Were a Baby	G		104	Jonas, Ann	William Morrow & Co.
Where Can It Be?	E		83	Jonas, Ann	William Morrow & Co.
Where Can We Go from Here?	F		54	Spinelle, Nancy Louise	Kaeden Books
Where's Al?	D		49	Barton, Byron	Houghton Mifflin
Where's My Daddy?	F			Watanabe, Shigeo	Putnam
Where's Spot?	E		65	Hill, Eric	Putnam
Where's the Puppy?	D			Christian, Cheryl et. al.	Checkerboard
Which Hat Today?	E		94	Ballinger, Margaret, and Gossett, R.	Scholastic
Who Am I?	E			Christensen, Nancy	Cartwheel Books
Who Goes Out on Halloween?	G			Alexander, Sue	Gareth Stevens
Who Will Be My Friends?	F		205	Hoff, Syd	Harper Trophy
Who Will Be My Mother?	E	8	156	Cowley, Joy	Wright Group/Story Box
Why Can't I Fly?	G		449	Gelman, Rita	Scholastic
William, Where Are You?	F		239	Gerstein, Mordicai	Random House
Willy's Hats	E		65	Stewart, Josie, and Salem, Lynn	Seedling
Winter Is Here	D		55	Weinberger, Kimberly	Scholastic
The Witch's Haircut	G	12	135	Wyvill, Mavis	Wright Group/Windmill
Worm Wrap	D	10	249		Sundance/AlphaKids
Yummy, Yummy	F			Grey, Judith	Troll
The Zoo in Willy's Bed	E		81	Sturnman Gorman, Kate	Seedling
Zoo Looking	G	7	149	Whitman, Candace	Mondo/Bookshop

Leveled Books–Transitional Readers

Title	Fountas and Pinnell	Reading Recovery® Level	Words	Author	Publisher/Series
Addie's Bad Day	J		566	Robins, Joan	HarperTrophy
Adventures of Snail at School	J			Stadler, John	HarperTrophy
Airport	I		116	Barton, Byron	HarperCollins
Albert the Albatross	I		191	Hoff, Syd	HarperCollins
All About	J	17	259		Modern Curriculum Press/ Ready Readers
All Tutus Should Be Pink	I		243	Brownrigg, Sheri	Scholastic
Allie's Basketball Dream	J		250+	Barber, Barbara,	Lee & Low Books
Alligators All Around	I		59	Sendak, Maurice	HarperCollins
Amalia and the Grasshopper	I		250+		Scholastic/ Guided Reading Program
And I Mean It Stanley	J		184	Bonsall, Crosby	HarperCollins
Andi's Wool	H	14	107	Cox, Rhonda	Richard C. Owen/ Books for Young Learners
Angus and the Cat	I		250+	Flack, Marjorie	Farrar, Straus, & Giroux
Annie's Pet	J		250+	Brenner, Barbara	Bantam Doubleday Dell
The Ant and the Grasshopper	I	15	231	Poole, Amy Lowry	Dominie Press/ Aesop's Fables
Apples and Pumpkins	I		185	Rockwell, Anne	Scholastic
Are You My Mother?	I		250+	Eastman, Philip D.	Random House
The Art Lesson			246	dePaola, Tomie	Putnam
Ask Mr. Bear	J		613	Flack, Marjorie	Aladdin Library
Away Went the Hat	I	15, 15, 18	260		Steck-Vaughn/New Way
The Awful Mess	H			Rockwell, Anne	Four Winds
Barney's Horse	I		250+	Hoff, Syd	HarperTrophy
Bear Shadow	J	18	489	Asch, Frank	Simon & Schuster
The Bear's Bicycle	I		185	McLeod, Emilie	Little, Brown
Because a Little Bug Went Ka-Choo	I		250+	Stone, Rosetta	Random House

Title	Fountas and Pinnell	Reading Recovery® Level	Words	Author	Publisher/Series
Bee My Valentine!	H		250+	Cohen, Miriam	Bantam Doubleday Dell
Ben and the Bear	I		250+	Riddell, Chris	Harper & Row
Benny Bakes a Cake	I			Rice, Eve	Greenwillow
Bertie the Bear	I		250+	Allen, Pamela	Coward
The Best Little Monkeys in the World	J		250+	Standiford, Natalie	Random House
Best Nest	J		250+	Eastman, Philip D.	Random House
Better Than TV	J		250+	Miller, Sara Swan	Bantam Doubleday Dell
Big Bad Rex	I		176	Erickson, Betty	Seedling
Big Dog, Little Dog	I		265	Eastman, Philip D.	Random House
The Big Hungry Bear	I		148	Wood, Don and Audrey	Scholastic
Big Max	J		250+	Platt, Kin	Harper Trophy
The Biggest Fish	I		254	Giles, Jenny	Rigby/PM Story Books
Bike Lesson	I		250+	Berenstain, Stan and Jan	Random House
Blackboard Bear	J		117	Alexander, Martha	The Penguin Group
The Boy Who Cried Wolf	J		140	Littledale, Freya	Scholastic
Building a House	H		83	Barton, Byron	William Morrow & Co.
The Busy Beavers	I		362	Randell, Beverly	Rigby/PM Story Books
Busy Buzzing Bumblebees and Other Tongue Twisters	I		250+	Schwartz, Alvin	Harper Trophy
Buzby	J		250+	Hoban, Julia	Harper Trophy
Buzz, Buzz, Buzz	H		162	Barton, Byron	Macmillan
Cabin in the Hills	J		349	Smith, Annette	Rigby/PM Story Books
The Cake That Mack Ate	H		189	Robart, Rose, and Kovalski, Maryann	Little, Brown
Camp Big Paw	J		250+	Cushman, Doug	Harper Trophy
Captain Cat	H		250+	Hoff, Syd	Harper Trophy
The Careful Crocodile	I		271	Randell, Beverly	Rigby/PM Story Books

Title	Fountas and Pinnell	Reading Recovery® Level	Words	Author	Publisher/Series
Cat Concert	J		250+	Bacon, Ron	Rigby/Literacy Tree
Cat in the Hat	J		250+	Dr. Seuss	Random House
The Cat with No Tail	I	15	137		Richard C. Owen/ Books for Young Learners
Cats and Mice	H		51	Gelman, Rita	Scholastic
Charlie Needs a Cloak	J		187	dePaola, Tomie	Prentice-Hall
Chicken in the Middle of the Road	J	16–18	478		Mondo/Bookshop
The Children of Sierra Leone	J	16	142		Richard C. Owen/ Books for Young Learners
City Mouse–Country Mouse	J		250+	Wallner, John	Scholastic
A Clean House for Mole and Mouse	H		201		Scholastic/Guided Reading Program
Clocks and More Clocks	J		374	Hutchins, Pat	Scholastic
The Color Wizard	J		250+	Brenner, Barbara	Bantam Doubleday Dell
Come and Have Fun	I			Hurd, Edith Thacher	HarperCollins
Come Out and Play, Little Mouse	H		198	Kraus, Robert	William Morrow & Co.
Could It Be?	J		250+	Oppenheim, Joanna	Bantam Doubleday Dell
Cow Up a Tree	H	13	215	Cowley, Joy	Rigby/Read Along
Coyote Plants a Peach Tree	I	16	233		Richard C. Owen/ Books for Young Learners
Crabbing Time	I	15	76		Richard C. Owen/ Books for Young Learners
The Crow and the Pitcher	I	15	265		Dominie Press/ Aesop's Fables
Curious George and the Ice Cream	J		250+	Rey, Margaret	Scholastic
Danny and the Dinosaur	J		250+	Hoff, Syd	Scholastic
Danny and the Dinosaur Go to Camp	H		250+	Hoff, Syd	HarperTrophy
A Day at the Races	H		85	Bauer, Roger	Kaeden Books
Days with Frog and Toad	J		250+	Lobel, Arnold	HarperTrophy
Detective Dinosaur	J		250+	Skofield, James	HarperTrophy

Title	Fountas and Pinnell	Reading Recovery® Level	Words	Author	Publisher/Series
Digging to China	H	13	108		Richard C. Owen/ Books for Young Learners
The Dinosaur Chase	I		240	Price, Hugh	Rigby/PM Story Books
The Dinosaur Who Lived in the Backyard	H		250+	Hennessy, Brendan G.	Scholastic
The Doctor Has the Flu	H	13	106		Modern Curriculum Press/Ready Readers
Dogs	I		116	Hutchins, Pat	Wright Group
Dogstar	J		250+	Edwards, Hazel	Rigby/Literacy 2000
Don't Be My Valentine– A Classroom Mystery	J		250+	Lexau, Joan M.	Harper Trophy
Don't Eat Too Much Turkey	J		250+	Cohen, Miriam	Bantam Doubleday Dell
Don't Touch	I		250+	Kline, Suzy	The Penguin Group
The Doorbell Rang	J	17	283	Hutchins, Pat	Scholastic
Dragon Gets By	I		250+	Pilkey, Dav	Orchard
Dragon's Fat Cat	I		250+	Pilkey, Dav	Orchard
Dragon's Halloween	I		250+	Pilkey, Dav	Orchard
Dragon's Merry Christmas	I		250+	Pilkey, Dav	Orchard Paperbacks
Dream in the Wishing Well	H		250+	Allen, R. V.	SRA/McGraw-Hill
Drummer Hoff	J		173	Emberley, Ed	Prentice-Hall
Eat Up, Gemma	I		463	Hayes, Sarah	Sundance
Edgar Badger's Balloon Day	I-J	18-20	864		Mondo/Bookshop
Egg to Chick	J		250+	Selsam, Millicent	Harper Trophy
Elephant and the Bad Baby	J		250+	Hayes, Sarah	Sundance
Emma's Problem	H	13	190	Parker, John	Rigby/Literacy 2000
The Enormous Turnip	H	14	431	Hunia, Fran	Ladybird Books
The Enormous Watermelon	H	14	304	Parkes, Brenda	Rigby/Traditional Tales
The Farmer and His Two Lazy Sons	J	17	250		Dominie Press/ Aesop's Fables

Title	Fountas and Pinnell	Reading Recovery® Level	Words	Author	Publisher/Series
Farmer Joe's Hot Day	J	17	406	Richards, Nancy Wilcox, and Zimmermann, Werner	Scholastic
Fat Cat	I		250+	Kent, Jack	Scholastic
Father Bear Comes Home	I	19	331	Minarik, Else H.	HarperCollins
Fern and Bert	H	14	375		Modern Curriculum Press/Ready Readers
The Fire Station	J		237		Pebble Books/Grolier
First Grade Takes a Test	J		250+	Cohen, Miriam	Bantam Doubleday Dell
Fix It	I		171	McPhail, David	The Penguin Group
Flip's Trick	H	14	134		Modern Curriculum Press/Ready Readers
The Flying Fish	H	14	215	Smith, Annette	Rigby/PM Extensions
Fox All Week	J		250+	Marshall, Edward	Puffin Books
Fox and His Friends	J		250+	Marshall, Edward	Puffin Books
Fox at School	J		250+	Marshall, Edward	Puffin Books
Fox Be Nimble	J		250+	Marshall, James	Puffin Books
Fox in Love	J		250+	Marshall, Edward	Puffin Books
Fox on Stage	J		250+	Marshall, James	Puffin Books
Fox on the Job	J		250+	Marshall, James	Puffin Books
Fox on Wheels	J		250+	Marshall, Edward	Puffin Books
Fox Outfoxed	J		250+	Marshall, James	Puffin Books
Fraidy Cats	J		250+	Krensky, Stephen	Scholastic
Franklin Plays the Game	J		250+	Bourgeois, Paulette, and Clark, Brenda	Scholastic
A Friend for Dragon	I		250+	Pilkey, Dav	Orchard Paperbacks
The Friendly Crocodile	I		218	Hiris, Monica	Kaeden Books
The Frog Prince	H	20	908		Wright Group/Sunshine
Froggy Learns to Swim	J		250+	London, Jonathan	Scholastic

Title	Fountas and Pinnell	Reading Recovery® Level	Words	Author	Publisher/Series
Fun at Camp	H	13	178		Troll/First Start
Funny Bones	J		250+	Ahlberg, Allan and Janet	Viking
George Shrinks	H		114	Joyce, William	HarperCollins
Geraldine's Big Show	I		250+	Keller, Holly	Scholastic
Ghosts! Ghostly Tales from Folklore	J		250+	Schwartz, Alvin	HarperTrophy
The Giant's Job	H		180	Stewart, Josie, and Salem, Lynn	Seedling
Gifts for Dad	H	14	178	Urmston, Kathleen, and Evans, Karen	Kaeden Books
Gingerbread Man	I		250+	Hunia, Fran	Ladybird Books
The Gingerbread Man	J	15	535	Parkes, Brenda	Rigby/PM Traditional Tales and Plays
Go Away, Dog	I		250+	Nodset, Joan	HarperCollins
Goha and His Donkey	I	15	114		Richard C. Owen/ Books for Young Learners
Goldilocks and the Three Bears	H	17	250+	Giles, Jenny	Rigby/PM Traditional Tales and Plays
Good News	I		250+	Brenner, Barbara	Bantam Doubleday Dell
Good-Bye Summer, Hello Fall	H	14	169		Modern Curriculum Press/Ready Readers
Goodnight, Moon	H		130	Brown, Margaret Wise	HarperCollins
Goodnight, Owl!	I		196	Hutchins, Pat	Macmillan
The Grandma Mix-Up	J		250+	McCully, Emily Arnold	HarperTrophy
Grandma's at Bat	J		250+	McCully, Emily Arnold	HarperTrophy
Grandpa, Grandma, and the Tracto	H	14	220		Modern Curriculum Press/Ready Readers
Granny and the Desperadoes	J		250+	Parish, Peggy	Simon & Schuster
Great Day for Up	J		180	Dr. Seuss	Random House

Title	Fountas and Pinnell	Reading Recovery® Level	Words	Author	Publisher/Series
The Great Snake Escape	J		250+	Coxe, Molly	HarperTrophy
Green Eggs and Ham	J		250+	Dr. Seuss	Random House
Grizzwold	I		250+	Hoff, Syd	HarperTrophy
The Gruff Brothers	I		250+	Hooks, William H.	Bantam Doubleday Dell
Hand, Hand, Fingers, Thumb	J		250+	Perkins, Al	Random House
Happy Birthday, Sam	I		213	Hutchins, Pat	Greenwillow
Harry and the Lady Next Door	J		250+	Zion, Gene	HarperTrophy
Hattie and the Fox	I		321	Fox, Mem	Bradbury/Trumpet
He Bear, She Bear	J		250+	Berenstain, Stan & Jan	Random House
Hedgehog Bakes a Cake	J		250+	McDonald, Maryann	Bantam Doubleday Dell
Hello, Cat You Need a Hat	I			Gelman, Rita	Scholastic
Hello, First Grade	I			Ryder, Joanne	Troll
Henny Penny	I		582	Galdone, Paul	Scholastic
Henry and Mudge and the Bedtime Thumps	J		250+	Rylant, Cynthia	Aladdin
Henry and Mudge and the Best Day of All	J		250+	Rylant, Cynthia	Aladdin
Henry and Mudge and the Careful Cousin	J		250+	Rylant, Cynthia	Aladdin
Henry and Mudge and the Forever Sea	J		250+	Rylant, Cynthia	Aladdin
Henry and Mudge and the Happy Cat	J		250+	Rylant, Cynthia	Aladdin
Henry and Mudge and the Long Weekend	J		250+	Rylant, Cynthia	Aladdin
Henry and Mudge and the Wild Wind	J		250+	Rylant, Cynthia	Aladdin
Henry and Mudge Get the Cold Shiver	J		250+	Rylant, Cynthia	Aladdin

Title	Fountas and Pinnell	Reading Recovery® Level	Words	Author	Publisher/Series
Henry and Mudge in Puddle Trouble	J		250+	Rylant, Cynthia	Aladdin
Henry and Mudge in the Family Tree	J		250+	Rylant, Cynthia	Aladdin
Henry and Mudge in the Green Time	J		250+	Rylant, Cynthia	Aladdin
Henry and Mudge in the Sparkle Days	J		250+	Rylant, Cynthia	Aladdin
Henry and Mudge Take the Big Test	J		250+	Rylant, Cynthia	Aladdin
Henry and Mudge Under the Yellow Moon	J		250+	Rylant, Cynthia	Aladdin
Henry and Mudge: The First Book	J		250+	Rylant, Cynthia	Aladdin
Hiccups for Elephant	I		250+	Preller, James	Scholastic
Hide-and-Seek with Grandpa	I		250+	Lewis, Rob	Mondo Publishing
A Hippopotamus Ate the Teacher	J		250+	Thaler, Mike	Avon Books
Hoketichee and the Manatee	I	15	113		Richard C. Owen/ Books for Young Learners
Hop on Pop	J		250+	Dr. Seuss	Random House
The Horse in Harry's Room	J		425	Hoff, Syd	HarperCollins
The House That Jack Built	J		250+	Peppe, Rodney	Delacorte
The House That Stood on Booker Hill	J	17	324		Modern Curriculum Press/Ready Readers
How Do I Put It On?	H			Watanabe, Shigeo	The Penguin Group
How Kittens Grow	J		250+	Selsam, Millicent	Scholastic
How the Mouse Got Brown Teeth	I	16	460		Mondo/Bookshop
How Turtle Raced Beaver	J	17	182	Davidson, Avelyn	Rigby/Literacy 2000
The Hungry Sea Star	I	14	69		Richard C. Owen/ Books for Young Learners
I Can Do It	I	13	200		Mondo/Bookshop
I Can Read with My Eyes Shut	J		250+	Dr. Seuss	Random House

Title	Fountas and Pinnell	Reading Recovery® Level	Words	Author	Publisher/Series
I Love to Sneeze	J		250+	Schecter, Ellen	Bantam Doubleday Dell
I Saw You in the Bathtub	J		250+	Schwartz, Alvin	HarperTrophy
I Was So Mad	J		232	Mayer, Mercer	Donovan
I Was Walking Down the Road	H		299	Barchas, Sarah	Scholastic
I'm a Good Reader	H	13	188		Dominie Press/ Carousel Readers
If I Had an Alligator	H			Mayer, Mercer	Dial
If I Were a Penguin	H		159	Goeneil, Heidi	Little, Brown
In a Dark, Dark Room	J		250+	Schwartz, Alvin	HarperTrophy
Insects	J		171	Maclulich, Carolyn	Scholastic
It's George!	H			Cohen, Miriam	Bantam Doubleday Dell
It's Not Easy Being a Bunny	I			Sadler, Marilyn	Random House
Jace, Mace and the Big Race	H			Gregorich, Barbara	School Zone
Jake and the Copycats	J		250+	Rocklin, Joanne	Bantam Doubleday Dell
Jamberry	J		111	Degen, Bruce	Harper & Row
Jessica in the Dark	I		362	Randell, Beverly	Rigby/PM Story Books
Jilliam Jiggs	J		250+	Gilman, Phoebe	Scholastic
Jim Meets the Thing	I		250+	Cohen, Miriam	Dell Publishing
Jim's Dog Muffins	I		250+	Cohen, Miriam	Dell Publishing
Jimmy Lee Did It	J		250+	Cummings, Pat	Lothrop
Joe and Betsy the Dinosaur	J		250+	Hoban, Lillian	HarperTrophy
Johnny Lions Book	J		250+	Hurd, Edith Thacher	HarperCollins
Jonathan Buys a Present	J		353	Smith, Annette	Rigby/PM Story Books
Just a Mess	I		206	Mayer, Mercer	Donovan
Just Grandma and Me	I		186	Mayer, Mercer	Donovan
Just Like Everyone Else	I			Kuskin, Karla	HarperCollins
Just Me and My Babysitter	H		182	Mayer, Mercer	Donovan

Title	Fountas and Pinnell	Reading Recovery® Level	Words	Author	Publisher/Series
Just Me and My Dad	H		161	Mayer, Mercer	Donovan
Just Me and My Puppy	H		190	Mayer, Mercer	Donovan
Just One Guinea Pig	I		339	Giles, Jenny	Rigby/PM Story Books
Kenny and the Little Kickers	J		250+	Mareollo, Claudio	Scholastic
Kick, Pass, and Run	J		250+	Kessler, Leonard	HarperTrophy
Kiss for Little Bear	J		250+	Minarik, Else H.	HarperTrophy
A Kiss for Little Bear	H		250+	Hoban, Tana	Scholastic
The Lad Who Went to the North Wind	J	20	796		Mondo/Bookshop
Last One in Is a Rotten Egg	J		250+	Kessler, Leonard	HarperTrophy
Leo the Late Bloomer	I		164	Kraus, Robert	Simon & Schuster
Let's Be Enemies	J		250+	Sendak, Maurice	Harper & Row
Liar, Liar, Pants on Fire	I		250+	Cohen, Miriam	Bantam Doubleday Dell
The Lighthouse Children	I		250+	Hoff, Syd	HarperTrophy
Little Bear	J		1664	Minarik, Else H.	HarperCollins
Little Bear's Best Friend	J		250+	Minarik, Else H.	HarperTrophy
Little Bear's Visit	J		250+	Minarik, Else H.	HarperTrophy
Little Black, a Pony	J		250+	Farley, Walter	Random House
Little Blue and Little Yellow	J		250+	Lionni, Leo	Scholastic
Little Chick's Friend Duckling	I		572	Kwitz, Mary Deball	HarperTrophy
Little Fireman	J		250+	Brown, Margaret Wise	HarperCollins
Little Fish That Got Away	I		250+	Cook, Bernadine	Scholastic
Little Gorilla	J		167	Bornstein, Ruth	Clarion
Little Mouse's Trail Tale	I	13	349	Vandine, JoAnn	Mondo/Bookshop
The Little Red Hen	I		416		Rigby/PM Traditional Tales and Plays
Little Red Riding Hood	H		250+	Hunia, Fran	Ladybird Books
Little Tuppen	I		250+	Galdone, Paul	Houghton Mifflin

Title	Fountas and Pinnell	Reading Recovery® Level	Words	Author	Publisher/Series
Look-Alike Animals	I		132		Scholastic/ Guided Reading Program
Lost in the Museum	I		250+	Cohen, Miriam	Bantam Doubleday Dell
Lots of Caps	I	15	205	Steck-Vaughn	New Way
Lottie Goat and Donny Goat			145		Modern Curriculum Press/Ready Readers
Lulu Goes to Witch School	J		250+	O'Connor, Jane	Harper Trophy
The Magic Fish	J		250+	Littledale, Freya	Scholastic/ Guided Reading Program
The Magic Fish	J		250+	Rylant, Cynthia	Scholastic
Marigold and Grandma on the Town	J		250+	Calmenson, Stephanie	Harper Trophy
Max	J		234	Isadora, Rachael	Macmillan
Meg and Mog	J		236	Nicoll, Helen	Viking
Mice at Bat	I		250+	Oechsli, Kelly	Harper Trophy
Mike Swam, Sink or Swim	J		250+	Heiligman, Deborah	Bantam Doubleday Dell
Milton the Early Riser	J		148	Kraus, Robert	Simon & Schuster
The Missing Necklace	H	14	231		Celebration Press/ Reading Unlimited
The Missing Tooth	J		250+	Cole, Joanna	Random House
Misty's Mischief	H		61	Campbell, Rod	Viking
Mitch to the Rescue	I		302	Smith, Annette	Rigby/PM Story Books
Mom's Secret	H		141		Scholastic/ Guided Reading Program
Monkey and Fire	J	18	372	Stott-Thornton, Janet	Rigby/Literacy Tree
Monster Bus	H	13	103		Dominie Press/ Monster Bus Series
Monster Bus Goes on a Hot Air Balloon Trip	I	16	254		Dominie Press/ Monster Bus Series
Monster Bus Goes to the Races	H	13	158		Dominie Press/ Monster Bus Series

Title	Fountas and Pinnell	Reading Recovery® Level	Words	Author	Publisher/Series
Monster Bus Goes to Yellowstone Park	I	15	259		Dominie Press/ Monster Bus Series
Monster Manners	J		250+	Cole, Joanna	Scholastic
Moon Boy	J		250+	Brenner, Barbara	Bantam Doubleday Dell
More Spaghetti, I Say!	H		250+	Gelman, Rita	Scholastic/ Guided Reading Program
Morris and Boris at the Circus	J		250+	Wiseman, Bernard	Harper Trophy
Morris Goes to School	J		250+	Wiseman, Bernard	Harper Trophy
Mouse Soup	J		1350	Lobel, Arnold	HarperCollins
Mouse Tales	J		1519	Lobel, Arnold	HarperCollins
The Mouse Who Wanted to Marry	J		250+	Orgel, Doris	Bantam Doubleday Dell
Mr. McCready's Cleaning Day	H		119	Shilling, Tracy	Scholastic
Mr. Putter and Tabby Bake the Cake	J		250+	Rylant, Cynthia	Harcourt Brace
Mr. Putter and Tabby Fly the Plane	J		250+	Rylant, Cynthia	Harcourt Brace
Mr. Putter and Tabby Pick the Pears	J		250+	Rylant, Cynthia	Harcourt Brace
Mr. Putter and Tabby Pour the Tea	J		250+	Rylant, Cynthia	Harcourt Brace
Mr. Putter and Tabby Walk the Dog	J		250+	Rylant, Cynthia	Harcourt Brace
Mrs. Brice's Mice	I		250+	Hoff, Syd	Harper Trophy
Mrs. Murphy's Crows	H	14	122		Richard C. Owen/ Books for Young Learners
My Best Friend	I			Hutchins, Pat	Greenwillow
My Brother, Ant	J		250+	Byars, Betsy	Viking
My Brown Bear Barney	H			Butler, Dorothy	William Morrow & Co.
My Cat	H		79	Taylor, Judy	Macmillan
My Father			194	Mayer, Laura	Scholastic
My Sloppy Tiger	I	16	217		Wright Group/Sunshine
The Mystery of the Missing Dog	J		250+	Levy, Elizabeth	Scholastic
Nana's Place	I		211	Gibson, Akimi, and Meyer, K.	Scholastic

Title	Fountas and Pinnell	Reading Recovery® Level	Words	Author	Publisher/Series
The Napping House	I		268	Wood, Don and Audrey	Harcourt
The New Baby Calf	H		240	Chase, Edith, and Reid, Barbara	Scholastic
Newt	J		250+	Novak, Matt	HarperTrophy
Nick Goes Fishing	I		123	Yukish, Joe	Kaeden Books
No Ball Games Here	H			Ziefert, Harriet	The Penguin Group
No Good in Art	I		250+	Cohen, Miriam	Bantam Doubleday Dell
No More Monsters for Me!	J		250+	Parish, Peggy	HarperTrophy
Noisy Nora	I		204	Wells, Rosemary	Scholastic
Norma Jean, Jumping Bean	J		250+	Cole, Joanna	Random House
Not Now! Said the Cow	J		250+	Demares, Chris	Bantam Doubleday Dell
Old Hat, New Hat	H			Berenstain, Stan and Jan	Random House
The Old Man's Mitten	I	19	378		Mondo/Bookshop
Oliver	H			Kraus, Robert	Simon & Schuster
One Bear All Alone	H		107	Bucknall, Caroline	Dial
Oscar Otter	J		250+	Benchley, Nathaniel	HarperTrophy
Otto the Cat	J		250+	Herman, Gail	Grosset & Dunlap
Our Polliwogs	I	15	91		Richard C. Owen/ Books for Young Learners
Owl at Home	J		1488	Lobel, Arnold	HarperCollins
Pack 109	J		164	Thaler, Mike	Scholastic
Peter's Chair	J		250+	Keats, Ezra Jack	HarperTrophy
A Picture for Harold's Room	H		550	Johnson, Crockett	HarperCollins
Pig William's Midnight Walk	H	14	354		Wright Group/Book Bank
Planning Dinner	H		260	Urmston, Kathleen, and Evans, Karen	Kaeden Books
The Popcorn Shop	J		250+	Low, Alice	Scholastic
Poppleton	J		250+	Rylant, Cynthia	Scholastic

Title	Fountas and Pinnell	Reading Recovery® Level	Words	Author	Publisher/Series
Poppleton and Friends	J		250+	Rylant, Cynthia	Scholastic
Poppleton Everyday	J		250+	Rylant, Cynthia	Scholastic
Poppleton Forever	J		250+	Rylant, Cynthia	Scholastic
Poppleton in Spring	J		250+	Rylant, Cynthia	Scholastic
Porcupine's Pajama Party	J		250+	Harshman, Terry Webb	Harper Trophy
The Pot of Gold	I	16	266		Celebration Press/ Reading Unlimited
Pretty Good Magic	J		250+	Dubowski, Cathy	Random House
The Princess and the Pea	I	17	304		Dominie Press/ Traditional Tales
Pterosaur's Long Flight	I		301	Price, Hugh	Rigby/PM Story Books
The Pumpkin House	J		250+	Carr, Roger Vaughan	Rigby/Literacy 2000
Put Me in the Zoo	H		250+	Lopshire, Robert	Random House
Quack, Said the Billy Goat	H		88	Causley, Charles	Harper & Row
The Quilt	I		165	Jonas, Ann	William Morrow & Co.
The Rabbit	H		59	Burningham, John	Crowell
Rabbit's Birthday Kite	J		250+	McDonald, Maryann	Bantam Doubleday Dell
Rain Puddle	J			Holl, Adelaide	William Morrow & Co.
Rapid Robert Roadrunner	H		125	Reese, Bob	Childrens Press
Ready, Set, Go	H		250+	Stadler, John	Harper Trophy
The Real-Skin Rubber Monster Mask	H			Cohen, Miriam	Bantam Doubleday Dell
The Rebus Bears	I		250+	Reit, Seymour	Bantam Doubleday Dell
Reflections	I			Jonas, Ann	William Morrow & Co.
Rescuing Nelson	J		369	Randell, Beverly	Rigby/PM Story Books
Robert and the Rocket	H				Scholastic/ Guided Reading Program
Robert Makes a Graph	H		160	Coulton, Mia	Kaeden Books

Title	Fountas and Pinnell	Reading Recovery® Level	Words	Author	Publisher/Series
Robert the Rose Horse	I			Heilbroner, Joan	Random House
Roller Skates	J		250+	Calmenson, Stephanie	Scholastic
Row, Row, Row Your Boat	J		250+	O'Malley Kevin	Bantam Doubleday Dell
Sam and the Firefly	J		250+	Eastman, Philip D.	Random House
Sam the Minuteman	J		250+	Benchley, Nathaniel	Harper Trophy
Sammy the Seal	H		250+	Hoff, Syd	Harper Trophy
Sammy's Supper	I	16	293		Celebration Press/ Reading Unlimited
Sarah and the Barking Dog	I		328	Giles, Jenny	Rigby/PM Story Books
See You In Second Grade	J		250+	Cohen, Miriam	Bantam Doubleday Dell
See You Tomorrow Charles	J		250+	Cohen, Miriam	Bantam Doubleday Dell
Seven Little Monsters	H		55	Sendak, Maurice	HarperCollins
Sharks	H	13	155		Modern Curriculum Press/Ready Readers
Shintaro's Umbrella	I	16	101		Richard C. Owen/ Books for Young Learners
The Show-and-Tell Frog	J		250+	Oppenheim, Joanna	Bantam Doubleday Dell
Silly Tilly's Valentine	J		250+	Hoban, Lillian	Harper Trophy
Silly Times with Two Silly Trolls	I		250+	Jewell, Nancy	Harper Trophy
Skates for Luke	I		346		Rigby/PM Story Books
SkyFire	J		250+	Asch, Frank	Scholastic
Small Pig	I		250+	Lobel, Arnold	Harper Trophy
Small Wolf	J		250+	Benchley, Nathaniel	Harper Trophy
Snow Day	I		250+	Bliss, Corinne Demas	Random House
The Snowy Day	J	18	319	Keats, Ezra Jack	Scholastic
So What?	I		250+	Cohen, Miriam	Bantam Doubleday Dell
Spooky Riddles	I			Brown, Marc	Random House
Spot's Birthday Party	I		97	Hill, Eric	Putnam

Title	Fountas and Pinnell	Reading Recovery® Level	Words	Author	Publisher/Series
Stanley	I		250+	Hoff, Syd	Harper Trophy
Starring First Grade	J		250+	Cohen, Miriam	Bantam Doubleday Dell
Stone Soup	J	17	250+	Hawes, Alison	Rigby/PM Traditional Tales and Plays
The Story of Chicken Licken	I		250+	Ormerod, Jan	Lothrop
The Surprise Party	J		250+	Proger, Annabelle	Random House
Sword in the Stone	J		250+	Maccarone, Grace	Scholastic
Teeny Tiny	I		250+	Bennett, Jill	Putnam
The Teeny Tiny Woman	J		369	Seuling, Barbara	Scholastic
Ten Apples Up on Top			250+	LaSieg, Theo	Random House
There's a Hippopotamus Under My Bed	J		250+	Thaler, Mike	Avon Books
There's a Nightmare in My Closet	I		153	Mayer, Mercer	The Penguin Group
There's an Alligator Under My Bed	J		250+	Mayer, Mercer	The Penguin Group
There's Something in My Attic	J		258	Mayer, Mercer	The Penguin Group
This Is the Bear	I		211	Hayes, Sarah and Craig H.	Harper & Row
This Is the Place for Me	I		250+	Cole, Joanna	Scholastic
The Three Billy Goats Gruff	I		549	Brown, Marcia	Harcourt Brace
The Three Little Pigs	H	13	392		Steck-Vaughn/ New Way
Tidy Titch	I		231	Hutchins, Pat	William Morrow & Co.
Toby and B. J.	I		307	Smith, Annette	Rigby/PM Story Books
Toby and the Accident	J		329	Smith, Annette	Rigby/PM Story Books
Toby and the Big Red Van	I		291	Smith, Annette	Rigby/PM Story Books
Toby and the Big Tree	I		298	Smith, Annette	Rigby/PM Story Books
Tom the TV Cat	J		250+	Heilbroner, Joan	Random House
Too Many Mice	J		250+	Brenner, Barbara	Bantam Doubleday Dell
Too Many Puppies	I			Brewater, Patience	Scholastic/ Guided Reading Program

Title	Fountas and Pinnell	Reading Recovery® Level	Words	Author	Publisher/Series
Too Many Rabbits	J		250+	Parish, Peggy	Bantam Doubleday Dell
Too Much Noise	J		250+	McGovern, Ann	Scholastic
Tool Box	H		144	Rockwell, Anne	Macmillan
The Toy Farm	I		311	Giles, Jenny	Rigby/PM Story Books
The Trek	I		158	Jonas, Ann	Greenwillow
Turtle Nest	H	13	84	Schaeffer, Lola	Richard C. Owen/ Books for Young Learners
Two Bear Cubs	H			Jonas, Ann	William Morrow & Co.
Two Silly Trolls	J		250+	Jewell, Nancy	Harper Trophy
Uncle Elephant	J		1784	Lobel, Arnold	HarperCollins
The Very Busy Spider	I		263	Carle, Eric	Philomel
The Very Hungry Caterpillar	H	18	237	Carle, Eric	Scholastic
Wake Me in Spring	J		301	Preller, James	Scholastic
We Are Best Friends	H		629	Aliki	William Morrow & Co.
We Just Moved!	I		250+	Krensky, Stephen	Cartwheel Books
We're Going on a Bear Hunt	I		363	Rosen, Michael	Macmillan
We're in Big Trouble, Black Board Bear	I		250+	Alexander, Martha	Penguin
Wet Grass	H	14	188	Melser, June	Wright Group/ Storybox
What Do You Hear When Cows Sing?	J		250+	Maestro, Marco and Giulio	Harper Trophy
What Game Shall We Play?	H		306	Hutchins, Pat	Sundance
What People Do	H	14	148		Sundance/Little Red Readers
Wheels on the Bus	I		362	Kovalski, Mary Ann	Little, Brown & Co.
Where Are You Going, Little Mouse?	H		148	Kraus, Robert	William Morrow & Co.
Where the Wild Things Are	J		339	Sendak, Maurice	HarperCollins
Where's Lulu?	I		250+	Hooks, William H.	Bantam

Title	Fountas and Pinnell	Reading Recovery® Level	Words	Author	Publisher/Series
Who Took the Farmer's Hat?	I		340	Nodset, Joan	HarperCollins
Who Wants One?	I			Serfozo, Mary	Simon & Schuster
Who's a Pest?	J		250+	Bonsall, Crosby	HarperCollins
Who's Afraid of the Dark?	I		250+	Bonsall, Crosby	HarperCollins
Who's in the Shed?	I	16	202	Parkes, Brenda	Rigby/Traditional Tales
Whose Mouse Are You?	H	13	98	Kraus, Robert	Simon & Schuster
Willie's Wonderful Pet	I		315	Cebulash, Mel	Scholastic
Wizard and Wart at Sea	J		250+	Smith, Janice Lee	HarperCollins
The Worst Show-and-Tell Ever	J		250+	Walsh, Rita	Troll
The Wrong-Way Rabbit	J			Slater, Teddy	Scholastic
Yes, Ma'am	H	14	125	Melser, June	Wright Group/ Read-Togethers
Yoo Hoo, Moon!	I		250+	Blocksma, Mary	Bantam
You Are Much too Small	J		250+	Boegehold, Betty	Bantam Doubleday Dell
You Can't Catch Me	J		250+	Oppenheim, Joanne	Houghton Mifflin
You'll Soon Grow in to Them, Titch	H	14	191	Hutchins, Pat	William Morrow & Co.

Leveled Books—Fluent Readers

Title	Fountas and Pinnell	Words	Author	Publisher/Series
Abby	M	250+	Hanel, Wolfram	North-South Books
Abe Lincoln's Hat	M	250+	Brenner, Martha	Random House
The Adventures of the Buried Treasure	L	250+	McArthur, Nancy	Scholastic
Afternoon on the Amazon	L	250+	Osborne, Mary Pope	Random House
Alexander and the Wind-up Mouse		250+	Lionni, Leo	Scholastic
Alfie's Gift	L	250+	Hilton, Nette	Rigby/Literacy 2000
Aliens Don't Wear Braces	M	250+	Dadey, Debbie, and Jones, Marcia	Scholastic
Aliens for Breakfast	M	250+	Etra, Jonathan	Random House
Aliens for Dinner	M	250+	Spinner, Stephanie	Random House
Aliens for Lunch	M	250+	Spinner, Stephanie, and Etra Jonathan	Random House
Alison's Puppy	K	250+	Bauer, Marion Dane	Hyperion
Alison's Wings	K	250+	Bauer, Marion Dane	Hyperion
All About Stacy	L	250+	Giff, Patricia Reilly	Bantam Doubleday Dell
All About Things People Do	K	250+	Rice, Melanie and Chris	Scholastic
All Star Fever	M	250+	Christopher, Matt	Little, Brown & Co.
Amalia and the Grasshopper	K	392	Tello, Jerry, and Krupinski, Loretta	Scholastic
Amelia Bedelia	L	250+	Parish, Peggy	Harper & Row
Amelia Bedelia and the Surprise Shower	L	250+	Parish, Peggy	Harper Trophy
Amelia Bedelia and the Baby	L	250+	Parish, Peggy	William Morrow & Co.
Amelia Bedelia Goes Camping	L	250+	Parish, Peggy	William Morrow & Co.
Amelia Bedelia Helps Out	L	250+	Parish, Peggy	Avon Camelot
Amelia Bedelia's Family Album	L	250+	Parish, Peggy	Harper Trophy
Angels Don't Know Karate	M	250+	Dadey, Debbie, and Jones, Marcia	Scholastic

Title	Fountas and Pinnell	Words	Author	Publisher/Series
Animal Tracks	L	250+	Dorros, Arthur	Scholastic
Annie Bananie Moves to Barry Avenue	L	250+	Komaiko, Leah	Bantam Doubleday Dell
The Art Lesson	M	246	dePaola, Tomie	Putnam
Arthur Accused!	M	250+	Brown, Marc	Little, Brown & Co.
Arthur and the Crunch Cereal Contest	M	250+	Brown, Marc	Little, Brown & Co.
Arthur and the Lost Diary	M	250+	Brown, Marc	Little, Brown & Co.
Arthur and the Popularity Test	M	250+	Brown, Marc	Little, Brown & Co.
Arthur and the Scare-Your-Pants-Off Club	M	250+	Brown, Marc	Little, Brown & Co.
Arthur Makes the Team	M	250+	Brown, Marc	Little, Brown & Co.
Arthur Rocks with Binky	M	250+	Brown, Marc	Little, Brown & Co.
Arthur's Back to School Day	K	250+	Hoban, Lillian	HarperTrophy
Arthur's Camp-Out	K	250+	Hoban, Lillian	HarperTrophy
Arthur's Christmas Cookies	K	250+	Hoban, Lillian	HarperTrophy
Arthur's Funny Money	K	250+	Hoban, Lillian	HarperTrophy
Arthur's Great Big Valentine	K	250+	Hoban, Lillian	HarperTrophy
Arthur's Honey Bear	K	250+	Hoban, Lillian	HarperCollins
Arthur's Loose Tooth	K	250+	Hoban, Lillian	HarperCollins
Arthur's Mystery Envelope	M	250+	Brown, Marc	Little, Brown & Co.
Arthur's Pen Pal	K	250+	Hoban, Lillian	HarperCollins
Arthur's Prize Reader	K	250+	Hoban, Lillian	HarperTrophy
Aunt Eater Loves a Mystery	K	250+	Cushman, Doug	HarperTrophy
Aunt Eater's Mystery Christmas	K	250+	Cushman, Doug	HarperTrophy
Aunt Eater's Mystery Vacation	K	250+	Cushman, Doug	HarperTrophy
Aunt Flossie's Hats (and Crab Cakes Later)	M	250+	Howard, Elizabeth	Scholastic
A Baby Sister for Frances	K	250+	Hoban, Russell	Scholastic
The Bad-Luck Penny	L	250+	O'Connor, Jane	Grosset & Dunlap
A Bargain for Frances	K	250+	Hoban, Russell	HarperTrophy
Baseball Ballerina	K	250+	Cristaldi, Kathryn	Random House

Title	Fountas and Pinnell	Words	Author	Publisher/Series
Baseball Flyhawk	M	250+	Christopher, Matt	Little, Brown & Co.
The Baseball Heroes	M	250+	Schultz, Irene	Wright Group
Baseball Pals	M	250+	Christopher, Matt	Little, Brown & Co.
The Basket Counts	M	250+	Christopher, Matt	Little, Brown & Co.
Bat Bones and Spider Stew	K	250+	Poploff, Michelle	Bantam Doubleday Dell
Bats	P	250+	Gordon, Anne	Rigby/Literacy 2000
Be Ready at Eight	K	250+	Parish, Peggy	Simon & Schuster/Aladdin
Beans on the Roof	L	250+	Byars, Betsy	Bantam Doubleday Dell
Bear at the Beach	K	250+	Carmichael, Clay	North-South Books
A Bear for Miguel	K	250+	Alphin, Elaine Marie	Harper Trophy
Bear Goes to Town	K	250+	Browne, Anthony	Doubleday
The Bears on Hemlock Mountain	M	250+	Dalgliesh, Alice	Aladdin
Beast and the Halloween Horror	M	250+	Giff, Patricia Reilly	Bantam Doubleday Dell
The Beast in Ms. Rooney's Room	M	250+	Giff, Patricia Reilly	Bantam Doubleday Dell
Beavers Beware!		250+	Brenner, Barbara	Bantam Doubleday Dell
Bedtime for Frances	K	250+	Hoban, Russell	Scholastic
The Beekeeper	M	250+	Maguiness, Jan	Rigby/Literacy 2000
The Berenstain Bears and the Missing Honey	M	531	Berenstain, Stan and Jan	Random House
The Berenstain Bears' Christmas	M	250+	Berenstain, Stan and Jan	Random House
The Berenstain Bears' Picnic	M	250+	Berenstain, Stan and Jan	RandomHouse
Best Friends for Frances	K	250+	Hoban, Russell	Scholastic
The Best Older Sister	L	250+	Choi, Sook Nyul	Bantam Doubleday Dell
The Best Teacher in the World	K	250+	Chardiet, Bernice, and Maccarone, Grace	Scholastic
The Best Way to Play	K	250+	Cosby, Bill	Scholastic
The Best Worst Day		250+	Graves, Bonnie	Hyperion

Title	Fountas and Pinnell	Words	Author	Publisher/Series
The Best-Loved Doll	L	250+	Caudill, Rebecca	Henry Holt & Co.
Big Al	L	250+	Clements, Andrew	Scholastic
The Big Balloon Race	K	250+	Coerr, Eleanor	HarperTrophy
The Big Fish	M	301	Yukish, Joe	Kaeden Books
The Big Sneeze	K	131	Brown, Ruth	Lothrop
Bigfoot Doesn't Square Dance	M	250+	Dadey, Debbie, and Jones, Marcia	Scholastic
Billy the Ghost and Me	L	250+	Greer, Greg, and Ruddick, Bob	HarperTrophy
A Birthday Bike for Brimhall	K	250+	Delton, Judy	Bantam Doubleday Dell
A Birthday for Frances	K	250+	Hoban, Russell	Scholastic
The Blind Man and the Elephant	K	250+	Backstein, Karen	Scholastic
Blue Ribbon Blues	M	250+	Spinelli, Jerry	Random House
Blueberries for Sal	M	250+	McCloskey, Robert	Scholastic
Bogeymen Don't Play Football	M	250+	Dadey, Debbie, and Jones, Marcia	Scholastic
Bony-Legs	K	250+	Cole, Joanna	Scholastic
A Book About Your Skeleton	M	250+	Gross, Ruth Belov	Scholastic
Bootsie Barker Ballerina	K	250+	Bottner, Barbara	HarperTrophy
Boundless Grace	M	250+	Hoffman, Mary	Scholastic
A Boy Named Boomer	K	250+	Esiason, Boomer	Scholastic
The Boy Who Cried Wolf		250+	Lawrence, Lucy	Rigby/Literacy 2000
The Boy Who Turned into a T.V. Set	L	250+	Manes, Stephen	Avon Camelot
Brad and Butter Play Ball!	M	250+	Hughes, Dean	Random House
Brain-in-a-Box	M	250+	Matthews, Steve	Sundance
Brave Maddie Egg	M	250+	Standiford, Natalie	Random House
Bread and Jam for Frances	K	250+	Hoban, Russell	Scholastic
Brenda's Private Swing	K	250+	Chardiet, Bernice, and Maccarone, Grace	Scholastic

Title	Fountas and Pinnell	Words	Author	Publisher/Series
Brigid Beware	L	250+	Leverich, Kathleen	Random House
Brigid Bewitched	L	250+	Leverich, Kathleen	Random House
Brigid the Bad	L	250+	Leverich, Kathleen	Random House
Brith the Terrible	M	250+	Cowley, Joy	Rigby/Literacy 2000
Buffalo Bill and the Pony Express	K	250+	Coerr, Eleanor	Harper Trophy
Bug Off!	L	250+	Dussling, Jennifer	Grosset & Dunlap
Bumps in the Night	K	250+	Allard, Harry	Bantam Doubleday Dell
The Buried Eye	M	250+	Schultz, Irene	Wright Group
Buster's Dino Dilemma	M	250+	Brown, Marc	Little, Brown & Co.
Button Soup	K	250+	Orgel, Doris	Bantam Doubleday Dell
The Cabbage Princess	K	250+	Cowley, Joy	Rigby/Literacy 2000
Cam Jansen and the Chocolate Fudge Mystery	L	250+	Adler, David	Puffin Books
Cam Jansen and the Mystery of the Babe Ruth Baseball	L	250+	Adler, David	Puffin Books
Cam Jansen and the Mystery of the Circus Clown	L	250+	Adler, David	Puffin Books
Cam Jansen and Mystery of the Dinosaur Bones	L	250+	Adler, David A.	Puffin Books
Cam Jansen and the Mystery at the Monkey House	L	250+	Adler, David	Puffin Books
Cam Jansen and the Mystery of Flight 54	L	250+	Adler, David	Puffin Books
Cam Jansen and the Mystery of the Gold Coins	L	250+	Adler, David	Puffin Books
Cam Jansen and the Mystery of the Monster Movie	L	250+	Adler, David	Puffin Books
Cam Jansen and the Mystery of the Television Dog	L	250+	Adler, David	Puffin Books
Cam Jansen and the Mystery of the U.F.O.	L	250+	Adler, David	Puffin Books
Cam Jansen and the Triceratops Pops Mystery	L	250+	Adler, David	Puffin Books
The Camp Knock Knock Mystery	K	250+	Douglas, Ann	Bantam Doubleday Dell
Camp Sink or Swim	M	250+	Davis, Gibbs	Random House

Title	Fountas and Pinnell	Words	Author	Publisher/Series
Camping with Claudine	K	250+	King, Virginia	Rigby/Literacy 2000
Can Do, Jenny Archer	M	250+	Conford, Ellen	Random House
Can I Have a Dinosaur?	L	250+	King, Virginia	Rigby/Literacy 2000
The Candy Corn Contest	L	250+	Giff, Patricia Reilly	Bantam Doubleday Dell
Cannonball Chris	L	250+	Marzollo, Jean	Random House
Caps for Sale	K	675	Slobodkina, Esphyr	Harper & Row
A Case for Jenny Archer	M	250+	Conford, Ellen	Random House
The Case of the Cat's Meow	K	250+	Bonsall, Crosby	Harper Trophy
The Case of the Cool-Itch Kid	L	250+	Giff, Patricia Reilly	Bantam Doubleday Dell
The Case of the Double Cross	K	250+	Bonsall, Crosby	Harper Trophy
The Case of the Dumb Bells	K	250+	Bonsall, Crosby	Harper Trophy
The Case of the Elevator Duck	M	250+	Brends, Polly Berrien	Random House
The Case of the Hungry Stranger	M	1358	Bonsall, Crosby	Harper Trophy
The Case of the Scaredy Cats	K	250+	Bonsall, Crosby	Harper & Row
The Case of the Two Masked Robbers	K	250+	Hoban, Lillian	Harper Trophy
Cass Becomes a Star	L	250+	Meadows, Graham	Rigby/Literacy 2000
The Cat Burglar	M	250+	Krailing, Tessa	Barron's Educational
Catch That Pass!	M	250+	Christopher, Matt	Little, Brown & Co.
Catcher with a Glass Arm	M	250+	Christopher, Matt	Little, Brown & Co.
The Catcher's Mask	M	250+	Christopher, Matt	Little, Brown & Co.
Center Court Sting	M	250+	Christopher, Matt	Little, Brown & Co.
Centerfield Ballhawk	M	250+	Christopher, Matt	Little, Brown & Co.
A Chair for My Mother	M	250+	Williams, Vera	Scholastic
Challenge at Second Base	M	250+	Christopher, Matt	Little, Brown & Co.
Chang's Paper Pony	L	250+	Coerr, Eleanor	Harper Trophy
Cherries and Cherry Pits	M	250+	Williams, Vera B.	Houghton Mifflin
Chicken Soup with Rice	M	310	Sendak, Maurice	HarperCollins
Chicken Sunday	M	205+	Polacco, Patricia	Scholastic

Title	Fountas and Pinnell	Words	Author	Publisher/Series
Chickens Aren't the Only Ones	K	250+	Heller, Ruth	Scholastic
Chipmunk at Hollow Tree Lane	K	250+	Sherrow, Victoria	Scholastic
The Circus Mystery	M	250+	Schultz, Irene	Wright Group
Clara and the Book Wagon	K	250+	Levinson, Nancy Smiler	Harper Trophy
Claudine's Concert	L	250+	King, Virginia	Rigby/Literacy 2000
Clifford, the Big Red Dog	K	241	Bridwell, Norman	Scholastic
Clifford, the Small Red Puppy	K	499	Bridwell, Norman	Scholastic
Clouds of Terror	L	250+	Welsh, Catherine A.	Carolrhoda Books
Cloudy with a Chance of Meatballs	M	250+	Barrett, Judy	Atheneum
The Clue at the Zoo	L	250+	Giff, Patricia Reilly	Bantam Doubleday Dell
The Clue in the Castle	M	250+	Schultz, Irene	Wright Group
Come Back, Amelia Bedelia	L	250+	Parish, Peggy	Harper & Row
The Comeback Challenge	M	250+	Christopher, Matt	Little, Brown & Co.
Commander Toad and the Big Black Hole	K	250+	Yolen, Jane	Putnam & Grosset
Commander Toad and the Dis-Asteroid	K	250+	Yolen, Jane	Putnam & Grosset
Commander Toad and the Intergalactic Spy	K	250+	Yolen, Jane	Putnam & Grosset
Commander Toad and the Planet of the Grapes	K	250+	Yolen, Jane	Putnam & Grosset
Commander Toad and the Space Pirates	K	250+	Yolen, Jane	Putnam & Grosset
Commander Toad and the Voyage Home	K	250+	Yolen, Jane	Putnam & Grosset
The Conversation Club	L	250+	Stanley, Diane	Aladdin
The Copper Lady	M	250+	Ross, Alice and Kent	Carolrhoda Books
Corduroy	K	250+	Freeman, Don	Scholastic
Count Your Money with the Polk Street School	M	250+	Giff, Patricia Reilly	Bantam Doubleday Dell
The Counterfeit Tackle	M	250+	Christopher, Matt	Little, Brown & Co.
Crackerjack Halfback	M	250+	Christopher, Matt	Little, Brown & Co.
Creep Show	L	250+	Dussling, Jennifer	Grosset & Dunlap
Cupid Doesn't Flip Hamburgers	M	250+	Dadey, Debbie, and Jones, Marcia	Scholastic

Title	Fountas and Pinnell	Words	Author	Publisher/Series
The Curse of the Cobweb Queen	L	250+	Hayes, Geoffrey	Random House
The Curse of the Squirrel	M	250+	Yep, Laurence	Random House
Cyclops Doesn't Roller-Skate	M	250+	Dadey, Debbie, and Jones, Marcia	Scholastic
Dabble Duck	K	250+	Leo Ellis, Anne	Harper Trophy
Dancing with the Indians	M	250+	Medearis, Angela Shelf	Scholastic
Dancing with the Manatees	K	250+	McNulty, Faith	Scholastic
Daniel's Dog	K	250+	Bogart, Jo Allen	Scholastic
Daniel's Duck	K	250+	Bulla, Clyde Robert	Harper Trophy
Darcy and Gran Don't Like Babies	K	250+	Cutler, Jane	Scholastic
A Day in Space	L	250+	Lord, Suzanne, and Epstein, Jolie	Scholastic
The Day Jimmy's Boa Ate the Wash	K	250+	Noble, Trinka H.	Scholastic
A Day of Ahmed's Secret	M	250+	Heide, Florence, and Gilliland, Judith	Scholastic
Day of the Dragon King	M	250+	Osborne, Mary Pope	Random House
The Day of the Rain	L	250+	Cowley, Joy	Dominie Press
The Day of the Snow	L	250+	Cowley, Joy	Dominie Press
The Day of the Wind	L	250+	Cowley, Joy	Dominie Press
The Deadly Dungeon	M	250+	Roy, Ron	Random House
December Secrets	L	250+	Giff, Patricia Reilly	Bantam Doubleday Dell
Deputy Dan and the Bank Robbers	L	250+	Rosenbloom, Joseph	Random House
Deputy Dan Gets His Man	L	250+	Rosembloom, Joseph	Random House
Desert Giant: The World of the Saguaro Cactus	L	250+	Bash, Barbara	Scholastic
The Diamond Champs	M	250+	Christopher, Matt	Little, Brown & Co.
The Diamond of Doom	M	250+	Schultz, Irene	Wright Group

Title	Fountas and Pinnell	Words	Author	Publisher/Series
Did You Carry the Flag Today, Charley?	M	250+	Caudill, Rebecca	Bantam Doubleday Dell
Dinosaur Babies	L	250+	Penner, Lucille Recht	Random House
Dinosaur Days	L	250+	Milton, Joyce	Random House
Dinosaur Hunters	L	250+	McMullan, Kate	Random House
Dinosaur Time	K	250+	Parish, Peggy	Harper & Row
Dinosaurs Before Dark	M	250+	Osborne, Mary Pope	Random House
Dirt Bike Racer	M	250+	Christopher, Matt	Little, Brown & Co.
Dirt Bike Runaway	M	250+	Christopher, Matt	Little, Brown & Co.
Do You Like Cats?	K	250+	Oppenheim, Joanne	Bantam Doublday Dell
The Dog That Pitched a No-Hitter	L	250+	Christopher, Matt	Little, Brown & Co.
The Dog That Stole Football Plays	L	250+	Christopher, Matt	Little, Brown & Co.
The Dog That Stole Home	L	250+	Christopher, Matt	Little, Brown & Co.
Dog-Gone Hollywood	L	250+	Sharmat, Marjorie Weinman	Random House
Dolphin	L	250+	Morris, Robert A.	Harper Trophy
Dolphins at Daybreak	M	250+	Osborne, Mary Pope	Random House
Don't Forget the Bacon	M	174	Hutchins, Pat	Puffin Books
Donkey	M	250+	Cianter, George	Rigby/Literacy 2000
Donkey Rescues	M	250+	Krailing, Tessa	Barron's Educational
Double Play at Short	M	250+	Christopher, Matt	Little, Brown & Co.
Double Trouble	M	250+	Lawrence, Lucy	Rigby/Literacy 2000
Dr. Jekyll, Orthodontist	M	250+	Greenburg, Dan	Grosset & Dunlap
Dracula Doesn't Drink Lemonade	M	250+	Dadey, Debbie	Scholastic
Dragon Breath	L	250+	O'Connor, Jane	Grosset & Dunlap
The Dragon's Birthday	L	250+	Mahy, Margaret	Rigby/Literacy 2000
Dragons Don't Cook Pizza	M	250+	Dadey, Debbie, and Jones, Marcia	Scholastic
The Dragons of Blueland	L	250+	Gannett, Ruth Stiles	Random House

Title	Fountas and Pinnell	Words	Author	Publisher/Series
Drinking Gourd	M	250+	Monjo, Ferdinand N.	Harper Trophy
The Duck in the Gun	M	250+	Cowley, Joy	Rigby/Literacy 2000
Eat!	M	250+	Kroll, Steven	Hyperion
Effie	K	250+	Allinson, Beverly	Scholastic
Egg	K	250+	Logan, Dick	Cypress
Elaine and the Flying Frog	K	250+	Chang, Heidi	Scholastic
Eliza the Hypnotizer	M	250+	Granger, Michelle	Scholastic
Elmer and the Dragon	M	250+	Gannett, Ruth Stiles	Random House
The Elves Don't Wear Hard Hats	M	250+	Dadey, Debbie, and Jones, Marcia	Scholastic
Elvis the Turnip . . . And Me	M	250+	Greenburg, Dan	Grosset & Dunlap
Emily Arrow Promises to Do Better This Year	M	250+	Giff, Patricia Reilly	Bantam Doubleday Dell
Emily Eyefinger	M	250+	Ball, Duncan	Aladdin
Everybody Cooks Rice	M	250+	Dooley, Norah	Scholastic
Families Are Different	K	250+	Pellegrini, Nina	Scholastic
Fancy Feet	M	250+	Giff, Patricia Reilly	Bantam Doubleday Dell
The Farmer in the Soup	K	250+	Littledale, Freya	Scholastic
The Fiddle and the Gun	M	250+	Mahy. Margaret	Rigby/Literacy 2000
Fighting Tackle	M	250+	Christopher, Matt	Little, Brown & Co.
The Fiji Flood		250+	Schultz, Irene	Wright Group
Finding Providence: The Story of Roger Williams	L	250+	Avi	Harper Trophy
First Flight	K	250+	Shea, George	Harper Trophy
Fish Face	M	250+	Giff, Patricia Reilly	Bantam Doubleday Dell
Five Funny Frights	K	250+	Stamper, Judith Bauer	Scholastic
Five True Dog Stories	M	250+	Davidson, Margaret	Scholastic
Five True Horse Stories	M	250+	Davidson, Margaret	Scholastic
A Flea Story	L	250+	Lionni, Leo	Scholastic
The Flight of the Union	L	250+	White, Tekla	Carolrhoda Books

Title	Fountas and Pinnell	Words	Author	Publisher/Series
Flower Girls #1: Violet	L	250+	Leverich, Kathleen	HarperTrophy
Flower Girls #2: Daisy	L	250+	Leverich, Kathleen	HarperTrophy
Flower Girls #3: Heather	L	250+	Leverich, Kathleen	HarperTrophy
Flower Girls #4: Rose	L	250+	Leverich, Kathleen	HarperTrophy
The Flower of Sheba	L	250+	Orgel, Doris, and Schecter, Ellen	Bantam Doubleday Dell
Fly Trap	L	250+	Anastasio, Dina	Grosset & Dunlap
Follow That Fish	K	250+	Oppenheim, Joanne	Bantam Doubleday Dell
Football Friends	L	250+	Marzollo, Jean, Dan, and Dave	Scholastic
Football Fugitive	M	250+	Christopher, Matt	Little, Brown & Co.
Four on the Shore	K	250+	Marshall, Edward	Puffin Books
The Fox Steals Home	M	250+	Christopher, Matt	Little, Brown & Co.
Frankenstein Doesn't Plant Petunias	M	250+	Dadey, Debbie	Scholastic
Frankenstein Doesn't Slam Hockey Pucks	M	250+	Dadey, Debbie, and Jones, Marcia	Scholastic
Frankenstein Moved on to the 4th Floor	M	250+	Levy, Elizabeth	Harper & Row
Franklin Goes to School	K	250+	Bourgeois, Paulette, and Clark, Brenda	Scholastic
Freckle Juice	M	250+	Blume, Judy	Bantam Doubleday Dell
Frog and Toad Are Friends	K	250+	Lobel, Arnold	Harper & Row
Frog and Toad Together	K	1927	Lobel, Arnold	HarperCollins
The Frog Prince	K	250+	Tarcov, Edith H.	Scholastic
The Frog Who Would Be King	M	250+	Walker, Kate	Mondo
Gargoyles Don't Drive School Buses	M	250+	Dadey, Debbie, and Jones, Marcia	Scholastic
The Gator Girls Book 2: The Rocking Reptiles	L	250+	Calmenson, Stephanie and Cole	Beech Tree Books
The Gator Girls	L	250+	Calmenson, Stephanie and Cole	Beech Tree Books

Title	Fountas and Pinnell	Words	Author	Publisher/Series
Genies Don't Ride Bicycles	M	250+	Dadey, Debbie, and Jones, Marcia	Scholastic
George and Martha	L	250+	Marshall, James	Houghton Mifflin
George and Martha Back in Town	L	250+	Marshall, James	Houghton Mifflin
George and Martha Encore	L	250+	Marshall, James	Houghton Mifflin
George and Martha One Fine Day	L	250+	Marshall, James	Houghton Mifflin
George and Martha Rise and Shine	L	250+	Marshall, James	Houghton Mifflin
George and Martha Round and Round	L	250+	Marshall, James	Houghton Mifflin
George the Drummer Boy	K	250+	Benchley, Nathaniel	Harper Trophy
George Washington's Mother	M	250+	Fritz, Jean	Scholastic
The Ghost in Tent 19	M	250+	O'Connor, Jim and Jane	Random House
A Ghost Named Wanda	M	250	Greenburg, Dan	Grosset & Dunlap
Ghost Town at Sundown	M	250+	Osborne, Mary Pope	Random House
Ghost Town Treasure	M	250+	Bulla, Clyde Robert	The Penguin Group
Ghosts Don't Eat Potato Chips	M	250+	Dadey, Debbie, and Jones, Marcia	Scholastic
Ghouls Don't Scoop Ice Cream	M	250+	Dadey, Debbie, and Jones, Marcia	Scholastic
The Giant Jam Sandwich	K	250+	Lord, John Vernon	Houghton Mifflin
Giants Don't Go Snowboarding	M	250+	Dadey, Debbie, and Jones, Marcia	Scholastic
Ginger Brown: The Nobody Boy	L	250+	Wyeth, Sharon	Random House
Ginger Brown: Too Many Houses	L	250+	Wyeth, Sharon	Random House
The Gingerbread Boy	L	1097	Galdone, Paul	Clarion
Go and Hush the Baby	K	250+	Byars, Betsy	Viking
The Golden Goose	M	250+	Parkes, Brenda	Rigby/Literacy 2000
Goliath and the Burglar	L	205+	Dicks, Terrance	Barron's Educational

Title	Fountas and Pinnell	Words	Author	Publisher/Series
Goliath and the Buried Treasure	L	250+	Dicks, Terrance	Barron's Educational
Goliath and the Cub Scouts	L	250+	Dicks, Terrance	Barron's Educational
Goliath at the Dog Show	L	250+	Dicks, Terrance	Barron's Educational
Goliath at the Seaside	L	250+	Dicks, Terrance	Barron's Educational
Goliath Goes to Summer School	L	250+	Dicks, Terrance	Barron's Educational
Goliath on Vacation	L	250+	Dicks, Terrance	Barron's Educational
Goliath's Birthday	L	250+	Dicks, Terrance	Barron's Educational
Goliath's Christmas	L	250+	Dicks, Terrance	Barron's Educational
Goliath's Easter Parade	L	250+	Dicks, Terrance	Barron's Educational
The Golly Sisters Go West	K	250+	Byars, Betsy	Harper Trophy
The Golly Sisters Ride Again	K	250+	Byars, Betsy	Harper Trophy
Good as New	L	250+	Douglass, Barbara	Scholastic
Good Driving, Amelia Bedelia	L	250+	Parish, Peggy	Harper & Row
Good Work, Amelia Bedelia	L	250+	Parish, Peggy	Avon Camelot
The Good-for-Nothing Dog	M	250+	Schultz, Irene	Wright Group
Grandma's at the Lake	K	250+	McCully, Emily Arnold	Harper Trophy
Grandpa Comes to Stay	K	1083	Lewis, Rob	Mondo
Grasshopper on the Road	L	250+	Lobel, Arnold	Harper Trophy
The Great Dinosaur Hunt		250+	Schultz, Irene	Wright Group
Great Ghosts	L	250+	Cohen, Daniel	Scholastic
Great-Grandpa's in the Litter Box	M	250+	Greenburg, Dan	Grosset & Dunlap
Greg's Microscope	K	250+	Selsam, Millicent	Harper Trophy
Gregory, the Terrible Eater	L	250+	Sharmat, Marjorie Weinman	Scholastic
Gremlins Don't Chew Bubble Gum	M	250+	Dadey, Debbie, and Jones, Marcia	Scholastic
Happy Birthday, Dear Duck	K	250+	Bunting, Eve	Clarion
Happy Birthday, Martin Luther King	L	250+	Marzollo, Jean	Scholastic

Title	Fountas and Pinnell	Words	Author	Publisher/Series
Happy Birthday, Moon	L	345	Asch, Frank	Simon & Schuster
Hard Drive to Short	M	250+	Christopher, Matt	Little, Brown & Co.
Harold and the Purple Crayon	K	660	Johnson, Crockett	Harper & Row
Harry and Willy and Carrothead	L	250+	Caseley, Judith	Scholastic
The Haunted Bike	L	250+	Herman, Gail	Grosset & Dunlap
The Haunted Halloween	M	250+	Schultz, Irene	Wright Group
The Headless Horseman	L	250+	Standiford, Natalie	Random House
Helen Keller	M	250+	Davidson, Margaret	Scholastic
Hello Creatures!	K	250+	Garland, Peter	Rigby/Literacy 2000
Hercules Doesn't Pull Teeth	M	250+	Dadey, Debbie, and Jones, Marcia	Scholastic
Here Comes the Strike Out	K	250+	Kessler, Leonard	Harper Trophy
The Hidden Hand	M	250+	Schultz, Irene	Wright Group
Hill of Fire	L	1099	Lewis, Thomas P.	HarperCollins
The Hit-Away Kid	M	250+	Christopher, Matt	Little, Brown & Co.
Home in the Sky	K	250+	Baker, Jeannie	Scholastic
Honey Bees	L	250+	Kahkonen, Sharon	Steck-Vaughn
Hoopstars: Go to The Hoop!	M	250+	Hughes, Dean	Random House
Hooray for the Golly Sisters!	K	250+	Byars, Betsy	Harper Trophy
Horrible Harry and the Ant Invasion	L	250+	Kline, Suzy	Scholastic
Horrible Harry and the Christmas Surprise	L	250+	Kline, Suzy	Scholastic
Horrible Harry and the Dungeon	L	250+	Kline, Suzy	Puffin Books
Horrible Harry and the Green Slime	L	250+	Kline, Suzy	Puffin Books
Horrible Harry and the Kickball Wedding	L	250+	Kline, Suzy	Puffin Books
Horrible Harry and the Purple People	L	250+	Kline, Suzy	Puffin Books
Horrible Harry in Room 2B	L	250+	Kline, Suzy	Puffin Books
Horrible Harry's Secret	L	250+	Kline, Suzy	Puffin Books
Hour of the Olympics	M	250+	Osborne, Mary Pope	Random House

Title	Fountas and Pinnell	Words	Author	Publisher/Series
House of the Horrible Ghosts	M	250+	Hayes, Geoffrey	Random House
How Do Plants Get Food?	L	250+	Goldish, Meish	Steck-Vaughn
How Much Does This Hold?	K	179	Coulton, Mia	Kaeden Books
How Much Is That Guinea Pig in the Window?	L	250+	Rocklin, Joanne	Scholastic
Howling at the Hauntly's	M	250+	Dadey, Debbie, and Jones, Marcia	Scholastic
Huberta the Hiking Hippo	L	250+	Cox, Daphne	Rigby/Literacy 2000
Hungry, Hungry Sharks	L	250+	Cole, Joanna	Random House
The Hunt for Pirate Gold	M	250+	Schultz, Irene	Wright Group
I Am Not Afraid	K	250+	Mann, Kenny	Bantam Doubleday Dell
I Can't, Said the Ant	M	250+	Cameron, Polly	Scholastic
I Hate Camping	M	250+	Petersen, P. J.	The Penguin Group
I Hate English	L	250+	Levine, Ellen	Scholastic
I Hate My Best Friend	L	250+	Rosner, Ruth	Hyperion
I Love the Beach	M	250+	Cartwright, Pauline	Rigby/Literacy 2000
I'm Out of My Body . . . Please Leave a Message	M	250+	Greenburg, Dan	Grosset & Dunlap
Ibis: A True Whale Story	K	250+	Himmelman, John	Scholastic
Ice Magic	M	250+	Christopher, Matt	Little, Brown & Co.
If You Give a Moose a Muffin	K	250+	Numeroff, Laura Joffe	HarperCollins
If You Give a Mouse a Cookie	K	291	Numeroff, Laura Joffe	HarperCollins
In the Clouds	M	250+	Reid, Susan	Rigby/Literacy 2000
In the Dinosaur's Paw	M	250+	Giff, Patricia Reilly	Bantam Doubleday Dell
The Invisible Dog	M	250+	King-Smith, Dick	Alfred A. Knopf
Invisible in the Third Grade	M	250+	Cuyler, Margery	Scholastic
Island Baby	M	250+	Keller, Holly	Scholastic
It's Halloween	K	250+	Prelutsky, Jack	Scholastic

Title	Fountas and Pinnell	Words	Author	Publisher/Series
It's Valentine's Day	K	250+	Prelutsky, Jack	Scholastic
Jack and the Beanstalk	K	250+	Weisner, David	Scholastic
Jamaica's Find	K	250+	Havill, Juanita	Scholastic
Jane Goodall and the Wild Chimpanzees	L	250+	Birnbaum, Bette	Steck-Vaughn
Jennifer Too	*	250+	Havill, Juanita	Hyperion
Jenny Archer to the Rescue	M	250+	Conford, Ellen	Little, Brown & Co.
Jenny Archer, Author	M	250+	Conford, Ellen	Little, Brown & Co.
Jilly the Kid	M	250+	Krailing, Tessa	Barron's Educational
A Job for Jenny Archer	M	250+	Conford, Ellen	Little, Brown & Co.
Joey's Head	L	250+	Cretan, Gladys	Simon & Schuster
Johnny Appleseed	K	250+	Moore, Eva	Scholastic
Johnny Long Legs	M	250+	Christopher, Matt	Little, Brown & Co.
Josefina Story Quilt	L	250+	Coerr, Eleanor	HarperTrophy
Junie B. Jones and a Little Monkey Business	M	250+	Park, Barbara	Random House
Junie B. Jones and Her Big Fat Mouth	M	250+	Park, Barbara	Random House
Junie B. Jones and Some Sneaky Peeky Spying	M	250+	Park, Barbara	Random House
Junie B. Jones and That Meanie Jim's Birthday	M	250+	Park, Barbara	Random House
Junie B. Jones and the Stupid Smelly Bus	M	250+	Park, Barbara	Random House
Junie B. Jones and the Yucky Blucky Fruitcake	M	250+	Park, Barbara	Random House
Junie B. Jones Has a Monster Under Her Bed	M	250+	Park, Barbara	Random House
Junie B. Jones Is a Beauty Shop Guy	M	250+	Park, Barbara	Random House
Junie B. Jones Is a Party Animal	M	250+	Park, Barbara	Random House
Junie B. Jones Is Not a Crook	M	250+	Park, Barbara	Random House
Junie B. Jones Loves Handsome Warren	M	250+	Park, Barbara	Random House
Junie B. Jones Smells Something Fishy	M	250+	Park, Barbara	Random House
Junior Gymnasts #2:Katie's Big Move	M	250+	Slater, Teddy	Scholastic
Just Us Women	K	250+	Caines, Jeannette	Scholastic
Kate Shelley and the Midnight Express	M	250+	Wetterer, Maragret	Carolrhoda Books

*No level available.

Title	Fountas and Pinnell	Words	Author	Publisher/Series
Katy and the Big Snow	L	250+	Burton, Virginia Lee	Scholastic
Kerri Strug: Heart of Gold	L	250+	Strug, Kerri, and Brown, Greg	Scholastic
The Kid Who Only Hit Homers	M	250+	Christopher, Matt	Little, Brown & Co.
Kids in Ms. Colman's Class: Author Day	M	250+	Martin, Ann M.	Scholastic
Kilmer's Pet Monster	L	250+	Dadey, Debbie, and Jones, Marcia	Scholastic
King Arthur	M	250+	Brown, Marc	Little, Brown & Co.
King, the Mice and the Cheese	K	250+	Gurney, Nancy	Random House
The Knight at Dawn	M	250+	Osborne, Mary Pope	Random House
Knights Don't Teach Piano	M	250+	Dadey, Debbie, and Jones, Marcia	Scholastic
Knock! Knock!	K	250+	Carter, Jack	Scholastic
A Know-Nothing Birthday	K	250+	Spirn, Michelle Sobel	HarperTrophy
The Know-Nothings	K	250+	Spirn, Michelle Sobel	HarperTrophy
The Last Puppy	K	244	Asch, Frank	Simon & Schuster
Lazy Lions, Lucky Lambs	M	250+	Giff, Patricia Reilly	Bantam Doubleday Dell
Leprechauns Don't Play Basketball	M	250+	Dadey, Debbie, and Jones, Marcia	Scholastic
Let's Get Moving	M	250+	Artis, Laura	Rigby/Literacy 2000
Let's Go Philadelphia!	M	250+	Giff, Patricia Reilly	Bantam Doubleday Dell
A Letter to Amy	K	250+	Keats, Ezra Jack	Harper & Row
The Lighthouse Mermaid	M	250+	Karr, Kathleen	Hyperion
Lily and Miss Liberty	M	250+	Stephens, Carla	Scholastic
Lionel and Louise	K	250+	Krensky, Stephen	Puffin Books
Lionel at Large	K	250+	Krensky, Stephen	Puffin Books
Lions at Lunchtime	M	250+	Osborne, Mary Pope	Random House
Little Chief	K	250+	Hoff, Syd	HarperCollins
Little Hawk's New Name	K	250+	Bolognese, Don	Scholastic
Little Lefty	M	250+	Christopher, Matt	Little, Brown & Co.

Title	Fountas and Pinnell	Words	Author	Publisher/Series
Little One Inch	K	384	Gibson, A., and Akiyam, M	Scholastic
Little Penguin's Tale	L	250+	Wood, Audrey	Scholastic
Little Polar Bear and the Brave Little Hare	K	250+	DeBeer, Hans	North-South Books
Little Runner of the Longhouse	K	250+	Baker, Betty	Harper Trophy
Little Soup's Birthday	K	250+	Peck, Robert	Bantam Doubleday Dell
The Little Spider		250+		Rigby/Literacy 2000
Little Swan	M	250+	Geras, Adele	Random House
Little Vampire and the Midnight Bear	L	250+	Kwitz, Mary Deball	Puffin Books
Little Walrus Rising	K	250+	Young, Carol	Scholastic
Little Witch Goes to School	K	250+	Hautzig, Deborah	Random House
Little Witch's Big Night	K	250+	Hautzig, Deborah	Random House
The Littles	M	250+	Peterson, John	Scholastic
The Littles and the Great Halloween Scare	M	250+	Peterson, John	Scholastic
The Littles and the Lost Children	M	250+	Peterson, John	Scholastic
The Littles and the Terrible Tiny Kid	M	250+	Peterson, John	Scholastic
The Littles and the Trash Tinies	M	250+	Peterson, John	Scholastic
The Littles Give a Party	M	250+	Peterson, John	Scholastic
The Littles Go Exploring	M	250+	Peterson, John	Scholastic
The Littles Go to School	M	250+	Peterson, John	Scholastic
The Littles Have a Wedding	M	250+	Peterson, John	Scholastic
The Littles Take a Trip	M	250+	Peterson, John	Scholastic
Locked in the Library!	M	250+	Brown, Marc	Little, Brown & Co.
Long Shot for Paul	M	250+	Christopher, Matt	Little, Brown & Co.
A Long Way to a New Land	L	250+	Sandin, Joan	Harper Trophy
The Long Way Westward	L	250+	Sandin, Joan	Harper Trophy
Look Who's Playing First Base	M	250+	Christopher, Matt	Little, Brown
Lost at the White House: A 1909 Easter Story	L	250+	Griest, Lisa	Carolrhoda Books
The Lucky Baseball Bat	M	250+	Christopher, Matt	Little, Brown & Co.

Title	Fountas and Pinnell	Words	Author	Publisher/Series
The Lucky Feather	L	250+	Cowley, Joy	Rigby/Literacy 2000
Lucky Last Luke	M	250+	Clark, Margaret	Sundance
Lucky Stars	L	250+	Adler, David	Random House
M & M and the Bad News Babies	K	250+	Ross, Pat	The Penguin Group
M & M and the Big Bag	K	250+	Ross, Pat	The Penguin Group
M & M and the Halloween Monster	K	250+	Ross, Pat	The Penguin Group
M & M and the Haunted House Game	K	250+	Ross, Pat	The Penguin Group
M & M and the Mummy Mess	K	250+	Ross, Pat	The Penguin Group
M & M and the Santa Secrets	K	250+	Ross, Pat	Puffin Chapters
M & M and the Super Child Afternoon	K	250+	Ross, Pat	The Penguin Group
The Mad Scientist	M	250+	Schultz, Irene	Wright Group
Madeline	K	250+	Bemelmans, Ludwig	Scholastic
Madeline's Rescue	K	250+	Bemelmans, Ludwig	Scholastic
The Magic Box	K	250+	Brenner, Barbara	Bantam Doubleday Dell
Magic Fish	L	870	Littledale, Freya	Scholastic
Magic Money	L	250+	Adler, David	Random House
Make Way for Ducklings	L	250+	McCloskey, Robert	Puffin Books
Man Out at First	M	250+	Christopher, Matt	Little, Brown & Co.
Manatee Winter	K	250+	Zoehfeld, Kathleen Weidnetz	Scholastic
Marcella	L	250+	McShane, Owen	Rigby/Literacy 2000
A Mare for Young Wolf	L	250+	Shefelman, Janice	Random House
Martians Don't Take Temperatures	M	250+	Dadey, Debbie and Jones, Marcia	Scholastic
Martin and the Teacher's Pet	K	250+	Chardiet, Bernice and Maccarone, Grace	Scholastic
Martin and the Tooth Fairy	K	250+	Chardiet, Bernice and Maccarone, Grace	Scholastic
Martin Luther King Day	L	250+	Lowery, Linda	Scholastic
Marvin Redpost: Alone in His Teacher's House	L	250+	Sachar, Louis	Random House

Title	Fountas and Pinnell	Words	Author	Publisher/Series
Marvin Redpost: Is He a Girl?	L	250+	Sachar, Louis	Random House
Marvin Redpost: Kidnapped at Birth?	L	250+	Sachar, Louis	Random House
Marvin Redpost: Why Pick on Me?	L	250+	Sachar, Louis	Random House
Mary Marony and the Chocolate Surprise	L	250+	Kline, Suzy	Bantam Doubleday Dell
Mary Marony and the Snake	L	250+	Kline, Suzy	Bantam Doubleday Dell
Mary Maroney Hides Out	L	250+	Kline, Suzy	Bantam Doubleday Dell
Mary Marony, Mummy Girl	L	250+	Kline Suzy	Bantam Doubleday Dell
Maybe Yes, Maybe No, Maybe Maybe	M	250+	Patron, Susan	Bantam Doubleday Dell
Me Too	K	136	Mayer, Mercer	Donovan
The Meanest Thing to Say	K	250+	Cosby, Bill	Scholastic
Meet M & M	K	250+	Ross, Pat	Puffin Chapters
Meet the Molesons	L	250+	Bos, Burny	North-South Books
Mermaid Island	L	250+	Frith, Margaret	Grosset & Dunlap
Mermaids Don't Run Track	M	250+	Dadey, Debbie, and Jones, Marcia	Scholastic
Michael Jordan	M	250+	Edwards, Nick	Scolastic
Midnight on the Moon	M	250+	Osborne, Mary Pope	Random House
Miracle at the Plate	M	250+	Christopher, Matt	Little, Brown & Co.
The Misfortune Cookie	M	250+	Greenburg, Dan	Grosset & Dunlap
Miss Nelson Has a Field Day	L	250+	Allard, Harry	Scholastic
Miss Nelson Is Missing	L	598	Allard, Harry	Houghton Mifflin
The Missing Fossil Mystery	L	250+	Herman, Emily	Hyperion
The Mitten	M	250+	Brett, Jan	Scholastic
Mog at the Zoo	L	250+	Nicoll, Helen	The Penguin Group
Mog's Mumps	L	250+	Nicoll, Helen	The Penguin Group
Molly the Brave and Me	K	250+	O'Connor, Jane	Random House
Molly's Pilgrim	M	250+	Cohen, Barbara	Dell
Molly's Pilgrim	M	250+	Cohen, Barbara	Bantam Doubleday Dell
Monster for Hire	M	250+	Wilson, Trevor	Mondo Publishing

Title	Fountas and Pinnell	Words	Author	Publisher/Series
The Monster from the Sea	K	250+	Hooks, William H.	Bantam Doubleday Dell
Monster Movie	K	250+	Cole, Joanna	Scholastic
Monster Rabbit Runs Amuck!	M	250+	Giff, Patricia Reilly	Bantam Doubleday Dell
Monsters Don't Scuba Dive	M	250+	Dadey, Debbie, and Jones, Marcia	Scholastic
The Monsters Next Door	L	250+	Dadey, Debbie, and Jones, Marcia	Scholastic
More Tales of Amanda Pig	K	1939	Van Leeuwen, Jean	The Penguin Group
More Tales of Oliver Pig	K	2052	Van Leeuwen, Jean	The Penguin Group
Mr. Gumpy's Motor Car	K	250+	Burningham, John	HarperCollins
Mr. Gumpy's Outing	L	283	Burningham, John	Henry Holt
Mrs. Huggins and Her Hen Hannah	K	250+	Dabcovich, Lydia	Dutton
Mrs. Jeepers' Batty Vacation	L	250+	Dadey, Debbie, and Jones, Marcia	Scholastic
Mummies Don't Coach Softball	M	250+	Dadey, Debbie, and Jones, Marcia	Scholastic
Mummies in the Morning	M	250+	Osborne, Mary Pope	Random House
The Mummy's Gold	L	250+	McMullan, Kate	Grosset & Dunlap
My Father's Dragon	M	250+	Gannett, Ruth Stiles	Random House
My Son, the Time Traveler	M	250+	Greenburg, Dan	Grosset & Dunlap
Mystery in the Night Woods	M	250+	Peterson, John	Scholastic
The Mystery of the Blue Ring	L	250+	Giff, Patricia Reilly	Bantam Doubleday Dell
The Mystery of the Dark Old House	M	250+	Schultz, Irene	Wright Group
The Mystery of the Missing Dog	M	250+	Schultz, Irene	Wright Group
The Mystery of the Pirate Ghost	L	250+	Hayes, Geoffrey	Random House
The Mystery of the Stolen Bike	M	250+	Brown, Marc	Little, Brown & Co.
The Mystery of the Talking Tail	M	250+	Clark, Margaret	Sundance
The Mystery of the Tooth Gremlin	L	250+	Graves, Bonnie	Hyperion
Nannies for Hire		250+	Hest, Amy	William Morrow & Co.

Title	Fountas and Pinnell	Words	Author	Publisher/Series
Nate the Great	K	250+	Sharmat, Marjorie Weinman	Bantam Doubleday Dell
Nate the Great and the Boring Beach Bag	K	250+	Sharmat, Marjorie Weinman	Bantam Doubleday Dell
Nate the Great and the Crunchy Christmas	K	250+	Sharmat, Marjorie Weinman	Bantam Doubleday Dell
Nate the Great and the Fishy Prize	K	250+	Sharmat, Marjorie Weinman	Bantam Doubleday Dell
Nate the Great and the Halloween Hunt	K	250+	Sharmat, Marjorie Weinman	Bantam Doubleday Dell
Nate the Great and the Lost List	K	250+	Sharmat, Marjorie Weinman	Bantam Doubleday Dell
Nate the Great and the Missing Key	K	250+	Sharmat, Marjorie Weinman	Bantam Doubleday Dell
Nate the Great and the Mushy Valentine	K	250+	Sharmat, Marjorie Weinman	Bantam Doubleday Dell
Nate the Great and the Musical Note	K	250+	Sharmat, Marjorie Weinman	Bantam Doubleday Dell
Nate the Great and the Phony Clue	K	250+	Sharmat, Marjorie Weinman	Bantam Doubleday Dell
Nate the Great and the Pillowcase	K	250+	Sharmat, Marjorie Weinman	Bantam Doubleday Dell
Nate the Great and the Snowy Trail	K	250+	Sharmat, Marjorie Weinman	Bantam Doubleday Dell
Nate the Great and the Sticky Case	K	250+	Sharmat, Marjorie Weinman	Bantam Doubleday Dell
Nate the Great and the Stolen Base	K	250+	Sharmat, Marjorie Weinman	Bantam Doubleday Dell
Nate the Great and the Tardy Tortoise	K	250+	Sharmat, Marjorie Weinman	Bantam Doubleday Dell
Nate the Great Goes Down in the Dumps	K	250+	Sharmat, Marjorie Weinman	Bantam Doubleday Dell
Nate the Great Goes Undercover	K	250+	Sharmat, Marjorie Weinman	Bantam Doubleday Dell

Title	Fountas and Pinnell	Words	Author	Publisher/Series
Nate the Great Saves the King of Sweden	K	250+	Sharmat, Marjorie Weinman	Bantam Doubleday Dell
Nathan and Nicholas Alexander	K	250+	Delacre, Lulu	Scholastic
Never Trust a Cat Who Wears Earrings	M	250+	Greenburg, Dan	Grosset & Dunlap
Next Time I Will		250+	Orgel, Doris	Bantam Doubleday Dell
Nice New Neighbors	K	250+	Brandenberg, Franz	Scholastic
Night of the Ninjas	M	250+	Osborne, Mary Pope	Random House
The Nine Lives of Adventure Cat	L	250+	Clymer, Susan	Scholastic
Nine True Dolphin Stories	M	250+	Davidson, Margaret	Scholastic
No Arm in Left Field	M	250+	Christopher, Matt	Little, Brown & Co.
No Copycats Allowed!	L	250+	Graves, Bonnie	Hyperion
No Fighting, No Biting!	K	250+	Minarik, Else H.	Harper Trophy
No Tooth, No Quarter!	K	250+	Buller, Jon	Random House
Now You See Me . . . Now You Don't	M	250+	Greenburg, Dan	Grosset & Dunlap
Oh, What a Daughter!	L	250+		Rigby/Literacy 2000
Old Enough for Magic	L	250+	Pickett, A.	Harper Trophy
The Old Man and the Bear	M	250+	Hanel, Wolfram	North-South Books
The Old Rocking Chair	M	250+	Root, Phyllis	Scholastic
Oliver and Amanda's Halloween	L	250+	Van Leeuwen, Jean	Puffin Books
The One Bad Thing About Father	M	250+	Monjo, Ferdinand N.	Harper Trophy
The One in the Middle Is the Green Kangaroo	M	250+	Blume, Judy	Bantam Doubleday Dell
One-Eyed Jake	M	547	Hutchins, Pat	William Morrow & Co.
Onion Sundaes	M	250+	Adler, David	Random House
Orca Song	K	250+	Armour, Michael C.	Scholastic
The Outside Dog	K	250+	Pomerantz, Charlotte	Harper Trophy
Over in the Meadow	L	375	Galdone, Paul	Simon & Schuster
Owl and the Pussy Cat	L	215	Lear, Edward	Scholastic

Title	Fountas and Pinnell	Words	Author	Publisher/Series
The Paint Brush Kid	M	250+	Bulla, Clyde Robert	Random House
Pajama Party	M	250+	Hest, Amy	William Morrow & Co.
The Pancake	K	250+	Lobel, Anita	Bantam Doubleday Dell
Parents' Night Fright	K	250+	Levy, Elizabeth	Scholastic
Patches	M	250+	Szymanski, Lois	Avon Camelot
The Peanut Butter Gang	K	250+	Siracusa, Catherine	Hyperion
Pedro's Journal: A Voyage with Christopher Columbus	L	250+	Conrad, Pam	Scholastic
Pee Wee Scouts	L	250+	Delton, Judy	Yearling
Pee Wee Scouts: Blue Skies, French Fries	L	250+	Delton, Judy	Bantam Doubleday Dell
Pee Wee Scouts: Book Worm Buddy	L	250+	Delton, Judy	Bantam Doubleday Dell
Pee Wee Scouts: Computer Clues	L	250+	Delton, Judy	Bantam Doubleday Dell
Pee Wee Scouts: Eggs with Legs	L	250+	Delton, Judy	Bantam Doubleday Dell
Pee Wee Scouts: Cookies and Crutches	L	250+	Delton, Judy	Bantam Doubleday Dell
Pee Wee Scouts: Fishy Wishes	L	250+	Delton, Judy	Bantam Doubleday Dell
Pee Wee Scouts: Greedy Groundhogs	L	250+	Delton, Judy	Bantam Doubleday Dell
Pee Wee Scouts: Grumpy Pumpkins	L	250+	Delton, Judy	Bantam Doubleday Dell
Perfect the Pig	L	250+	Jeschke, Susan	Scholastic
Pet Sitter Plus Five	L	250+	Springstubb, Tricia	Scholastic
Peter and the North Wind	K	250+	Littledale, Freya	Scholastic
Phantoms Don't Drive Sports Cars	M	250+	Dadey, Debbie, and Jones, Marcia	Scholastic
Picking Apples and Pumpkins	L	250+	Hutchings, A. and R.	Scholastic
Pickle Puss	L	250+	Giff, Patricia Reilly	Bantam Doubleday Dell
Pied Piper	L	250+	Hunia, Fran	Ladybird Books
The Pied Piper of Hamelin	K	250+	Hautzig, Deborah	Random House
Piggle	K	250+	Bonsall, Crosby	HarperCollins
Pinky and Rex	L	250+	Howe, James	Simon & Schuster

Title	Fountas and Pinnell	Words	Author	Publisher/Series
Pinky and Rex and the Bully	L	250+	Howe, James	Simon & Schuster
Pinky and Rex and the Double-Dad Weekend	L	250+	Howe, James	Simon & Schuster
Pinky and Rex and the Mean Old Witch	L	250+	Howe, James	Simon & Schuster
Pinky and Rex and the New Baby	L	250+	Howe, James	Simon & Schuster
Pinky and Rex and the New Neighbors	L	250+	Howe, James	Simon & Schuster
Pinky and Rex and the Perfect Pumpkin	L	250+	Howe, James	Simon & Schuster
Pinky and Rex and the School Play	L	250+	Howe, James	Simon & Schuster
Pinky and Rex and the Spelling Bee	L	250+	Howe, James	Simon & Schuster
Pinky and Rex Get Married	L	250+	Howe, James	Simon & Schuster
Pioneer Bear	L	250+	Sandin, Joan	Random House
Pirates Don't Wear Pink Sunglasses	M	250+	Dadey, Debbie, and Jones, Marcia	Scholastic
Pirates Past Noon	M	250+	Osborne, Mary Pope	Random House
Play Ball, Amelia Bedelia	L	250+	Parish, Peggy	Harper & Row
Pocket for Corduroy	K	250+	Freeman, Don	Scholastic
Polar Bears Past Bedtime	M	250+	Osborne, Mary Pope	Random House
Pony Trouble	L	250+	Gasque, Dale Blackwell	Hyperion
The Pooped Troop	L	250+	Delton, Judy	Bantam Doubleday Dell
The Postcard Pest	M	250+	Giff, Patricia Reilly	Bantam Doubleday Dell
The Powder Puff Puzzle	L	250+	Giff, Patricia Reilly	Bantam Doubleday Dell
Princess Josie's Pets	L	250+	Macdonald, Maryann	Hyperion
A Prize for Purry	K	250+	Slater, Janet	Rigby/Literacy 2000
Puppets	K	250+	Trussell-Cullen, Alan	Rigby/Literacy 2000
The Puppy Who Wanted a Boy	L	250+	Thayer, Jane	Scholastic
Purple Climbing Days	M	250+	Giff, Patricia Reilly	Bantam Doubleday Dell
The Quilt Story	L	250+	Johnston, Tony, and dePaola, Tomie	Scholastic

Title	Fountas and Pinnell	Words	Author	Publisher/Series
Rabbit Stew	L	250+		Modern Curriculum Press/First Chapters
Rabbits	M	250+	Meadows, Graham	Rigby/Literacy Tree
Rapunzel	L	250+	Beck, Jennifer	Rigby/Literacy 2000
Rats on the Range	M	250+	Marshall, James	Puffin Books
Rats on the Range and Other Stories	M	250+	Marshall, James	The Penguin Group
Rats on the Roof and Other Stories	M	250+	Marshall, James	The Penguin Group
Red Ribbon Rosie	M	250+	Marzollo, Jean	Random House
Return of Rinaldo, The Sly Fox	M	250+	Scheffler, Ursel	North-South Books
Return of the Third-Grade Ghost Hunters	M	250+	Maccarone, Grace	Scholastic
The Riddle of the Red Purse	L	250+	Giff, Patricia Reilly	Bantam Doubleday Dell
Rinaldo the Sly Fox	M	250+	Scheffler, Ursel	North-South Books
Rip-Roaring Russell	M	250+	Hurwitz, Johanna	The Penguin Group
Rise and Shine, Mariko-chan	K		Tomioka, Chiyoko	Scholastic
Rollo and Tweedy and the Ghost at Dougal Castle	K	250+	Allen, Laura Jean	HarperTrophy
Ruby the Copycat	K	250+	Rathman, Peggy	Scholastic
Russell and Elisa	M	250+	Hurwitz, Johanna	The Penguin Group
Russell Rides Again	M	250+	Hurwitz, Johanna	Puffin Books
Russell Sprouts	M	250+	Hurwitz, Johanna	Puffin Books
Sable		250+	Hesse, Karen	Henry Holt
Sadie and the Snowman	L	250+	Morgan, Allen	Scholastic
Sam Who Never Forgets	K	281	Rice, Eve	William Morrow & Co.
Sam's Glasses	M	250+	Basser, Megan	Rigby/Literacy 2000
Sandy's Suitcase	K		Edwards, Elsy	SRA/McGraw-Hill
Santa Claus Doesn't Mop Floors	M	250+	Dadey, Debbie	Scholastic
Say "Cheese"	L	250+	Giff, Patricia Reilly	Bantam Doubleday Dell
The Schoolyard Mystery	L	250+	Levy, Elizabeth	Scholastic

Title	Fountas and Pinnell	Words	Author	Publisher/Series
Science–Just Add Salt	L	250+	Markle, Sandra	Scholastic
Scruffy	K	250+	Parish, Peggy	Harper Trophy
Scrunder Goes Wandering	M	250+	Krailing, Tessa	Barron's Educational
The Search for the Lost Cave	M	250+	Schultz, Irene	Wright Group
Second Grade–Friends Again!	M	250+	Cohen, Miriam	Scholastic
Secondhand Star	L	250+	Macdonald, Maryann	Hyperion
The Secret at the Polk Street School	M	250+	Giff, Patricia Reilly	Bantam Doubleday Dell
The Secret of Foghorn Island	K	250+	Hayes, Geoffrey	Random House
The Secret of the Monster Book	M	250+	Schultz, Irene	Wright Group
The Secret of the Old Oak Trunk	M	250+	Schultz, Irene	Wright Group
The Secret of the Song	M	250+	Schultz, Irene	Wright Group
The Secret Soldier	L	250+	McGovern, Ann	Scholastic
The Selfish Giant	L	250+	Wilde, Oscar	Rigby/Literacy 2000
Shadow Over Second	M	250+	Christopher, Matt	Little, Brown & Co.
Sheila Rae, the Brave	K	250+	Henkes, Kevin	Scholastic
Shipwreck Saturday	K	250+	Cosby, Bill	Scholastic
Shortest Kid in the World	K	250+	Bliss, Corinne Demas	Random House
Shortstop From Tokyo	M	250+	Christopher, Matt	Little, Brown & Co.
Shorty	M	250+	Rule, Christine	Rigby/Literacy 2000
Show Time at the Polk Street School	M	250+	Giff, Patricia Reilly	Bantam Doubleday Dell
Six Foolish Fisherman	L	715	Elkin, Benjamin	Childrens Press
Skateboard Tough	M	250+	Christopher, Matt	Little, Brown & Co.
Skeletons Don't Play Tubas	M	250+	Dadey, Debbie, and Jones, Marcia	Scholastic
Slam Dunk Saturday	M	250+	Marzollo, Jean	Random House
The Smallest Cow in the World	K	250+	Paterson, Katherine	Harper Trophy

Title	Fountas and Pinnell	Words	Author	Publisher/Series
Snaggle Doodles	M	250+	Giff, Patricia Reilly	Bantam Doubleday Dell
Snake Alarm	M	250+	Krailing, Tessa	Barron's Educational
Snow Goes to Town	L	250+	Beames, Margaret	Rigby/Literacy 2000
Snow White and Rose Red	K	250+	Hunia, Fran	Ladybird Books
The Snowball War	K	250+	Chardiet, Bernice	Scholastic
Snowshoe Thompson	K	250+	Smiler Levinson, Nancy	Harper Trophy
Soap Soup and Other Verses	K	250+	Kuskin, Karla	Harper Trophy
Soccer Cousins	K	250+	Marzollo, Jean	Scholastic
Soccer Mania	M	250+	Tamar, Erika	Random House
Soccer Sam	M	250+	Marzollo, Jean	Random House
Solo Girl	M	250+	Pinkey, Andrea Davis	Hyperion
Sound, Heat and Light: Energy at Work	L	250+	Berger, Melvin	Scholastic
Space Dog and Roy		250+	Standiford, Natalie	Random House
Space Dog and the Pet Show	L	250+	Standiford, Natalie	Random House
Space Dog in Trouble	L	250+	Standiford, Natalie	Random House
Space Dog the Hero	L	250+	Standiford, Natalie	Random House
Space Rock	K	250+	Buller, Jon	Random House
Spectacular Stone Soup	M	250+	Giff, Patricia Reilly	Yearling
The Spider and the King	L	250+	Krueger, Carol	Rigby/Literacy 2000
Spider Man	M	250+	Patterson, Peter J.	Rigby/Literacy 2000
Spoiled Rotten	L	250+	DeClements, Barthe	Hyperion Press
Spy Down the Street	M	250+	Schultz, Irene	Wright Group
The Spy in the Attic		250+	Scheffler, Ursel	North-South Books
The Spy on Third Base	M	250+	Christopher, Matt	Little, Brown & Co.
Squanto and the First Thanksgiving	L	250+	Celsi, Teresa	Steck-Vaughn
Stacy Says Good-bye	M	250+	Giff, Patricia Reilly	Bantam Doubleday Dell

Title	Fountas and Pinnell	Words	Author	Publisher/Series
Stan the Hot Dog Man	K	250+	Kessler, Ethel and Leonard	HarperTrophy
Star	M	250+	Simon, Jo Ann	Random House
Statue of Liberty	L	250+	Penner, Lucille Recht	Random House
Stop, Stop	M	250+	Hurd, Edith Thacher	HarperCollins
The Story of Hungbu and Nolbu	K	802		Mondo/Bookshop
Strike Out!	M	250+	Howard, Tristan	Scholastic
Sunny-Side Up	M	250+	Giff, Patricia Reilly	Bantam Doubleday Dell
Sunset of the Sabertooth	M	250+	Osborne, Mary Pope	Random House
Supercharged Infield	M	250+	Christopher, Matt	Little, Brown & Co.
Surprise Party	K	333	Hutchins, Pat	Macmillan
Surprises	L	250+	Hopkins, Lee Bennett	HarperTrophy
The Tale of Peter Rabbit	L	250+	Potter, Beatrix	Scholastic
Tales of Amanda Pig	L	250+	Van Leeuwen, Jean	Puffin Books
Teach Us, Amelia Bedelia	L	250+	Parish, Peggy	Scholastic
Teacher's Pet	L	250+	Dicks, Terrance	Scholastic
Teddy Bears Cure a Cold	K		Gretz, Susanna	Scholastic
Thank You, Amelia Bedelia	L	250+	Parish, Peggy	Harper & Row
That Fat Hat	K	250+	Barkan, Joann	Scholastic
That's a Laugh! Four Funny Fables	M	250+	Bryan, Phillip	Rigby/Literacy 2000
Things That Go: Traveling Alphabet	L	250+	Reit, Seymour	Bantam Doubleday Dell
This Is My House	L	250+	Dorros, Arthur	Scholastic
Three Bears	K	873	Galdone, Paul	Clarion
Three Billy Goats Gruff	K	478	Stevens, Janet	Harcourt Brace
The Three Blind Mice Mystery	L	250+	Krensky, Stephen	Bantam Doubleday Dell
Three by the Sea	K	250+	Marshall, Edward	Puffin Books
Three Days on a River in a Red Canoe	K	250+	Williams, Vera B.	Scholastic
Three Ducks Went Wandering	K	250+	Roy, Ron	Clarion

Title	Fountas and Pinnell	Words	Author	Publisher/Series
Three Little Pigs	L	919	Galdone, Paul	Houghton Mifflin
The Three Little Pigs	L	250+	Marshall, James	Scholastic
Three Smart Pals	L	250+	Rocklin, Joanne	Scholastic
Three Stories You Can Read to Your Cat	K	250+	Miller, Sara Swan	Houghton Mifflin
Three Stories You Can Read to Your Dog	K	250+	Miller, Sara Swan	Houghton Mifflin
Through Grandpa's Eyes	L	250+	MacLachlan, Patricia	Harper Trophy
Through the Medicine Cabinet	M	250+	Greenburg, Dan	Grosset & Dunlap
Tight End	M	250+	Christopher, Matt	Little, Brown & Co.
Tom Edison's Bright Idea	M	250+	Keller, Jack	Steck-Vaughn
Too Hot to Handle	M	250+	Christopher, Matt	Little, Brown
Too Many Babas	K	250+	Croll, Carolyn	Harper Trophy
Touchdown for Tommy	M	250+	Christopher, Matt	Little, Brown & Co.
Treasure Hunting	M	250+	Pascoe, Gwen	Rigby/Literacy 2000
Treasure of the Lost Lagoon	K	250+	Hayes, Geoffrey	Random House
Trees Belong to Everyone	L	250+	Noonah, Diana	Rigby/Literacy 2000
Triplet Trouble and the Bicycle Race	L	250+	Dadey, Debbie, and Jones, Marcia	Scholastic
Triplet Trouble and the Class Trip	L	250+	Dadey, Debbie, and Jones, Marcia	Scholastic
Triplet Trouble and the Cookie Contest	L	250+	Dadey, Debbie, and Jones, Marcia	Scholastic
Triplet Trouble and the Field Day Disaster	L	250+	Dadey, Debbie, and Jones, Marcia	Scholastic
Triplet Trouble and the Pizza Party	L	250+	Dadey, Debbie, and Jones, Marcia	Scholastic
Triplet Trouble and the Red Heart Race	L	250+	Dadey, Debbie, and Jones, Marcia	Scholastic
Triplet Trouble and the Runaway Reindeer	L	250+	Dadey, Debbie, and Jones, Marcia	Scholastic

Title	Fountas and Pinnell	Words	Author	Publisher/Series
Triplet Trouble and the Talent Show Mess	L	250+	Dadey, Debbie, and Jones, Marcia	Scholastic
Trixie and the Cyber Pet	M	250+	Krailing, Tessa	Barron's Educational
Trolls Don't Ride Roller Coasters	M	250+	Dadey, Debbie, and Jones, Marcia	Scholastic
True Stories About Abraham Lincoln	M	250+	Gross, Ruth Belov	Scholastic
The True Story of Balto: The Bravest Dog Ever	L	250+	Standiford, Natalie	Random House
Turkey Trouble	M	250+	Giff, Patricia Reilly	Bantam Doubleday Dell
The Turkeys' Side of It	M	250+	Smith, Janice Lee	Harper Trophy
Two Foolish Cats	K	250+		Rigby/Literacy 2000
Two Plus One Goes A.P.E.	L	250+	Springstubb, Tricia	Scholastic
The Two Runaways	M	250+	Schultz, Irene	Wright Group
Tyler Toad and Thunder	M	250+	Crowe, Robert	Dutton
Unicorns Don't Give Sleigh Rides	M	250+	Dadey, Debbie, and Jones, Marcia	Scholastic
The Upside-Down Reader	L	250+	Gruber, Wolfram	North-South Books
Vacation Under the Volcano	M	250+	Osborne, Mary Pope	Random House
The Valentine Star	M	250+	Giff, Patricia Reilly	Bantam Doubleday Dell
Vampire Trouble	L	250+	Dadey, Debbie, and Jones, Marcia	Scholastic
Vampires Don't Wear Polka Dots	M	250+	Dadey, Debbie, and Jones, Marcia	Scholastic
A Very Strange Dollhouse	L	250+	Dussling, Jennifer	Grosset & Dunlap
Viking Ships at Sunrise	M	250+	Osborne, Mary Pope	Random House
The Volcano Goddess Will See You Now	M	250+	Greenburg, Dan	Grosset & Dunlap
Wacky Jacks	L	250+	Adler, David	Random House
Wagon Wheels	K	250+	Brenner, Barbara	Harper Trophy
Wake Up, Emily, It's Mother's Day	M	250+	Giff, Patricia Reilly	Yearling
Walter the Warlock	M	250+	Hautzig, Deborah	Random House

Title	Fountas and Pinnell	Words	Author	Publisher/Series
Watch Out! Man-eating Snake	L	250+	Giff, Patricia Reilly	Bantam Doubleday Dell
Wax Museum	L	250+	Cook, Donald	Grosset & Dunlap
We Scream for Ice Cream	K	250+	Chardiet, Bernice, and Maccarone, Grace	Scholastic
Weather Poems for All Seasons	L	250+	Hopkins, Lee Bennett	Harper Trophy
Werewolves Don't Go to Summer Camp	M	250+	Dadey, Debbie, and Jones, Marcia	Scholastic
Whales–The Gentle Giants	L	250+	Milton, Joyce	Random House
What Kind of Babysitter Is This?	L	250+	Johnson, Dolores	Scholastic
What Next, Baby Bear?	L	313	Murphy, Jill	Dial
What's Cooking, Jenny Archer?	M	250+	Conford, Ellen	Little, Brown & Co.
When I Get Bigger	K	205	Mayer, Mercer	Donovan
When the Giants Came to Town	L	250+	Leonard, Marcia	Scholastic
When Will We Be Sisters?	K	250+	Kroll, Virginia	Scholastic
Where Are the Bears?	K	250+	Winters, Kay	Bantam Doubleday Dell
Where Is the Bear?	K	250+	Nims, Bonnie	Whitman
Whistle for Willie	L	380	Keats, Ezra Jack	The Penguin Group
Who Sank the Boat?	K	219	Allen, Pamela	Coward
Who's Afraid of the Big, Bad Bully?	K	250+	Slater, Teddy	Scholastic
Who's in Love with Arthur?	M	250+	Brown, Marc	Little, Brown & Co.
The Wind Blew	L	169	Hutchins, Pat	Puffin Books
Wingman on Ice	M	250+	Christopher, Matt	Little, Brown & Co.
Witches Don't Do Backflips	M	250+	Dadey, Debbie, and Jones, Marcia	Scholastic
The Wizard of Oz	L	903	Hunia, Fran	Ladybird Books
Wizards Don't Need Computers	M	250+	Dadey, Debbie, and Jones, Marcia	Scholastic
Wolf and the Seven Little Kids	L	250+	Hunia, Fran	Ladybird Books

Title	Fountas and Pinnell	Words	Author	Publisher/Series
Wolves of Willoughby Chase	L	250+	Aiken, Joan	Bantam Doubleday Dell
Wonder Kid Meets the Evil Lunch Snatcher	M	250+	Duncan, Lois	Little, Brown & Co.
The World's Greatest Toe Show	M	250+	Lamb, Nancy, and Singer, Muff	Troll
Write Up a Storm with the Polk Street School	M	250+	Giff, Patricia Reilly	Bantam Doubleday Dell
The Year Mom Won the Pennant	M	250+	Christopher, Matt	Little, Brown & Co.
Young Wolf's First Hunt	M	250+	Shefelman, Janice	Random House
Zack's Alligator	K	250+	Mozelle, Shirley	Harper Trophy
Zack's Alligator Goes to School	K	250+	Mozelle, Shirley	Harper Trophy
Zap! I'm a Mind Reader	M	250	Greenburg, Dan	Grosset & Dunlap
Zero's Slider	M	250+	Christopher, Matt	Little, Brown & Co.
Zombies Don't Play Soccer	M	250+	Dadey, Debbie, and Jones, Marcia	Scholastic

Dynamic Grouping

Grouping in Guided Reading

Guided reading is dependent on the teacher being aware of each child's competencies, interests, and experiences; being able to determine the supports and challenges offered by a book; and accepting the role of supporting learning rather than directing learning (Mooney, 1990).

Guided reading provides primary classroom teachers with a powerful teaching tool—flexible grouping. No longer do students have to be assigned to a semipermanent group based on perceived ability; rather, there are options in which students can travel between groups based on an ongoing assessment process that recognizes their reading growth and development and provides them with relevant reading materials that encourage an active engagement with text.

Following are two grouping options you may wish to consider as elements of your guided reading program.

Whole-class Guided Reading

Involving your students in a whole-class guided reading activity uniformly exposes them to important reading strategies. A whole-class guided reading activity has many benefits for the classroom teacher. Routman (1991) provides several advantages, which are summarized below:

• Teachers moving from traditional basal reading instruction into guided reading instruction can use the activity as a transitional stage.

• The activity assists in the management of instruction time.

> **G**uided reading is dependent on the teacher being aware of each child's competencies, interests, and experiences; being able to determine the supports and challenges offered by a book; and accepting the role of supporting learning rather than directing learning.

• Conducting a whole-class guided reading activity can help teachers get to know their students, particularly at the start of the school year, and learn their strengths and weaknesses.

• Teachers can gradually introduce the concepts of guided reading to children who may be used to more traditional reading practices.

• This type of activity helps the teacher model appropriate reading techniques and encourages open discussion through the use of open-ended questions.

• Whole-class guided reading activities promote the enjoyment of literature and provide a comfortable segue into small-group activities.

Small-group Guided Reading

Small groups are a very important part of the guided reading program. They offer children opportunities for active participation in the reading process, engage students in reading strategies, provide a match between reading ability and text difficulty, and offer a structure for developing and increasing reading proficiency. The emphasis is on the interaction between teacher and students and between students and text. The ultimate goal is to help beginning readers develop a sense of independence in reading that will carry over into their subjects and other aspects of their lives.

Small groups also provide opportunities to focus on the specific instructional needs of individual learners. These needs, assessed through formal and informal means (see Unit 5), provide you with a unique opportunity to teach skills in context—to help students see the relevance of selected skills in authentic reading materials. Some lessons can be planned in advance while others are unscripted and evolve out of teachable moments as students interact with a specific piece of literature.

Individualized Guided Reading

Guided reading strategies can be presented to students in a one-to-one format. A student is led through an introduction to a self-selected piece of literature (at his or her appropriate level), is engaged in the five stages of a guided reading lesson, and participates in conferences with the teacher. The same procedures and processes that are in place in a small-group session can be used with individual students. The disadvantage would be that the student does not have the opportunity to discuss and share a book with others who have also read the same book.

Individualized guided reading can be done when a particular student has an interest or desire to pursue a selected book on a selected topic. It is appropriate for use after students have become thoroughly comfortable with the practices and procedures of small-group guided reading lessons. It is equally appropriate for students to use a previously demonstrated strategy with a book of their own choosing, for example, a book they have selected from the classroom library or school library.

Individualized guided reading instruction can also be used as a passage from small-group work to independent reading. It provides a support structure for children to assume a measure of independence and self-reliance in reading. It's important to keep in mind that individualized guided reading is only an adjunct to the overall guided reading program—it is not a replacement for the small-group lessons that are the foundation of the program.

> *Individualized guided reading is only an adjunct to the overall guided reading program.*

Alternate Grouping Strategies

Guided reading provides you with a framework for conducting relevant and meaningful reading instruction. It is not a *way* to teach reading; neither is it a *method* of teaching reading. Rather, it is a structure upon which you can begin to build focused and directed lessons that are part of a balanced reading program.

Following are several alternative grouping strategies that can be integrated into your overall guided reading program.

• **Strategy Group:** Assign students to a single group that works with a single reading strategy. Students may need initial instruction in the strategy or may require added reinforcement for a previously introduced strategy. It is not essential, nor is it necessary, for all students to be at the same stage or level of reading proficiency.

• **Interest Group:** Students are assigned to a group based on a common interest (dinosaurs, ladybugs, bears, and so on). Interests can be assessed using interest inventories or other informal means. In this grouping strategy, students may all use the same reading strategy in a variety of books related to a common interest, or they may all use the same book (based on an identified interest) with an assortment of strategies. The advantage is that students are intrinsically motivated by materials that have a high interest value.

• **Skill Group:** Students may temporarily need a specific phonemic awareness, phonics, or vocabulary skill. They can be grouped together for a short period of time to receive instruction and opportunities to try out the skill in a specific book or piece of literature at a particular stage of reading.

• **Random Group:** Students can be assigned to a guided reading group at random. The advantage of this approach is that students can determine their own groups and work together to apply a technique or strategy to a book they select.

In using these multiple grouping options, you will note that they can be effectively used as a follow-up to a whole-group guided reading activity. If you are just beginning the concept of guided reading, you may wish to start off with a whole-group lesson and then try one of the alternate options, including small-group instruction. Such options increase your teaching effectiveness and the learning opportunities for children.

Grouping Considerations

Here are several ideas you may wish to consider when planning guided reading groups in your classroom:

Consideration	Description	Factors
Group size	Traditionally, guided reading groups range from two to five students. However, the flexibility within guided reading allows you to structure groups based on several factors.	• Number of students in the class • Number of available individual copies of a book • Need for a specific strategy
Formation	The formation of groups is primarily driven by assessment. Maintaining an ongoing system of running records, for example, will help you in assigning and re-assigning students to various groups.	• Continuous use of assessment • Interest • Strategy • Skill • Number of times available to meet during the week
Movement between groups	Guided reading groups are never static. Students should be placed in groups where the reading materials offer them few challenges—challenges that can be met with relevant strategies and a support structure offered by the teacher.	• Accuracy rate • Self-correction rate • Level of comprehension • Individual student needs
Number of groups	There is no minimum or maximum number of groups for any classroom. You will have to determine your level of comfort with many groups in concert with a select number of strategies for any single group. It is not necessary to have one reading group for every level of reader in your classroom.	• Books available • Strategies needed • Materials • Physical layout of room • Personal management skills
Group maintenance	There is no minimum or maximum amount of time for a group to stay together. The critical decisions to be made are: What is the purpose of the group? and When will the purpose be accomplished? The answer to those questions will determine how long a group should remain intact. Time frames may range from one day to two weeks.	• Needs of a group • Instructional time available for guided reading • Purpose of the group • Assessment results

The success of any guided reading group, as well as any modifications or alterations you may wish to incorporate into your classroom procedures, depends upon one factor: *routines*. Students must be well-instructed and practiced in the routines and expectations of each grouping format *before* they are assigned to those groups. This may take several weeks at the beginning of the school year, but the rewards later in the year will be well worth the time and effort. Provide your students with sufficient training in the demands, expectations, behaviors, and routines of group work. Post charts and posters in the classroom reminding them of those expectations. Take time at the beginning of each week to go over those routines to ensure that they are fully ingrained. Each type of group will have different expectations. Make sure students are aware of those well before they are assigned to a particular grouping format.

Keep in mind that groups may form, re-form, and disperse. Some individuals may come and go within a group as the needs of the group change as well as the individual needs of specific group members change. There are many grouping strategies available that can keep your guided reading program fresh and dynamic.

Strategies for Success

Traditional vs. Transactional Teaching

Many teachers subscribe to the notion that reading involves an active and energetic relationship between the reader and the text. That is, the reader-text relationship is reciprocal and involves the characteristics of the reader as well as the nature of the materials. This philosophy of reading, often referred to as a *transactional approach to reading*, is based on the seminal work of Louise Rosenblatt (1978) and has particular applications for teachers building effective student-based reading programs. As you might expect, it serves as a foundation for the construction, implementation, and effectiveness of balanced reading programs. Here are some principles of reading instruction (adapted from Rosenblatt, 1978) particularly useful for classroom teachers seeking to implement effective guided reading practices:

1. Reading is a lived-through experience or event. The reader evokes the text, bringing a network of past experiences with the world, language, and other texts.

2. The meaning is neither in the reader nor in the text, but in the reciprocal transaction between the two.

3. There is no single correct reading of a literary text.

4. In any specific reading activity, given agreed-upon purposes and criteria, some readings or interpretations are more defensible than others.

We all have our own unique backgrounds of experience that we bring to any reading material. As a result, we will all have our own interpretation of that material—one that may or may not be similar to the interpretations of others reading the same text. Reading a piece of literature opens up interpretive possibilities for children and provides opportunities for

> *R*eading a piece of literature opens up interpretive possibilities for children and provides opportunities for extending that literature in personal and subjective ways.

extending that literature in personal and subjective ways.

Encouraging children to become actively and meaningfully engaged with text demands a systematic approach to reading instruction. Traditional practices (e.g., Directed Reading Activity) have placed the burden of responsibility on the shoulders of teachers who directed much of the learning and much of the interpretation of textual material. Current views (e.g., transactional views) place a great deal of responsibility on the shoulders of students. Two models are illustrated in the following table.

Traditional vs. Transactional Teaching

Traditional Directed Reading Activity	**Transactional** Guided Reading Paradigm
Readiness and Motivation • Teacher sets purpose for reading • Teacher talk predominates • Teacher discusses vocabulary and predetermined concepts • No writing is involved	*Before (Book Orientation)* • Students make predictions about story • Teacher helps activate prior knowledge • Students share in flexible grouping formats • Students establish purposes for reading
Oral/Silent Reading • Students read silently • Students sometimes read in round robin situations	*During (Independent Reading)* • Students read silently • Students relate what they are reading to prior experiences • Teacher carefully observes students • Students attend to prompts (as needed) • Students focus on appropriate reading strategies
Follow-up Activities • Students answer comprehension questions (with predetermined answers) • Teacher selects writing topics • Teacher teaches specific skills	*After (Responding and Rereading)* • Students discuss and share what they have read • Students engage in problem-solving activities • Students participate in self-initiated activities • Students achieve success

Source: Adapted from Pincus, 1986.

The transactional approach to reading instruction is significant because it emphasizes three critical and interrelated stages in the reading process. Together, these stages are essential in the comprehension and appreciation of all types of reading materials:

Before Reading: Processes designed to link students' background knowledge and experiences to the text

During Reading: Processes designed to help students read constructively and interact with text

After Reading: Processes designed to deepen and extend students' responses to text

The emphasis (at all stages and levels) is on the development of appropriate reading strategies. Strategies are those mental processes that readers use (independently) to obtain meaning from text. Mature readers use a wide variety of strategies to comprehend written

> *The purpose of a reading program is to assist children in comprehending what they read.*

material. Beginning readers must be taught necessary strategies in order to ascend through the various stages of reading development. The purpose of a reading program is to assist children in comprehending what they read.

Strategies in Place

Many teachers are curious about the reading strategies that should be in place at each level of the guided reading process. Knowing the strategies that an individual student should master at a particular level will assist you in developing appropriate instructional activities for every student in your class. By the same token, you will be able to move students to higher levels when you are aware of the strategies they should master at a previous level.

An additional advantage of knowing what strategies students should have at each level is that it provides you with some incredible teaching opportunities. Instead of grouping students only by their respective reading level(s), you can now group individuals by strategies. For example, if you have several students who may need some instructional time working on predicting, you can organize an ad hoc predicting group. You may have children in that group from more than one reading level—however, the advantage is that this process opens up some new teaching opportunities for you as well as additional learning opportunities for your students. It's important to remember that grouping is not permanent. Students are assigned to groups based on any number of factors and circumstances. Those factors and circumstances change and evolve over time. So too, must groups change and evolve in terms of their emphasis, focus, and composition of individuals.

The charts on pages 177–178 provide a list of specific strategies that should be mastered at each reading level. Keep in mind that this chart is fluid—the horizontal lines between levels and strategies are flexible and dynamic. Don't assume that students must master all of the strategies at a single level before they are eligible to move up to the next level. The intent is to offer you some markers by which you can gauge (in general terms) the progress of students throughout your guided reading program. Students at any level will exhibit a majority of the strategies described, but not necessarily all of them.

Strategies Mastered at Each Level

Guided Reading in Grades K–2	Guided Reading Fountas & Pinnell, (1996)	Reading Recovery® Level	Strategies In Place
Emergent Reader	A	1	Knows that there is a message in printed materials Knows front, back, top, bottom of a book Can do a return sweep
	B	2	Can match voice to print Knows the difference between pictures and text Can point to selected words as they are said
	C	3	Uses picture clues Knows the difference between a letter and a word Can read and interpret illustrations
		4	Is able to use some letter sounds Is in the beginning stages of predicting Uses pictures and illustrations to interpret text
	D	5	Recognizes pattern and repetition of text Understands and uses rhyming words Uses oral language to connect to print
		6	Uses beginning letter sounds Uses ending letter sounds Has developed a collection of high-frequency words
Early Reader	E	7	Uses text patterns to make predictions Has mastered concepts of print Obtains information from print (rather than exclusively from illustrations)
		8	Recognizes and uses initial consonants Checks text predictions with illustrations
	F	9	Begins to use multiple sources of information about text (meaning, structure, graphophonics) Recognizes and uses punctuation
		10	Recognizes and uses a bank of high-frequency words Is able to recall repeated words
	G	11	Can check and confirm words using beginning, middle, and ending letters Recognizes similarities in sentence patterns Recognizes differences in sentence patterns
		12	Can read with some phrasing Can read with some fluency Can self-correct oral errors Continues to increase bank of sight words Uses self-monitoring techniques to assess comprehension

Strategies Mastered at Each Level

Guided Reading in Grades K–2	Guided Reading Fountas & Pinnell, (1996)	Reading Recovery® Level	Strategies in Place
Transitional Reader	H	13	Is able to use multiple sources of information Can make predictions and confirm/reject them while reading When encountering a difficult word, can skip it and go on
		14	Recognizes little words inside big words Uses and reads many punctuation marks Is able to retell important parts of a story
	I	15	Is able to read longer sections of text Is able to read more complex sections of text Is aware of story structure
		16	Continues to increase self-monitoring techniques Can self-correct words that don't make sense Is aware of structural cues to figure out unknown words
		17	Is able to integrate visual, contextual, and syntactic cues to determine unfamiliar words Can engage in active discussions about what is read
	J	18	Continues to integrate visual, contextual, and syntactic cues to determine unfamiliar words Reads with phrasing and fluency Has a sufficient bank of high-frequency words
		19	Can read independently for longer periods of time Can follow a plot line over several pages Attempts a variety of reading strategies
Fluent Reader	K	20	Can recall significant story events Is able to detect and correct reading errors Can problem-solve unfamiliar words
	L		Is able to make inferences about text Monitors reading for understanding Reads with sophisticated fluency
	M		Is able to tap into a variety of reading strategies Can establish own purposes for reading Is able to monitor and adjust reading rate
	N		Has a large storehouse of sight words Is able to revisit text to support interpretations Can synthesize information Uses and understands figurative language Comfortable in taking risks while reading

Instructional Strategies

Guided reading is strategic. One of the primary objectives of guided reading is assisting children in understanding and integrating the behaviors of accomplished readers. This is done through explanations or demonstrations of those behaviors by the teacher, gradually releasing responsibility for those behaviors to a group of students, and supporting and encouraging readers as they begin to use those behaviors. Teachers assist young readers in becoming independent thinkers who are able to use a variety of strategies to comprehend increasingly difficult texts.

Guided reading rests on the notion that children's literature can be an effective vehicle for teaching necessary reading strategies. Teachers will want to use that literature in ways that stimulate literacy development and conceptual understandings in a host of contexts. There are two factors that determine the intent and direction of a guided reading lesson—the needs of students in a leveled group and the challenges of the text they are about to read.

The following lists of techniques and strategies can be used with specific books and reading selections, and with a wide range of students in your classroom. They can have a significant impact on your overall guided reading program and on the developing reading abilities of every child.

Universal Strategies (for all stages)

On the next page is a list of strategies used by many readers in various types of texts. Not all of these ideas should be used with a single book or group of books. Instead, the intent is to offer you a selection from which you can choose and begin to build meaningful and lasting experiences with all kinds of literature—with single or multiple guided reading groups. This is not intended to be a finite list, but a collection of successful strategies used by other teachers. You can begin to create dynamic lesson plans that assist your students in becoming competent and energetic readers.

> *One of the primary objectives of guided reading is assisting children in understanding and integrating the behaviors of accomplished readers.*

Strategy	Description/Explanation	Questions/Prompts
Background knowledge	Background knowledge forms the foundation and structure for all reading experiences. What readers know affects what they can learn.	"What does this remind you of?" "Is this similar to anything you've read before?" "I like the way you remembered that other story." "How are you and this character similar?"
Predicting	Based on what readers know, they make educated guesses about what will happen or what will make sense in a story. Good readers are constantly predicting.	"What do you think will happen next?" "What else do you think we will learn?" "Don't forget how the pictures give us some clues." "You're making some good guesses about the story."
Mental imagery	Good readers create "mind pictures" as they read. Visualizing the characters, elements, or events of a story is critical to overall comprehension.	"Close your eyes. What do you see in the picture in your head?" "Can you create a picture of this in your mind?"
Monitor	Good readers keep track of their reading. They know when something isn't right or doesn't make sense.	"What did you see?" "How did you know that wasn't right?" "Is something not working?" "I like the way you're able to keep track of your reading."
Using "fix-up" tools	Accomplished readers are constantly correcting as they read. They may need to reread a passage, stop and match illustrations and text, or ask for assistance when something is too difficult.	"What do you think will make this right?" "You stopped here. Why?" "How can I help you understand this?" "Did you reread the word/sentence?" "Remember how we did this in the other book?"
Confirm	Readers need confirmation that what they read is understood. They use a trio of information sources (meaning, structure, and visual/graphophonics) to ensure that they are comprehending what they are reading.	"How do you know you are correct?" "Is there a way you can check to see if you are right?" "How can we find out?" "I liked the way you checked that out."
Important ideas	Good readers are able to separate important from unimportant information in text. They can identify critical details and separate them from extraneous material.	"What is the most important idea here?" "What is the main idea?" "Why do you think this is important?" "I like the way you find important ideas."

Strategy	Description/Explanation	Questions/Prompts

Search	Good readers search through the three sources of information (M, S, V) in order to make sense of what they read. Beginning readers may over-rely on a single source (visual/graphophonics, for example) to the exclusion of the other two.	"Here is what we read:
		  1. Does it make sense? (M)
		  2. Does it sound right? (S)
		  3. Does it look right? (V)"
		"What are some others ways we can figure this out?"
		"Don't forget to look at/for _____."

Drawing conclusions; making inferences	Good readers are able to pull together all the information in a text as they read. They are able to make educated guesses about the content of text throughout the reading process.	"What is happening here?" "What makes you think that?" "How did you arrive at that idea?" "You're using some good thinking skills here."
Comparing and contrasting	Readers must be able to compare and contrast what they are reading to other information (background knowledge, other texts). This helps them to expand their knowledge base.	"How is this similar to what we read before?" "Is this different or the same as _____?" "Remember that other story?" "Let's see if we can do a Venn diagram."
Check	Three questions that are in the back of every reader's mind are: "Does this make sense?" "Does this sound right?" and "Does this look right?" This is an internal process that comes about as readers have more and more experiences with books. Helping developing readers use a multiplicity of M, S, and V skills is a critical element in overall reading development.	"Is there another way we could figure this out?" "You seem to use _____; is there something else we could do?" "What do you think would make sense?" "What do you think would sound right?" "What do you think would look right?" "Good. You went back to see if that word made sense."
Summarizing	Good readers are able to pull together all that they have read into an inclusive statement. Their comprehension is based on their ability to summarize setting, characters, plot, theme, and point of view into a single statement.	"What was this about?" "Can you combine everything we read into one sentence?" "What would you tell someone else about this story?" "It sounds like you can tell someone at home what this story is about."

Specific Strategies (by stage)

The strategies listed below have been organized within each of the four stages. They will provide you with many selections to use with the literature shared in a guided reading lesson. This does not imply that each strategy can or should be used only with readers at the stage in which the strategy is listed. These strategies are developmental in nature and can be appropriate across stages. You are encouraged to match the strategies listed with the books you share and with the developing reading abilities of your students.

Emergent Readers

- Using pictures/illustrations to predict a story
- Focusing on the beginning and end of words
- Tracking print
- Noting patterns in text
- Chunking sounds together
- Problem-solving new words
- Detecting and correcting errors

Early Readers

- Chunking words into phrases
- Monitoring
- Self-correcting
- Paying attention to spelling patterns
- Using all three cueing systems together
- Skip and return
- Problem-solving new words
- Detecting and correcting errors
- Maintaining fluency

Transitional Readers

- Using a story map
- Rereading to clarify meaning
- Beginning to use graphic organizers
- Determining character traits
- Oral retelling
- Using a character map
- Dramatizing a story or book
- Understanding and following the plot of a story
- Constructing a before and after chart
- Problem-solving new words
- Detecting and correcting errors
- Maintaining fluency

Fluent Readers

- Using features of the text to aid comprehension
- Constructing and using K-W-L charts
- Extracting information from charts, graphs, maps, and other visuals
- Understanding figurative language
- Writing summaries of books
- Creating visual responses to what is read
- Making accurate predictions
- Determining the objectivity of an author
- Getting the gist of a story from an initial preview
- Problem-solving new words
- Detecting and correcting errors
- Maintaining fluency

More Strategies

One of the primary goals of your guided reading program is to help your students along the road to independent reading. This can best be accomplished when students are provided with the tools (e.g., strategies) that allow them to become less teacher-dependent and more reading independent. Obviously, as they begin their journey along this road, they will need your guidance and assistance.

This journey can be facilitated with strategic reading practices. Earlier you read about some of the universal strategies to which students must be exposed in order to facilitate their literacy progress, no matter what stage they are in. You've also seen lists of strategies that are appropriate for each of the four stages of literacy growth. What follows is a series of strategic methods that have been proven to assist children in developing an interactive relationship with text. These methods have been designed to promote a variety of reading strategies and higher levels of comprehension.

▶ Semantic Webbing

One method used as a framework for making links between prior knowledge and knowledge encountered in text is Semantic Webbing. Semantic Webbing is a graphic display of students' words, ideas, and images combined with textual words, ideas, and images. A semantic web helps students comprehend text by activating their background knowledge, organizing new concepts, and discovering the relationships between the two. A divergent semantic web includes the following steps:

1. Select a word or phrase that is central to the story and write it on the chalkboard.

2. Encourage students to think of as many words as they can that relate to the central word. Record these on separate sheets or on the chalkboard.

3. Ask students to identify categories that encompass one or more of the recorded words.

4. Write category titles on the board. Students then share words from their individual lists or the master list that are appropriate for each category. Write words under each category title.

5. Encourage students to discuss their word placements. Students can also make predictions about story content.

6. After students have read the story, they can add new words or categories to the web. They can modify other words or categories, depending upon the information learned from the story.

An Inside Look Alison Verde uses Semantic Webbing throughout her guided reading lessons for individual books she wishes to explore with her students. For the book *Bringing the Rain to Kapiti Plain* by Verna Aardema (Fluent), Alison wrote the word *Africa* on the chalkboard and invited the students in a guided reading group of five individuals to brainstorm all the words and concepts they knew. After the chalkboard had been covered with words, Alison invited students to work in two small mini-groups to organize the words into several selected categories and to provide a title for each category. Afterward, she asked each mini-group to record their categories on the board and to explain their choice of words within groupings to the entire group. Discussion then centered on selecting the most representative categories. A master web, developed by the students, was drawn on the chalkboard.

Alison wrote the identified category titles in white chalk and recorded the items selected for each category on the radiating spokes in yellow chalk.

During the course of the book, as students were reading about Ki-pat's exploits, they added more words and ideas to the master web in pink chalk. Students were able to see the relationships that can exist between their background knowledge (yellow chalk) and the knowledge they were learning within the book (pink chalk).

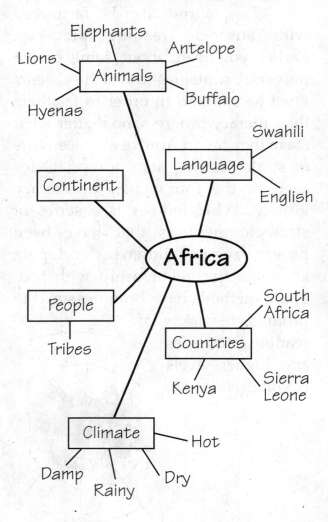

Student Motivated Active Reading Technique (S.M.A.R.T)

S.M.A.R.T. is a comprehension strategy providing students opportunities—both expository and narrative—to become personally involved in reading. Self-initiated questions and concept development underscore the utility of S.M.A.R.T. throughout a wide range of reading situations and abilities.

S.M.A.R.T., which is appropriate for individuals as well as small and large groups, can be organized as follows:

1. Select a book, story, or reading selection for the group to discuss.

2. Record the title of the book on the chalkboard and encourage the group members to ask questions. Record all questions.

3. The group makes predictions about the content of the selection. Students decide on questions that are most appropriate for exploration.

4. Examine any illustrations found in the book or story and propose additional questions. The initial prediction is modified or altered according to information shared on the illustrations.

5. The group reads the selection while looking for answers to the recorded questions. New questions may be generated for discussion as well. As students find answers in the text, the individual or group talks about them and attempts to arrive at mutually satisfying responses.

6. The procedure continues throughout the remainder of the selection. Upon completion of the book, the class discusses all recorded questions and answers provided in the selection. The group decides on appropriate answers. Questions that were not answered from the text are also shared. Encourage students to refer back to the book to answer them.

Concept Cards

Concept Cards allow students to tap into their background knowledge about the topic of a book, share that information with classmates, and make predictions about the content of a piece of literature. At the same time, students can manipulate their vocabulary and share ideas related to word study and comprehension of text. Although this strategy works particularly well with nonfiction materials, it can also be used with narrative text.

1. Before students read a book, select fifteen to twenty-five words from the book. It is preferable to have words from the front, middle, and back of the book. Include words with which you know students are familiar, words essential to comprehension of text, and a few unknown words.

2. Print each set of words on index cards and distribute the set to a guided reading group.

3. Invite students to assemble the cards into categories of their own choosing (without telling them a specific number of categories or the number of word cards that should be in each). Encourage students to place words in categories according to their own knowledge of those words or their predictions of how those words might be used in the text.

4. Invite students to share the various categories and provide rationale for the placement of word cards within specific groups.

5. Invite students to read the book, looking for the words on the index cards. After reading, encourage students to rearrange cards into new categories based on the information learned from the text. Afterward, invite students to discuss reasons for any rearrangements and compare their placements with those they did in the pre-reading stage.

An Inside Look Brenda Peltner is a first-grade teacher in Colorado Springs, Colorado. She has always enjoyed reading the "Sheep" series of books by Nancy Shaw to her students. In preparation for a guided reading lesson with an early reader group, Brenda prepared several sets of concept cards for the book *Sheep on a Ship*. She selected words from the book, including words her students were familiar with, as well as additional vocabulary important to their overall comprehension. The words Brenda used with the group are listed on the chart below.

sheep	sail	ship	trip	waves
sails	flap	map	nap	clouds
storm	rains	hails	slosh	slide
collide	whip	sagging	chop	mast
raft	craft	drifts	lifts	port

▶ Mental Imagery

Mental Imagery is the creation of pictures in the reader's mind prior to, during, or after reading. With appropriate modifications and extensions, you can use this technique with all types of readers, all types of reading materials, and at all stages of the reading process.

A process of mental imagery helps readers construct mind pictures that serve as an aid in comprehension and as a way to tie together predictions, background knowledge, and textual knowledge in a satisfying experience. Once images are created and colored by a reader's experiences, they become a permanent part of long-term memory. Just as important, they assist in the development of independent readers who are connected to the books they read.

Mental Imagery is more a developmental process than a single instructional strategy. Students need to be exposed to four basic stages throughout the reading program (and throughout the school year) in order to effectively integrate mental imagery as a personal reading strategy. Following are the four basic stages of mental imagery, along with some sample activities:

1. Provide students with opportunities to create images of concrete and tangible objects.
- Visualize a three-dimensional object
- Visualize a variety of objects

2. Encourage students to visualize and recall familiar objects, scenes, or past experiences outside of the classroom.
- Visualize a familiar room
- Imagine playing with a favorite object

3. Provide students with opportunities to listen to high imagery stories that utilize common experiences or knowledge.
- Share an unfamiliar story with good description and action.
- Illustrate selected parts of a story.

4. Encourage students to begin to create their own mental images as they read stories.
- Describe character emotions and feelings after reading.
- Explain possible scenery for a play.

An Inside Look Rafe Lauber is a first-grade teacher in Oakland, California. He has incorporated Mental Imagery in a variety of curricular activities. He has discovered that when students have sufficient opportunities to generate their own mental images prior to the reading of a book, their recall of significant events as well as their overall comprehension of the story increases significantly. "My Mental Imagery activities are fairly structured," Rafe states. "I don't use them for every book, but over the years I've been able to construct a variety of pre-reading imagery activities that help students 'get into' the theme or plot of a book. Later, in our post-reading discussions, I find that students have a better grasp of the material and are more personally involved in it."

Following is a Mental Imagery activity Rafe used prior to having his students read the book *Where the Wild Things Are* by Maurice Sendak (Transitional):

Close your eyes. Create a picture in your mind of a tropical island. Imagine that you are standing in the middle of the island. Imagine that you are standing on a very large and very green island. Imagine that you are standing on a beach on that island. Now, imagine that you are suddenly surrounded by many strange creatures. There are some weird critters. There are marvelous beasts with big eyes and long teeth. Several are covered with long bushy hair. Imagine that they are not scary. Imagine that they want to play with you. They are friendly creatures. Think about what you would like to say to them. Imagine yourself talking to these creatures. Now pretend that the creatures want to make you their leader. Imagine yourself in charge of all these big-eyed creatures. Now imagine that you and the creatures dance around. Imagine some of the games you could play. Imagine yourself having lots of fun. Everybody is happy. Everybody is smiling. Everybody is laughing—you and all the friendly monsters.

After reading this to his students, Rafe invited them to open their eyes and describe the images each one created in her or his head. Rafe pointed out the similarities and differences in the images and notes how everyone's mental image was personal and colored by her or his own experiences. Then Rafe encouraged students in a guided reading group to read the book *Where the Wild Things Are*. Upon completion, he provided students opportunities to compare their pre-reading images with those depicted in the book.

Mental Imagery works particularly well when the following guidelines are made part of the entire process:

1. Students need to understand that their images are personal and are affected by their own backgrounds and experiences.

2. There is no right or wrong image for any student.

3. Provide students with sufficient opportunities to create their images prior to any discussion.

4. Provide adequate time for students to discuss the images they develop.

5. Assist students in image development through a series of open-ended questions (e.g., "Tell us more about your image." or "Can you add some additional details?").

► K-W-L

K-W-L (Ogle, 1986) is a three-step framework that helps students access appropriate information in expository writing. It takes advantage of students' background knowledge and helps demonstrate relationships between that knowledge and the information in text.

K-W-L (What I **K**now, What I **W**ant to Learn, What I **L**earned) involves students in three major cognitive steps—accessing their background knowledge about a topic, determining what students would like to learn about that subject, and evaluating what was learned about the topic. The following steps provide an outline for helping students begin to read expository text:

1. Invite students to talk about what they already know about the topic of the text. Write this information on a section of the chalkboard entitled K—What we Know.

2. Encourage students to categorize this information. This can be done through a grouping strategy such as Semantic Webbing. Record the grouping on the chalkboard.

3. Invite students to make predictions about the types of information the text will contain. These predictions should be based on their background knowledge as well as the categories of information elicited in Step 2.

4. Encourage students to generate their own questions about the text. They can discuss these questions while you record their responses on a section of the board entitled W—What we Want to learn.

5. Invite students to read the text and record any answers to their questions. Students may wish to do this individually or in pairs.

6. Upon completion of the text, provide students with an opportunity to discuss the information learned and how that data relates to their prior knowledge. Record this information on a section of the board entitled L—What we Learned. Talk about questions posed for which no information was found in the text. Help students discover other sources for satisfying their inquiries.

A blank K-W-L Strategy Chart appears on page 200.

► Possible Sentences

Possible Sentences (Moore and Moore, 1986) is an exciting reading strategy that assists students in 1) learning new vocabulary, 2) generating appropriate story predictions, 3) developing individual (or group) purposes for reading, and 4) stimulating their intellectual curiosity about a book or story. It is a strategy appropriate for all types of expository material and revolves around a five-part lesson plan:

1. List essential vocabulary from the book. Pre-select these words and present them to students on sheets of paper or on the chalkboard. For example, Carol Rice, a first-grade teacher in Columbia, South Carolina, assigned the book *The Very Hungry Caterpillar* by Eric Carle (Transitional) to two separate guided reading groups. Before students read the book, she provided them with duplicated sheets on which she typed the following terms:

egg	leaf
Sunday	morning
pop!	caterpillar
apple	hungry
ate	plums
oranges	cupcake
stomachache	better

2. Invite students to select at least two words from the list and construct a sentence they think might be in the book. On the chalkboard, Carol recorded each of the sentences given by the students exactly as they were dictated. Below are three sentences generated by the students :

Once upon a time there was a *hungry caterpillar.*

In the *morning* he *ate* a *cupcake.*

He also *ate* an *apple.*

3. Ask students to read the book in order to check the accuracy of the sentences generated.

4. Evaluate each of the sentences in terms of the information presented in the book. Carol's students discussed their sentences, and she encouraged them to eliminate, revise, or modify them in light of the information learned from the book. At times, students will need to reread portions of the book in order to confirm or alter their original predictions.

5. After evaluating the original sentences, encourage students to generate additional sentences using the selected vocabulary. As Carol's students generated new sentences, she checked them against the original story for accuracy.

Possible Sentences allows students to integrate important vocabulary and their predictive abilities in a worthwhile activity. This strategy assists students in developing connections between prior knowledge and textual knowledge while incorporating a variety of language skills. Although Possible Sentences was originally designed to help students focus on expository materials, it is equally successful with selected narrative books as well. In addition, this strategy provides some important pre-lesson assessment information that can be addressed later in the reading process.

► Directed Reading-Thinking Activity (DRTA)

The DRTA (Stauffer, 1969) is a comprehension strategy that stimulates students' critical thinking of text. It is designed to allow students to make predictions, think about those predictions, verify or modify the predictions with text, and stimulate a personal involvement with many different kinds of reading material.

DRTAs are guided by three essential questions, which are inserted throughout the reading and discussion of a book. These include:

"What do you think will happen next?" (Using prior knowledge to form hypotheses)

"Why do you think so?" (Justifying predictions; explaining one's reasoning)

"How can you prove it?" (Evaluating predictions; gathering additional data)

Vacca and Vacca (1989) outline a series of general steps for the DRTA.

1. Begin with the title of the book or with a quick survey of the title, subheads, illustrations, and so on. Ask students, "What do you think this story (or book) will be about?" Encourage students to make predictions and to elaborate on the reasons for making selected predictions ("Why do you think so?").

2. Have students read to a predetermined logical stopping point in the text (locate this before students read). This point can be a major shift in the action of the story, the introduction of a new character, or the resolution of a story conflict.

3. Repeat the questions from step 1. Some of the predictions will be refined, some will be eliminated, and new ones will be formulated. Ask students, "How do you know?" to encourage clarification or verification. Redirect questions to several students (if working in a group situation).

4. Continue the reading to another logical stopping point. Again, ask questions similar to those above.

5. Continue through to the end of the text. Make sure the focus is on large units of text, rather than small sections, which tend to upset the flow of the narrative and disrupt adequate comprehension. As students move through the text, be sure to encourage thoughtful contemplation of the text, reflective discussion, and individual purposes for reading.

▶ MM & M (Metacognitive Modeling and Monitoring)

MM & M provides readers with an opportunity to see inside the mind of a reader going through the reading process. In essence you serve as a model of efficient reading—demonstrating for students the thought processes and mental activities used while reading. When struggling readers are made aware of the strategies readers use (inside their heads) then they can emulate those strategies for themselves.

In this strategy you select a reading selection and begin to think out loud, verbalizing what is going on inside your head as you read. Since you serve as the most significant role model for students in all their academic endeavors, your talking while reading gives them some firsthand experiences with reading as a thinking process—processes they can begin to incorporate into their schema.

I. Make predictions. (Demonstrate the importance of making hypotheses.)

"From this title, I predict that this story will be about a missing ring and a haunted house."

"In the next chapter, I think we'll find out how the two twins were able to sail to the other side of the lake."

"I think this next part will describe what the thief took from the dresser drawer."

2. Describe your mental images. (Show how mental pictures are formed in your head as you read.)

"I can see a picture of an old man walking down a country lane with his dog at his side."

"I'm getting a picture in my mind of a sparsely furnished apartment with very small rooms."

"The picture I have in my mind is that of a very short girl with curly red hair and a face full of freckles."

3. Share an analogy. (Show how the information in the text may be related to something in one's background knowledge.)

"This is like the time I had to take my daughter to the hospital in the middle of the night."

"This is similar to the time I first learned to ski in Colorado and kept falling down all the time."

"This seems to be like the day we had to take our family dog to the veterinarian because he was sick."

4. Verbalize a confusing point.
(Show how you keep track of your level of comprehension as you read.)

"I'm not sure what is happening here in the story."

"This is turning out a little differently than I expected."

"I guess I was correct in my original prediction."

5. Demonstrate "fix-up" strategies. (Let students see how you repair any comprehension problems.)

"I think I need to reread this part of the story."

"Maybe this word is explained later in the story."

"Now that part about the fishing rod makes sense to me."

These five steps can and should be modeled for students in several different kinds of reading material. As you read and model, allow students opportunities to interject their thoughts about what may be going on in their heads as they listen to the selection. Your goal will be to have students internalize these processes and be able to do them on their own in all kinds of reading material.

▶ Answer First!

Answer First! is a questioning strategy that encourages and stimulates thinking at higher levels of comprehension. It allows you to direct students to more sophisticated levels of comprehension through the careful and judicious sequencing of questioning skills. This strategy has proven to be quite successful with all types of readers and is a particularly worthwhile addition to the work of any guided reading group. In fact, it can be used as either an individual activity or a small-group activity with equal results.

In Answer First!, you invite a guided reading group to read a selected book or text. In advance of the reading, you design a series of answers (see below) which you duplicate on sheets of paper. Upon completion of the book, students must formulate questions based on the material they've read. The questions should be posed so as to generate the answers on the Answer First! sheet.

An Inside Look Following is an example using a fictitious story about turtles. This story was created by Jennifer Bowker, a first-grade teacher near Sarasota, Florida. Jennifer wanted to introduce her students to this strategy through a story she wrote so that they would not be influenced by a book or author they may have previously read. After students were comfortable with this strategy, Jennifer planned to present it to guided reading groups as part of their discussion and interpretation of selected books. She prepared the answers that follow the selection ahead of time. They were given to students after they read the passage. Jennifer gave them the responsibility for creating appropriate questions for each answer. She encouraged students to share and discuss possible questions in their groups before deciding on an appropriate question for each designated response.

Note that in the example, the answers previously determined by Jennifer begin at the literal level of cognition and progressively move students to higher levels of cognition (comprehension, application, analysis, synthesis, evaluation) in a systematic way. This is the major advantage of this guided reading strategy—students can begin to read and interpret various forms of reading material at increased levels of understanding. Jennifer and many other teachers have successfully used Answer First! with both fiction and nonfiction materials and across a wide range of student abilities. This often results in students who are able to generate their own questions at higher levels of cognition.

Turtle Time

Have you seen a turtle? Turtles live in the sea. Some turtles live on land. Land turtles are called tortoises. Some turtles are old. They can be 200 years old. Turtles are heavy. They can weigh 500 pounds. That's heavier than a grown man! One turtle is the leatherback turtle. It can weigh 1000 pounds. Wow!

Turtles may sleep in the winter. They dig into the sand. They slow down their breathing. They slow down their heart. Then, they sleep for a long time. They don't move. They don't eat.

Turtles are very slow. They are not fast. Some turtles can swim fast. But they can't walk fast. Turtles eat slowly. They chew their food slowly. They need to eat a lot. They may eat most of the day.

Turtle eggs are slow, too. They may take a year to hatch. The babies are in danger. They must crawl to the sea. Sometimes other animals catch them. Only a few make it to the water. Turtles have a hard life.

Question:_____
    Answer: It is a turtle that lives on land.
Question:_____
    Answer: More than a grown man.
Question:_____
    Answer: They sleep for a long time.
Question:_____
    Answer: It must eat a lot of food each day.
Question:_____
    Answer: Turtles have a hard life.

▶ Cloze Technique

In the Cloze Technique, you prepare sentences or paragraphs in which selected words have been omitted. For example, you may wish to delete every fifth or every tenth word, or you may wish to delete all the nouns or all the adjectives from a chapter in a book.

When you have decided on the words to be deleted from the piece, you retype it, leaving blank spaces for the deleted words (make each blank the same length so that students cannot infer words based solely on their length). You can then use the retyped piece with students as part of a guided reading lesson. The advantage of Cloze is that it allows you to focus on specific grammatical concepts within the context of a familiar and contextually appropriate piece of writing. Students are then encouraged to work together or by themselves to replace the missing words with words that make sense in the selection.

 An Inside Look On the right is a Cloze piece developed by Cynthia Ermond for her second-grade students. She took a portion of text from the book *In One Tidepool: Crabs, Snails, and Salty Tails* by Anthony D. Fredericks (Fluent) and retyped it onto a sheet of acetate for use on the overhead projector. As she prepared the piece, she deleted selected nouns and replaced each one with a blank of ten spaces. She then projected the story sample onto the screen and invited students in one guided reading group to contribute nouns that would help restore a sense of meaning to the original story. (Cynthia was not interested in having students replicate the exact words she had deleted from the text, but wanted them to focus on a specific part of speech within a familiar book.)

Here is a _____ with pounding waves,

Sea-splashed _____ and hidden _____,

With _____ gliding out of reach

And clumps of _____ tossed on the _____.

This is where a _____ lay,

Crowded with _____ on a summer's _____.

In One Tidepool: Crabs, Snails and Salty Tails by Anthony D. Fredericks. Nevada City, CA: Dawn, 2002

▶ Story Map

This "organizer" helps students determine the essential elements of a well-crafted story. Not only can students focus on important details (e.g., setting, characters, problem, and so on), but they begin to see how these parts of a story are woven together. Equally significant is the fact that most well-written stories present some sort of problem for the main character or characters to solve. Students can begin to understand this writing technique by analyzing the elements of a story.

Provide individual copies of page 201 to the members of a guided reading group (an alternative plan would be to offer one sheet to the entire group; one student is the designated scribe while all group members contribute ideas). Encourage students to complete the form either while reading the story or (more appropriately) upon the completion of the story. Be sure to provide sufficient opportunities for students to share and discuss their respective interpretations of the story. It is not essential that students all arrive at the same conclusions, but rather that they have adequate opportunities to talk about theme.

▶ What If

Many of the questions we typically ask our students are of the literal or factual variety. There is an enormous body of research which suggests that students (at any grade) need to be exposed to a larger proportion of higher-level, divergent, and creative thinking questions. By doing so, we are ensuring that our students will be able to approach any reading task with a creative spirit, thus ensuring a dynamic interpretation of text.

One of the most effective strategies for promoting an active engagement with text is "What Iffing." In this strategy, take some of the questions that you would normally ask students at the conclusion of a guided reading passage and tag the two words "What if" to the front of each question.

There are no right or wrong answers with "What Iffing." Students are given opportunities to play with language and the possibilities that might exist within a story or beyond that story. Students' divergent thinking is stimulated and enhanced in a wide variety of reading materials.

Following is a sample list of "What if" questions for the story *The Three Little Pigs.*

What if the story were *The Three Little Wolves*?

What if all three houses had been made of brick?

What if the wolf had asthma?

What if the story had taken place in the city?

What if there was an army of pigs?

What if the story was told from the wolf's point of view? (Of course, this could lead to a discussion of *The True Story of the Three Little Pigs* by Jon Scieszka.)

You will notice that "What if" questions encourage and stimulate the generation of multiple queries and responses. Its advantage lies in the fact that all students are encouraged to participate and all responses can be entertained and discussed.

▶ Story Frames

A Story Frame (Fowler, 1982) is a basic outline of a story that is designed to help the reader or writer organize his or her thoughts about a story. A "frame" consists of a series of extended blanks (similar in nature to the cloze procedure) that are linked together by transition words or phrases. A Story Frame differs from a cloze in that students are provided longer blanks to complete and are given more latitude in selecting appropriate words or phrases.

When completed, Story Frames can serve as discussion starters for the components of good stories as well as an outline for students who need a support structure for the creation of their own stories. Obviously, the intent is not to have all students arrive at an identical story, but provide them with the freedom they need to create stories within appropriate grammatical contexts. The following examples offer some Story Frames you may find appropriate for your classroom.

Story Frame

This story is about _____

_____

_____ who is an important character.

_____ tried to _____

_____

_____

_____.

The story ends when _____

_____

_____

_____

Plot Frame

In this story the problem starts when _____

_____

After that _____

Next, _____

Then, _____

The problem is finally solved when _____

_____

_____

_____

Information Frame

This story was written to teach us about _____
_____
_____.

One important fact I learned was _____
_____.

Another fact I learned was _____
_____.

A third important fact I learned was _____
_____.

If I were to remember one important thing from this story, it would be
_____

because _____
_____.

Character Analysis Frame

_____ is an important character in this story.
_____ is important because _____
_____.

Once, he/she _____
_____

Another time, _____
_____

I think that _____ is _____

because _____
_____

He/she is also _____

because _____.

Name _____ **Date** _____

Book _____

K-W-L Strategy Chart

K–What we Know	**W**–What we Want to Learn	**L**–What we Learned and Still Need to Learn

Story Map

Name _____ **Date** _____

Title: _____

Setting:

Characters: _____
_____

Problem:

Event 1: _____

Event 2: _____

Event 3: _____

Event 4: _____

Solution:

Theme: _____

Questions and Prompts

Helping students attain a measure of independence in reading is one of the major goals of the guided reading program. This is accomplished through the use of books matched to each reader's instructional reading level combined with strategies and activities that stimulate and encourage young learners to master the conventions of print. Guided reading provides children with enjoyable, successful opportunities to read for meaning.

> *One of the most significant ways we can assist children in the development of independent reading abilities is through the use of questions and prompts.*

One of the most significant ways we can assist children in the development of independent reading abilities is through the use of questions and prompts. These instructional devices have been used by teachers for many years, but they achieve a unique potency when used as a significant and integrated element of guided reading. There is growing evidence that these elements can have the most profound effect on students' reading growth and development. When used with the strategies described in this unit, questions and prompts offer children a thoroughly integrated strategic approach to reading.

Questions

Consider the fact that a typical elementary teacher may ask as many as 400 questions per day of his or her students. Reading researchers have postulated that as much as 80 percent of the questions typically asked of children are of the literal/factual/memorization type. This information is important because students tend to read and think based on the types of questions they anticipate receiving from their teacher. If we wish our students to become actively engaged in the dynamics of text, we need to provide them with questions that model those dynamics. When students hear questions at higher levels of cognition or that embody high levels of problem-solving, they will be better prepared to integrate those strategies into their reading repertoire. We can assist our students throughout their reading instruction by providing them with *models of thought*. These models take the form of the questions we typically ask during the course of the day or that can be easily integrated into the discussions and routines of the five stages of a guided reading lesson.

A description of some questioning strategies follows. These can be easily imported into any book discussion or group sharing activity. All of these suggestions are strategic in nature; they provide children in grades K–2 with "in-the-head" processes they can use to focus on and understand text.

Process Questions

Process questions are those designed to assist children in making their own decisions and arriving at their own solutions to problems. When the responsibility for learning is kept with the student and facilitated by the teacher, higher levels of involvement, appreciation, and understanding result.

Process	Sample Questions
Observing	What have you noticed so far? How are your observations similar to Bill's? What else have you observed? How would you explain what you read?
Classifying	What category or group does this belong in? How is this related to _____?
Inferring	Why do you believe that? Can you give an explanation for your choice?
Predicting	How do you think this will turn out? Can you make some guesses? Why are you saying that?

Prior Knowledge and Purpose-Setting Questions

Before embarking on a guided reading lesson, it is vital that you know what type of background information and the level of that information your students are bringing to the lesson. Questioning, when it is planned and sequential, can yield valuable information on what your students know about a topic. While you may be tempted to use close-ended questions, consider instead a series of open-ended questions at the beginning of a lesson. These questions will appear less threatening and may yield more useful data about your students' background information. For example, let's say you were about to share the book *Frog and Toad Are Friends* by Arnold Lobel with a transitional guided reading group. Here are some prior knowledge questions you may want to pose:

"Where would you expect to find frogs or toads?"

"How are frogs and toads similar?"

"What do you like most about frogs or toads?"

These questions are nonthreatening, but can provide you with important background data while alerting students to some book concepts.

Purpose-setting questions, on the other hand, allow students to focus on the objectives of the lesson. It is important that students understand the direction a guided reading lesson is to take so that they can become active participants. Purpose-setting questions allow students to define the limits of a lesson, making it specific and purposeful. For example, instead of saying, "Today's book will be about a hen" (*Rosie's Walk* by Pat Hutchins [Early Reader]), it might be more appropriate to help students focus by asking questions such as, "What can you tell me about hens, chickens, or foxes?" or "Does anyone know some of the things a chicken might do during the day?" Questions such as these alert students to the fact that the upcoming book will deal with life in a barnyard. As you have probably noticed from the two examples, purpose-setting questions can also be used as prior knowledge questions. Not only do you notify students about the direction for the selected book; you allow them to share their background information on the subject—information necessary to your monitoring process.

Open-ended Questions

Open-ended questions are useful when you are attempting to create a responsive atmosphere. Students can respond with reasonable confidence that their answers will not be wrong. This type of question serves as an excellent motivator, encouraging students to use their individual backgrounds to think about a global situation. When you use open-ended questions, you are not asking for something that requires memorization or a one-to-one association.

Examples of Open-ended Questions

What do you see?
Can you make a prediction?
Can you suggest a way to group these together?
What might be another way of thinking about this?
How are these similar?
Are there other ways of looking at this?
How would you explain this to a friend?
When would you use this?
What do you think will happen next?
Why is this important to know?

One distinctive advantage of open-ended questions is the fact that they invite other types of questions. For example, when you ask students open-ended questions, you usually get a variety of responses. Then, by following up with some probing questions, you open up new and exciting dimensions for students to examine and explore. There are three purposes for asking probing questions: 1) they can be used to elicit clarification of a student's answer ("Could you explain that in another way?"); 2) they can solicit new information to extend or build upon a student's response ("Now that you've discussed the characteristics of the main character, how can you use that information to describe other characters in the story?"); and 3) they redirect or restructure a student's response in a more productive direction ("That might be one way of looking at it, but how would that apply to the book we read yesterday?"). It's important to note that probing questions send a powerful signal to students. Question-asking is more than you asking one question and expecting one response. Rather, the message is that questioning can and should be an interactive exchange of information and investigation.

Metacognitive Questions

Metacognition is thinking about one's thinking. When students are given opportunities to think about the thought processes that are going on in their heads, they are provided with some wonderful insights into how all readers approach written material as well as how they might arrive at their own conclusions or solutions. When students are aware of their thinking, they will understand more of what is taking place in a book or story.

The goal of asking students appropriate metacognitive questions is to gradually release your responsibility of question-asking and place it in the hands of the students. You can enhance and facilitate the metacognitive process by posing questions that help students "look inside their heads." You will be giving them a valuable skill—not just in reading, but for all other content areas as well. Metacognitive questions can be used at any time during a guided reading lesson. They are an important and critical element in strategic reading.

Teacher-Posed Metacognitive Questions

1. Is this story similar to anything you may have read before?

2. What were you thinking when you read this part of the story?

3. What have we learned so far?

4. What is the most important part of this section?

5. Did you change your mind about anything after reading this part of the story?

6. Do you have any other questions about this book that have not been answered so far?

7. What did you do when you didn't understand that word in the story?

8. What new information are you learning?

9. How did you know it was _____?

10. What do you know that isn't right?

Prompts

One of the most powerful teaching tools we can use with students during a guided reading lesson is prompting. Prompting involves assisting children in using various reading strategies and sources of information while reading a book or story. To effectively use this technique, you must have the strategy for the lesson in mind and know where you are going with the lesson. In addition, you must possess the ability to think on your feet when students are not headed in the proper direction. This requires you to be aware of the feedback students are providing both verbally and nonverbally.

As teachers, we need to be aware of two basic concerns while students are engaged in guided reading activities:

- Is the student using appropriate sources of information while reading?

- What sources of information are being neglected?

Our response to the first question can guide us in developing appropriate probes that help students zero in on all the information sources at their disposal. The answer(s) to the second question can guide us in redirecting students' thinking and attention to alternate information resources (sometimes referred to as "fix-up" strategies). The prompts we use throughout a guided reading lesson are powerful focusing techniques that alert children to specific elements of the reading process and ways in which they can assume a measure of control over what and how they read.

Universal Strategy	Suggested Prompts
Monitor	Did you notice something wrong? What was it? How did you know it was _____? Show me where it wasn't correct. I like the way you noticed something wasn't right.
Search	What do you think isn't right on this page? What do you know that isn't right? Can you show me where the difficulty is? Point to the problem. What do you think this should be? Is there anything on the page that will help you?
Predict	What do you think will happen next? What do you think it should be (letter, word)? What would make sense here?
Check	What did you see? Check to see if what you read makes sense (M). Check to see if what you read sounds right (S). Check to see if what you read looks right (V). What do you think should be here? I like the way you found that.
Confirm	Are you right? How do you know? Can you explain that to me? How could you prove that? What did you do to make that right?
Self-correct	How do you know you're right? Can you find something that isn't right on that page? I like how you made that right all by yourself.

Source: Adapted from Schulman and Payne, 2000.

A variety of prompts are both necessary and critical. Over-reliance on one type of prompt may cause children to focus only on one particular element or cue (M, S, V) of reading. Students may then neglect other cues necessary for a complete and thorough understanding of the material. For example, the use of many visual/graphophonic prompts may cause students to over-rely on those cues to the exclusion of other reading cues. Again, the key is to help students see all the elements inherent in strategic reading. This can be accomplished through a liberal sprinkling of various prompts within all guided reading lessons.

The chart on the previous page provides you with a selection of prompts that encourage the use of universal reading strategies. These are also delineated in the previous unit.

The judicious use of prompts integrated throughout a guided reading experience provides students with important focusing information that helps them "take charge" of their own reading development. This encourages independence in reading while underscoring the strategies necessary to reading comprehension. The eventual goal is to help students take over these mental processes for themselves.

Strategy Planning Guides

The Strategy Planning Guides on pages 208–211 can be used to help you plan appropriate instruction and activities for selected guided reading groups. Duplicate these guides and have them available whenever you work on lesson plans for selected groups of students. By checking off the necessary strategies, you will be able to select appropriate books, activities, questions, and prompts that can help you maximize your instructional time as well as the learning opportunities for your students.

Information recorded in the Comments/Observations section of these sheets can be useful in helping you decide whether to maintain the members of a group or transfer individual students to other groups. This data can easily be carried over to individual student portfolios as a way of recording progress throughout the program.

Strategy Planning Guide
Emergent Reader Level

Date: _____   **Time:** _____

Group Members:

1. _____   4. _____

2. _____   5. _____

3. _____   6. _____

Universal Strategies: ← (✓ one or more) → **Emergent Reader Strategies:**

❑ Using background knowledge

❑ Predicting

❑ Forming mental imagery

❑ Monitoring

❑ Using fix-up tools

❑ Confirming

❑ Identifying important ideas

❑ Searching

❑ Drawing conclusions/inferences

❑ Comparing/contrasting

❑ Checking

❑ Summarizing

❑ Predicting with pictures

❑ Identifying beginnings/ends of words

❑ Tracking print

❑ Noting patterns in text

❑ Chunking sounds together

❑ Problem-solving new words

❑ Detecting and correcting errors

Comments/Observations:

1.	4.
2.	5.
3.	6.

Strategy Planning Guide
Early Reader Level

Date: _____   **Time:** _____

Group Members:

1. _____   4. _____

2. _____   5. _____

3. _____   6. _____

Universal Strategies: ← (✓ one or more) → **Early Reader Strategies:**

❑ Using background knowledge
❑ Predicting
❑ Forming mental imagery
❑ Monitoring
❑ Using fix-up tools
❑ Confirming
❑ Identifying important ideas
❑ Searching
❑ Drawing conclusions/inferences
❑ Comparing/contrasting
❑ Checking
❑ Summarizing

❑ Chunking words into phrases
❑ Self-correcting
❑ Identifying spelling patterns
❑ Using all three cueing systems
❑ Using Skip and Return
❑ Problem-solving new words
❑ Detecting and correcting errors
❑ Maintaining fluency

Comments/Observations:

1.	4.
2.	5.
3.	6.

Strategy Planning Guide
Transitional Reader Level

Date: _____ **Time:** _____

Group Members:

1. _____ 4. _____

2. _____ 5. _____

3. _____ 6. _____

Universal Strategies: ◄ (✓ one or more) ► **Transitional Reader Strategies:**

❏ Using background knowledge   ❏ Story mapping
❏ Predicting   ❏ Rereading to clarify meaning
❏ Forming mental imagery   ❏ Using graphic organizers
❏ Monitoring   ❏ Identifying character traits
❏ Using fix-up tools   ❏ Oral retelling
❏ Confirming   ❏ Character mapping
❏ Identifying important ideas   ❏ Dramatizing a story/book
❏ Searching   ❏ Following the plot
❏ Drawing conclusions/inferences   ❏ Using a Before and After chart
❏ Comparing/contrasting   ❏ Problem-solving new words
❏ Checking   ❏ Detecting and correcting errors
❏ Summarizing   ❏ Maintaining fluency

Comments/Observations:

1.	4.
2.	5.
3.	6.

Strategy Planning Guide
Fluent Reader Level

Date: _____   **Time:** _____

Group Members:

1. _____   4. _____

2. _____   5. _____

3. _____   6. _____

Universal Strategies: ← (✓ one or more) → **Fluent Reader Strategies:**

❑ Using background knowledge   ❑ Identifying text features

❑ Predicting   ❑ Using K–W–L strategy charts

❑ Forming mental imagery   ❑ Utilizing charts, graphs, maps, and visuals

❑ Monitoring   ❑ Recognizing figurative language

❑ Using fix-up tools   ❑ Preparing a book summary

❑ Confirming   ❑ Creating a visual response

❑ Identifying important ideas   ❑ Making predictions

❑ Searching   ❑ Determining author objectivity

❑ Drawing conclusions/inferences   ❑ Story previewing

❑ Comparing/contrasting   ❑ Problem-solving new words

❑ Checking   ❑ Detecting and correcting errors

❑ Summarizing   ❑ Maintaining fluency

Comments/Observations:

1.	4.
2.	5.
3.	6.

Literacy Centers

The Importance of Literacy Centers to Guided Reading

One of the issues many teachers struggle with is the quality of instructional time for students who are not part of guided reading groups. Their concerns center on the time when they are working with a small group of students in a planned guided reading lesson. Teachers frequently ask, "How can I develop powerful independent activities and practices that will reinforce strategies taught in small-group situations?" The response revolves around the development of literacy centers, or those opportunities for children to work apart from the teacher while the teacher is working with a small guided reading group.

It is apparent from a survey of the research (Baumann, Hoffman, Duffy-Hester, & Ro, 2000; Ford & Opitz, 2002) as well as in conversations with teachers across the United States and Canada that student time away from the teacher was a significant concern of many educators. The research and classroom observations have concluded that a significant portion (up to 70 percent) of a student's time in a guided reading program is spent in activities that do not directly involve the teacher. In more traditional classroom configurations this would imply a round-robin reading session with a teacher and a small group of students, along with workbook or skill sheet activities completed by other students at their desks.

The success of guided reading as an instructional practice certainly depends on the implementation of a classroom structure that provides teachers with opportunities to work effectively with small groups of readers while keeping other readers independently engaged in meaningful literacy learning activities (Kane, 1995). In many classrooms teachers have used literacy centers (also called learning centers) as a practice and part of their guided reading programs.

> *Teachers frequently ask, "How can I develop powerful independent activities and practices that will reinforce strategies taught in small group situations?"*

Creating literacy centers and effectively implementing them into the overall structure of the reading program is a constant and continuing challenge for many teachers.

Ford and Opitz (2002) have presented five important considerations that will ensure the success of literacy centers. These are summarized below:

1. Students cannot be assigned to literacy centers without adequate instruction on how to be independent learners. One teacher interviewed for this book indicated that she spends the first two months of school teaching her first graders how to work by themselves on independent activities. She uses that time to carefully assess children's skills as well as their needs as they would relate to the use of literacy centers. For example, these might include learning how to work with a partner, learning how to operate a tape player and headphones, learning how to use a pocket chart, or learning how to record ideas in a personal journal. As teachers identify these needs (individually and collectively) in their students, it is suggested that they plan a four-part mini-lesson focused on each need:

- A focus (purpose for the lesson)

- An explanation in which children are provided with the information related to the stated purpose

- Role-playing, which gives students opportunities for guided practice

- Direct application, which provides children with time to use the information as they complete their center activities for the day

2. Teachers need to consider specific types of activities for independent work. The critical question becomes, "What specific activities do children need that will advance their knowledge about literacy?" Embodied within that larger question is a series of mini-questions that can help in formulating appropriate centers. These may include one, some, or all of the following:

- Do students need to write a response to something they have read?

- Do students need to listen to a story on tape as they follow along in a book?

- Do students need to work with a classmate to practice and refine a comprehension strategy?

- Do students need to engage in sustained silent reading activities?

- Do students need to expand their concepts of print skills?

- Do students need to develop speaking/reading skills with readers theatre?

- Do students need to understand the relationship between illustrations and text through art activities?

The fundamental question that needs to be addressed as you respond to these questions is: "What activities will require students to become actively engaged in their literacy development?"

3. One operational plan that can help you in designing appropriate centers can be your state or district standards. Centers can be constructed that focus on designated competencies as outlined in these curricular guides. Obviously, not all standards can be easily translated into literacy centers, nor should they be. However, a thoughtful and careful perusal of those standards can be a productive component of your overall guided reading plan.

4. Two key considerations for the development of literacy centers revolve around the perception of those centers by children. Students must have the answers to two questions both prior to and during their participation in a specific center. These are:

- Will I be successful in this activity?

- Will my participation in this activity be valued?

These two questions focus on the affective dimension of any instructional activity, particularly those designed for center use. They tap into the needs of all learners—children as well as adults. Indeed, they are questions that ultimately determine the importance of a skill or activity for a learner and how well that skill will become integrated into the learner's cognitive functioning. Knowing where your students are—in terms of skills or abilities and celebrating their accomplishments—will ultimately determine your success with literacy centers.

> **K**nowing where your students are—in terms of skills or abilities and celebrating their accomplishments—will ultimately determine your success with literacy centers.

5. Some final guidelines that will ensure the success of literacy centers are:

- Consider centers that will cause the least disruption to your instructional activities.

- Operate centers with minimal transition time.

- Encourage equitable use of activities by all students.

- Include a simple accountability form for each center.

- Consider simple centers rather than elaborate ones.

- Build the centers around established classroom routines and expectations.

Following are some additional considerations for establishing literacy centers in your classroom:

- Start the school year with three or four centers. As students become comfortable with routines, gradually increase the number of centers.

- The success of your centers can be assured by teaching your students familiar routines (how to move between centers, how to work cooperatively). Plan on devoting several weeks at the beginning of the year on teaching these routines.

- Consider the physical placement and arrangement of centers in your room. Students need to be able to move to and between centers with minimal disruption and time.

- Post a set of directions in each center. Plan time to share and discuss each set of directions and/or routines with students as part of your introductory mini-lesson (see above).

- Create a daily schedule of activities as well as center monitoring devices and spend time each day reviewing these plans with students.

- Consider assigning students to selected centers as well as offering students opportunities to select centers on their own.

- Talk with students about the amount of time necessary to engage in or complete the activities within a center. It is not critical for students (particularly in the beginning stages of reading) to complete all the activities within a center.

- Establish a procedure or routine that will allow students to signal when they are having difficulty with a specific center activity.

- Provide regular opportunities for students to discuss what went well at one or more centers as well as what might be done to improve a center.

- As you finish with one guided reading group and before you move on to another, take a few minutes to walk the room to observe students working at center activities.

- Create centers that are comprised of extending activities related directly to the books shared during guided reading lessons rather than busy work.

Suggested Literacy Centers

Remember that two key factors that will assist you in developing appropriate centers for your classroom are simplicity and routines. The following centers stay the same (routine), but the activities that are housed in a particular center can be modified, replaced, or added to throughout the school year (simplicity).

Each of the following center ideas is divided into four subsections. These include: 1) a brief description of the center, 2) the value of the center to the guided reading program, 3) some design considerations, and 4) suggested activities. It is not necessary to use all of the centers or all of the instructional suggestions. It is a good idea to continuously assess the needs of your students throughout the year. Determine the appropriateness of literacy centers (or the activities within a center) with students' developing reading abilities. Centers should not be added to the reading program without adequate instruction and familiarity.

> **R**emember that two key factors that will assist you in developing appropriate centers for your classroom are simplicity and routines.

Listening Center

A Listening Center offers children a unique opportunity to integrate two of the language arts. Reading and listening are combined into an enjoyable and productive format that supports and extends the guided reading program. Students can begin to make a connection between the sounds of language and the written form of that language.

Value
- Stimulates active involvement with text
- Improves listening and reading comprehension
- Brings books and stories to life
- Allows for personal interpretations of text
- Supports the integrated language arts
- Provides opportunities for students to do something with what they hear
- Provides students with models of good reading

Design Considerations
- Select an area that is furthest away from the guided reading instructional area.
- Provide a simple and easy-to-operate tape player.
- Provide multiple headphones for students to use.

- Thoroughly train students in the operation of the tape player and positioning of the headphones.
- When possible, record stories in your own voice (rather than using commercial tapes).
- Record stories at a rate commensurate with students' reading fluency.
- Record stories and books that will be part of guided reading lessons.

Suggested Activities

- Invite students to warm up with a guided reading book at the listening center.
- Invite students to review a guided reading book at the listening center.
- Invite students to listen to a guided reading book after receiving instruction on specific reading strategies.
- Allow students to listen to a story several times over a period of several days.
- Provide opportunities for students to orally read and record their own stories (see Readers Theatre Center on page 221).

- Allow students to listen just for pleasure.
- Invite students to listen to a story and then retell it to another student.

ABC/Spelling Center

An ABC/Spelling Center provides a unique opportunity for students to work independently on visual/graphophonic skills. Students can engage in various matching activities in which they manipulate both the sounds and letters of the English language.

Value

- Allows students to work independently on specific phonics skills
- Allows students to manipulate the basic elements of language
- Allows students to learn to match phonemes and graphemes
- Gives students a chance to learn spelling conventions

Design Considerations

- Provide appropriate manipulation space on a table or desk.
- Provide a variety of letter sizes (uppercase, lowercase).
- Provide a variety of letter materials (cardboard, magnetic, plastic, wood, and so on).
- Provide words from a book for students to duplicate.
- Provide opportunities for students to work in teams.

Suggested Activities

- Encourage students to spell their names.
- Invite students to spell or reconstruct words from a selected book or story.
- Designate a letter or word of the day for students to duplicate in the center.
- Invite students to "spell the room."
- Invite students to create their own letters for inclusion in the center.
- Invite students to share a favorite word from the story and spell it in the center.

Art Center

An Art Center encourages children to focus on one of the most important beginning reading strategies—the connection between text and illustrations. As children engage in a variety of books and genres, they begin to develop understandings about the cues inherent in pictures, illustrations, and photographs. Providing creative outlets for students to express themselves through art assists them in making the transition from visual cues to spoken cues to written cues.

Value

- Students can develop personal responses to literature
- Enhances the development of an important multiple intelligence (see page 232)
- Creates connections between pictures and words
- Extends guided reading activities in imaginative ways
- Is personally fulfilling and enriching

Design Considerations

- Provide a wide variety of art materials.
- Assemble the materials in well-labeled boxes or baskets.
- Instruct students on how to obtain and replace materials.
- Allow children free choice of materials.
- Provide smocks, aprons, and other protective wear as necessary.
- Provide examples of text/illustration matches for display.
- Post student work prominently in the center.

Suggested Activities

- Invite students to duplicate illustrations from a favorite book.
- Provide the text from a book and invite students to create a matching illustration.
- Invite students to label pictures and illustrations.
- Ask students to include speech balloons for book characters.

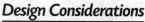

- Invite students to write descriptive sentences (from a guided reading book) on their illustrations.
- Bind student illustrations into a class book.
- Invite students to work together to create "Buddy Books."

Writing Center

One of the most valuable parts of the classroom literacy program is the opportunity to integrate writing into the curriculum. Writing provides children with another form of expression. It is a natural and normal connection to guided reading in that children have multiple opportunities to use some of their reading strategies in another context.

Value
- Fosters critical thinking
- Demonstrates the interrelationships between all language arts
- Promotes organization of ideas
- Allows for expressive thought
- Places a personal value on words and their use
- Stimulates application of print conventions
- Highlights process writing (pre-writing, drafting, revising, editing, publishing)

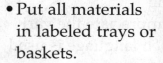

Design Considerations
- Provide a large, expansive area.
- Offer a wide variety of writing tools (pencils, markers, pens, crayons, colored pencils).
- Offer many types of recording possibilities (paper, cardboard, construction paper, journals, and so on).
- Provide writing-related tools (stapler, paper clips, scissors, glue, date stamp, and so on).
- Put all materials in labeled trays or baskets.
- Provide a check out/check in system for all materials.

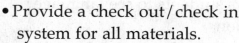

Suggested Activities
- Invite children to retell favorite stories.
- Allow students to create labels for various classroom items.
- Allow students to create a set of directions for a game.
- Invite students to write their names using various materials.
- Invite students to write a letter or create a list.
- Allow students to create their own poetry, rewrite a story, or create a vocabulary list.
- Allow students to keep a journal or diary.

Reading Around the Room Center

This particular center is less a center than it is an opportunity for students to become more aware of their surroundings. Fill your classroom with signs, posters, letters, words, sentences, and items to be read of every shape, size, and dimension.

Value

- Immerses students in the sights and sounds of language
- Supports the immersion principle of language learning
- Helps students appreciate the various ways in which language is used
- Allows students to see language in action
- Gives students a chance to make connections between the language in a book and the language that is used in normal everyday activities

Design Considerations

- Provide a central location for students to begin.
- Provide appropriate writing materials.
- Post/use words selected from specific guided reading texts.
- Use the students' own language.
- Cover every available classroom space with words and letters.
- Invite students to create their own signs and postings for the classroom.
- Provide students with pointers (long and short) to use.

Suggested Activities

- Invite students to work with a partner to locate specific words/letters. One student can point to a word while the other reads the word.
- Reverse the roles on a regular basis.
- Invite students to "write the room"—copying down selected letters and/or words.
- Allow students to read language experience stories.
- Invite students to read alphabet charts.
- Invite students to read several different versions of their own names posted throughout the room.
- Invite students to read appropriate materials posted in pocket charts.

Readers Theatre Center

Readers Theatre is a storytelling device that stimulates the imagination and promotes all of the language arts. It is an oral interpretation of a piece of literature read in a dramatic style. Readers theatre helps children understand and appreciate the richness of language, the ways in which to interpret that language, and how language can be a powerful vehicle for the comprehension and appreciation of different forms of literature.

Value
- Stimulates curiosity and enthusiasm for literature
- Facilitates the development of critical and creative thinking
- Focuses on all the language arts
- Gives children opportunities for personal investment in literature
- Helps children learn about plot, theme, setting, point of view, and characterization
- Helps children learn that reading can be a shared activity
- Enhances the development of communication skills
- Enhances positive self-concepts

Design Considerations
- Provide a variety of simple props.
- Provide one script per student.
- Highlight each actor's part.
- Provide several opportunities to practice before a production.
- Emphasize reading the script, not memorizing it.

Suggested Activities
- Allow students to do a readers theatre adaptation of a guided reading book.
- Allow students to read a script independently or with a partner.
- Invite students to work together to prepare their own script using a familiar story.
- Allow students to listen to a readers theatre presentation on tape while following along with a script.
- Invite students to practice and present a script to the class, or to make an audio tape of a script.
- Use a readers theatre script as a guided reading text.

The following script can be included in a Readers Theatre Center. Consider it an example of the languaging offerings that can become part of this valuable literacy endeavor.

Readers Theatre Script (Fluent Stage)

Hey, Diddle, Diddle, the Cat and the Fiddle, the Cow Just Can't Get Over the Moon

Staging: The Narrator stands at a lectern or podium. Each of the other characters can be standing in a loose semicircle or seated in chairs.

Cow
X

Cat
X

Dog
X

Dish
X

Spoon
X

Narrator
X

Narrator: Once upon a time there was this cow. The cow was part of a Mother Goose story. Have you heard it? It goes something like this: Hey, diddle, diddle, the cat and the fiddle, the cow jumped over the moon, and so on. Well, to tell the truth, the cow really didn't jump over the moon. Let's listen and find out why.

Cow: Hey, guys, we've got a real problem. Someone is going to write a Mother Goose rhyme about us. In order for it to rhyme ,they're going to have me jump over the moon. Can you believe that?

Cat: That's unbelievable, Cow. Why would they want you to jump over the moon?

Cow: Well, I think they needed a word that would rhyme with *spoon*.

Spoon: Hey, don't blame me. I'm going to run away with the dish.

Dish: Yeah, that's right. But, you see, the writers couldn't figure out any words that would rhyme with *dish* except for *wish* and *fish*. And I know they don't want anyone running away with a fish.

Spoon: That's why they had to put me at the end of that line.

Dog: Yeah, they sure couldn't put me at the end of a line. What would I rhyme with? *Hog? Frog? Jog?*

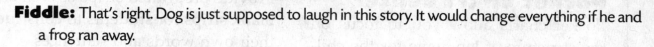

Fiddle: That's right. Dog is just supposed to laugh in this story. It would change everything if he and a frog ran away.

Cat: Hey, wait a minute. How is a dish able to talk?

Dish: Don't worry. This is just a Mother Goose rhyme. All kinds of things, from plates to pancakes, can talk in these stories. Don't let it bother you.

Cat: O.K.

Cow: Now, wait a second, guys. We're getting away from my problem.
How am I going to fly over the moon? I'm not a space shuttle, you know.
And I'm not the lightest animal in the world. So, what do I do?

Spoon: Maybe we could invent some kind of rocket launcher to get you up in space.

Cow: Do we look like scientists? How are we going to invent a rocket launcher?

Dog: Well, we can talk so we must be pretty smart.

Dish: Yeah, but just not smart enough to get big old Bossy here up into space and up and over the moon.

Cat: So, what are we going to do?

Cow: I guess we are just going to have to let the writer use his imagination to get me over the moon and back safely so that I can rhyme with my friend the spoon.

Narrator: And so it was. The cow was just too big to get over the moon in real life. But, the writer made up a real neat poem that made you think that the cow could actually jump that high. And this is what he wrote:

> Hey, diddle, diddle, the cat and the fiddle,
> The cow jumped over the moon;
> The little dog laughed to see such sport,
> And the dish ran away with the spoon.

Cow: Hey, thanks a lot, guys!

From *Tadpole Tales and Other Totally Terrific Treats for Readers Theatre* by Anthony D. Fredericks (Englewood, CO: Teacher Ideas Press, 1997), pp. 42–45. Used by permission of the author.

Pocket Chart Center

Pocket charts allow you to focus on the structure of language for the children in your class. You may wish to devote attention to the various language patterns that exist in the books and stories you share with students and compare those patterns to the oral language used by individuals. Pocket charts allow for a great deal of flexibility and can enhance the teaching of the ways in which language works.

Value
• Enhances cooperation
• Engages students in a hands-on, minds-on activity
• Promotes student independence
• Provides students with opportunities to see the relationships between oral and written language

Design Considerations
• If possible, provide several pocket charts for students to use.
• Post one or more pocket charts on the wall (where they cannot be pulled down).
• Provide one or more pocket charts for students to use at a table, desk, or other flat area.
• Instruct students on the procedures to use in placing word or sentence strips in the pockets.
• Provide opportunities for students to work independently as well as in small groups.

• Provide preprinted strips as well as blank strips for students to construct their own words and sentences.

Suggested Activities
• Invite students to reconstruct the words in a story sentence, poem, or song.
• Allow students to dictate a sentence to you. Print each word on a separate card for the student to reconstruct in a pocket chart.
• Ask one student to read a sentence from a book while another places the pre-printed words in a pocket chart.
• Invite a small group of students to place words in a pocket chart to create a sentence and then locate that sentence in the accompanying book.
• Allow students to construct rebus (picture) sentences.
• Invite students to build words from a book using specific phonic elements.

Free Reading Center

The ultimate goal of guided reading is to assist children in becoming independent readers. Students who have opportunities to select books on their own and read those books using the skills and strategies taught in the classroom reading program are provided with a genuine gift. Not only do they see the value of reading instruction; they have valid opportunities to utilize those newfound abilities in meaningful ways.

Value
- Enables students to become independent readers
- Enables students to use reading strategies in a variety of self-selected texts
- Gives children easy access to texts
- Allows students to extend guided reading skills in various ways
- Presents reading as a personal endeavor
- Gives students time, by themselves, to read

Design Considerations
- Fill the center with books from all genres.
- Provide carpet squares, rugs, and chairs.
- Provide a quiet space away from the busy classroom.

- Provide a timer so that students can read for a set period of time.
- Make the center as colorful and as print-rich as possible with signs ("Our Favorite Authors"), lists (books, genres), posters ("Good Readers Gather Here"), and other indicators.

Suggested Activities
- Allow students to read silently or with a partner.
- Allow students to select books from the classroom library.
- Allow students to warm up for guided reading with a matching book, or to extend a guided reading lesson with a similar book (theme, level, author, genre, and so on).
- Invite students to read with an older student or an adult volunteer.
- Invite students to keep a list of books read in a journal or individual notebook.

Drama/Storytelling Center

Drama provides children with many opportunities to bring the books and stories they read to life. It is an opportunity to share with children divergent and creative interpretations. Children begin to understand reading as a personal interpretation that can be enhanced by one's experiences and imagination.

Value

- Enables students to interpret literature in a variety of ways
- Enhances cooperative learning skills
- Allows children to use their imaginations in a host of activities
- Enhances students' oral language and listening skills
- Encourages appreciation of stories through multiple sharing activities
- Provides opportunities for students to be creative, imaginative, and inventive
- Integrates speaking and listening skills

Drama in the Classroom

Drama and storytelling are natural extensions of the guided reading program. They enhance the listening comprehension and appreciation of children, they magnify the role of reading and literature throughout the entire curriculum, they serve as a vital foundation for process writing, and they offer many opportunities for children to use books in personally satisfying ways. Following are some suggested drama/storytelling preparations:

1. Invite students to select a book or story that will interest both them and their audience. Their enthusiasm for a story is important in helping the audience enjoy the story, too.

2. Encourage students to practice a story several times before presenting it to a group and to discuss the characters, settings, and events within the story.

3. Students may wish to consider how they might animate the story using hand gestures, facial expressions, or body movements.

4. Encourage students to practice different accents, voice inflections, and loud and soft speech patterns to help make characters come alive.

5. Consider the use of simple puppets as a way to animate the story. Individual puppets can be made for selected characters, or generic puppets can be made and used in a variety of storytelling presentations.

6. Invite students to promote their storytelling time. Children may wish to create announcements, advertisements, or proclamations about an upcoming storytelling time. They can post advertisements in the classroom, throughout the halls, or in a school newspaper.

7. Consider the use of simple props (other than puppets) to use during the telling of a story, such as a paper boat, a magnifying glass, or camera.

8. After the telling of a story, invite the students to discuss the story with class members. Students may wish to discuss their favorite parts, what they liked most about the main character, or how they might prepare a sequel for the story.

Making Puppets

Not only do puppets allow children to animate a book or story, but they also provide opportunities for the audience to become personally involved in the story through the actions and reactions of selected characters. Following are some simple designs you and your students can use to construct appropriate storytelling puppets:

Tongue Depressor Puppet

Draw the face of the puppet on a tongue depressor. Attach fabric for clothes. Add pipe cleaner arms.

Finger Puppet

Cut off the fingers of a glove. Use yarn, buttons, sequins, and other art materials to create a face on each finger.

Rubber Glove Puppet

Draw a face, hair, and other attributes on a clear latex glove.

Paper Bag Puppet

Paint a face on the bag. Yarn and other materials can be used to decorate the bag.

Spoon Puppet

Attach some material to a large serving spoon. Glue eyes, nose, and mouth on the back of the spoon.

Sock Puppet

Glue pieces of fabric, yarn, buttons, sequins, and other art materials to a sock. Colored markers can also be used.

Simple Shape Puppet

Glue simple shapes together to form a head, body, arms, legs, and other attributes. Attach to a craft stick.

Cup Puppet

Turn cup upside down. Cut a hole in each side of the cup. Create a face and add hair. Insert fingers in holes for arms

Pop-up Puppet

Place a dowel in the center of a paper cup. Attach a puppet made from paper or fabric scraps to the end of the dowel. Pop the puppet in and out of the cup.

Design Considerations

- Provide students with a variety of materials for the construction of puppets.
- Provide a variety of costumes (hats, masks, old clothing, shoes, etc.).
- Provide boxes and other items that can be turned into houses, buildings, and related structures.
- Provide drawing, marking, and coloring tools (crayons, paints, markers, etc.) for students to design props, scenes, or book settings.
- Encourage students to work together to interpret a story or book.
- Consider an older student or adult volunteer to assist with the construction of materials.
- Provide opportunities for student groups to share their productions with others.

Suggested Activities

(See *Drama in the Classroom* on page 226 for additional ideas.)

- Invite students to create one or more of the puppets described in the table on page 227.

- Invite students to create their own original puppets.
- Create a staging set (e.g., the bottom cut out of a cardboard box or a plywood puppet stage that has been painted and hung with curtain material).
- Videotape productions for later showing.
- Invite students to turn traditional show and tell into a dramatic sharing of a favorite book.
- Invite students to develop a favorite book into a readers theatre production.

Buddy Reading Center

Buddy reading allows children to work together in pairs to share and discuss a favorite story or book. Its advantage is that children begin to understand that reading, speaking, and listening are all related and can be integrated into meaningful and purposeful literacy activities. Students can share their developing competencies with a member of their peer group in a highly supportive environment.

Value

- Enhances listening skills
- Teaches cooperative learning techniques
- Engages students in discussing text
- Helps students assume a measure of independence in language learning
- Gives students an eager and receptive audience

Design Considerations

- Provide a quiet area where students can work.
- Train students in advance about the importance of sharing and listening.
- Fill the center with books appropriate for students' reading levels.
- Students can be randomly assigned to the center, or select their own buddies.
- Use a special rug or several carpet squares.

Suggested Activities

- Students can have identical copies of a book and read it to each other.
- Students can have two different books and share them with each other.
- One student can read the first page of a book, and the other student can read the second page, and so on.
- One student can read a book aloud while the other points to the accompanying illustrations.
- One student can read a book aloud while the other points to the matching words.
- Reading buddies can read a book together silently or out loud.

Poetry Center

Poetry activities provide students with unique opportunities to play with language. Children gravitate naturally to rhyming simply because it illustrates how fun words can be.

Value

- Helps children experience the playfulness of language
- Allows children to participate in a wide variety of extention activities
- Helps children begin to understand the similarities between words
- Gives students a chance to develop an appreciation for the sounds in words
- Reinforces guided reading activities

Poetry activities provide students with unique opportunities to play with language.

Design Considerations

- Provide large print poems for students to read with a pointer.
- Post pocket charts that encourage manipulation.
- Provide collections of favorite poems in a notebook or binder.
- Assemble a class book of poems.
- Glue favorite poems on stiff cardboard for posting.
- Make audio recordings of poems and provide written versions for students to follow along.
- Provide rhyming word pairs on index cards for students to create and assemble their own simple poems.
- Provide poems from a variety of favorite authors (Shel Silverstein, Jack Prelutsky, and so on).

Suggested Activities

- Cut apart poems shared in a guided reading lesson (divide into stanzas, sentences, or individual words) for students to re-assemble.
- Put a large collection of poems in a basket or bin for free reading.
- Invite students (individually or with a buddy) to reconstruct a poem for posting in the classroom.
- Color-code individual words in a poem for students to build their own poems (e.g., green words are used at the start of a sentence, blue words at the end, and so on.).
- Provide poems in a Cloze format for students to fill in the missing words.
- Use Story Frames for students to create longer poems.
- Provide poetry collections for students to read during free reading.

- Invite parents or other volunteers to create an ongoing series of poetry tapes for students to listen to.
- Glue familiar poems to cardboard and cut apart into jigsaw puzzles. Invite students to reconstruct them.

Big Book Center

This center is an extension of the activities and processes that take place during guided reading lessons. However, in this center, your role can be taken over by one or more students, who will have a unique opportunity to use teacher materials (e.g., big books) and emulate you or replicate the activities shared during guided reading.

Value

- Allows students to use familiar materials
- Gives students practice using familiar routines
- Gives students unique opportunities to extend guided reading concepts through independent work
- Allows students to use large-print materials, which can be seen by all members of a group
- Engages students in cooperative learning activities

Design Considerations

- Provide a wide assortment of big books.
- Provide opportunities for students to practice manipulating the big books using teacher skills (e.g., opening the cover of the book, turning a page, pointing to selected words, and so on).
- Provide small pointers for children to use.
- In addition to big books, consider reproducing text on acetate sheets and projecting them on a wall for students to read.
- Provide students with a set of laminated cards on which you have outlined the things you do during guided reading so that students may emulate them.
- Provide books with which students are familiar or have used in guided reading sessions.

Suggested Activities

- Encourage students to work in small groups to discuss a book shared during guided reading.
- Ask students to focus on a specific literary feature of the story (e.g., character, setting, point of view).
- Invite students to share and discuss what they enjoyed about a book.
- Ask students to retell the story in their own words.
- Invite students to compare and contrast two big books.
- Invite students to use word frames to highlight selected words.
- Invite students to use sticky notes to mask selected words, phrases, punctuation, illustrations, and so on.

Literacy Centers and Multiple Intelligences

Literacy centers offer many opportunities for students to actively engage in a constructivist approach to learning. They provide meaningful learning opportunities tailored to students' needs and interests. Children are given the chance to make important choices about what they learn as well as about how they learn it. Literacy centers provide the means to integrate essential components of the guided reading program through a variety of learning opportunities and ventures.

Incorporated into literacy centers are opportunities for students to build upon one or more of their intelligences. It's important to remember that individuals differ in the strength (or weakness) of each of the eight intelligences in isolation as well as in combination. For example, some individuals learn best through linguistic means, others are more kinesthetic learners, and still others are spatial learners. No two people learn in the same way, nor should they be taught in the same way.

Individuals possess these eight intelligences in varying degrees:

I. Verbal-Linguistic Intelligence

involves ease in producing language and sensitivity to the nuances, order, and rhythm of words. Individuals who are strong in verbal-linguistic intelligence love to read, write, and tell stories.

Literacy Center Activities: Writing, reading, storytelling, speaking, debating

2. Logical-Mathematical Intelligence

relates to the ability to reason deductively or inductively and to recognize and manipulate abstract patterns and relationships. Individuals who excel in this intelligence have strong problem-solving and reasoning skills and ask questions in a logical manner.

Literacy Center Activities: Problem-solving, patterning, showing relationships

3. Musical-Rhythmic Intelligence

encompasses sensitivity to the pitch, timbre, and rhythm of sounds as well as responsiveness to the emotional implications of these elements of music. Individuals who remember melodies or recognize pitch and rhythm exhibit musical intelligence.

Literacy Center Activities: Composing, singing, listening to music

4. Visual-Spatial Intelligence includes

the ability to create visual-spatial representations of the world and to transfer them mentally or concretely. Individuals who exhibit spatial intelligence need a mental or physical picture to best understand new information. They are strong in drawing, designing, and creating things.

Literacy Center Activities: Painting, drawing, pretending, imagining

5. Bodily-Kinesthetic Intelligence

involves using the body to solve problems, make things, and convey ideas and emotions. Individuals who are strong in this intelligence are good at physical activities, eye-hand coordination, and have a tendency to move around, touch things, and gesture.

Literacy Center Activities: Role-playing, movement

6. Intrapersonal Intelligence entails

the ability to understand one's own emotions, goals, and intentions. Individuals strong in intrapersonal intelligence have a strong sense of self, are confident, and can enjoy working alone.

Literacy Center Activities: Thinking strategies, focusing, metacognitive techniques, silent reflection

7. Interpersonal Intelligence refers

to the ability to work effectively with other people and to understand them and recognize their goals and intentions. Individuals who exhibit this intelligence thrive on cooperative work, have strong leadership skills, and are skilled at organizing, communicating, and negotiating.

Literacy Center Activities: Communicating, receiving feedback, collaborating, cooperating

8. Naturalist Intelligence includes

the capacity to recognize flora and fauna, to make distinctions in the natural world, and to use this ability productively in activities such as farming and biological science.

Literacy Center Activities: Reading and listening to nonfiction

The research on multiple intelligences has revealed that teaching aimed at sharpening one kind of intelligence will carry over to others. There is also mounting evidence that learning opportunities that involve a variety of intelligences allow students to take advantage of their preferred intelligence(s) as well as strengthen weaker intelligences. Literacy centers stimulate the development of all eight intelligences.

Literacy centers also provide you with many opportunities to combine the intelligences of your students with the resources, information, and guided reading principles of your entire reading curriculum. Literacy centers celebrate multiple intelligences, offering learning opportunities that provide students with a meaningful and balanced approach to guided reading.

Literacy Center Planning Materials

On the following pages, you will find several forms that are useful for managing students' visits to the literacy centers in your classroom. Following is a description of each:

Literacy Center Icons (pp. 235–237):

These pages include an icon for each literacy center suggested in this unit. You can use the icons to identify the centers in your classroom. Simply make a copy of it from this book, then color it using colored pencils or markers (students will probably enjoy doing this for you). Laminate the icon and post it in your classroom.

My Weekly Literacy Center Sheet (p. 238):

This form will help your students monitor their progress through the literacy centers in your classroom. Provide a new one for each child at the beginning of the week. Make copies of the small icons from pages 235-237 and ask children to cut out the icons and paste them on their sheet.

Literacy Center Status Sheet (p. 239):

This is a recording sheet that will assist you in monitoring student progress through your classroom literacy centers. List student names down the left-hand column. Place a check mark in the appropriate column after a student has completed the required activity.

Literacy Center Icons

Listening Center

Art Center

ABC/Spelling Center

Writing Center

Literacy Center Icons

Reading Around the Room Center

Pocket Chart Center

Readers Theatre Center

Free Reading Center

Literacy Center Icons

Drama/Storytelling Center

Poetry Center

Buddy Reading Center

Big Book Center

My Weekly Literacy Center Sheet

Name: _____   **Week Number:** _____

Show the centers you work in each day.

Monday: _____

Tuesday: _____

Wednesday: _____

Thursday: _____

Friday: _____

Literacy Center Status Sheet

Name: _____   **Week Number:** _____

Literacy Centers

Students	A	B	C	D	E	F	G	H	I	J	K	L
1.												
2.												
3.												
4.												
5.												
6.												
7.												
8.												
9.												
10.												
11.												
12.												
13.												
14.												
15.												
16.												
17.												
18.												
19.												
20.												
21.												
22.												
23.												
24.												
25.												

A = Listening Center
B = ABC/Spelling Center
C = Art Center
D = Writing Center

E = Reading Around the Room Center
F = Readers Theatre Center
G = Pocket Chart Center
H = Free Reading Center

I = Drama/Storytelling Center
J = Buddy Reading Center
K = Poetry Center
L = Big Book Center

Organizing and Managing Your Classroom

Key Factors for Success

The success of your guided reading program depends on two key components: the layout of your classroom and your management of the time available for instruction. The traditional arrangement of a teacher's desk at the front of the room and equally spaced rows of desks sweeping to the back of the room does not foster or encourage student participation or involvement in the demands and structures of a well-rounded guided reading program. The following factors will facilitate guided reading principles throughout the school year:

Factor	Description
Time	Time devoted at the very beginning of the school year to fostering group interaction and establishing class rules and routines will create more time for instruction throughout the remainder of the school year.
Responsibility	Student responsibility for the organization and management of books and other materials in the classroom is important.
Environments	Learning environments must recognize that teacher and student needs may differ and those differences need to be discussed in an atmosphere of trust and support.
Cooperative Learning	Many opportunities for cooperative learning and feedback should take place throughout the school day.
Community of Learners	Establishing a community of learners is essential for guided reading practices to be successful and sustaining.
Physical Organization	The physical organization of the classroom must encourage appropriate behavior by separating areas of high activity from areas requiring quiet concentration and solitude.
Resource Materials	There should be a decentralized placement of resource and reference materials throughout the classroom. This supports numerous activities taking place simultaneously.

The Basics of Classroom Layout

Effective integration of guided reading practices throughout your reading curriculum requires the creation of classroom areas where children can congregate to collaborate on projects that support the goals of guided reading. Children need to surround themselves with a print-rich environment that signals the significance of reading as a normal and natural occurrence of the school day. There is no single physical arrangement or structure that can generate a successful classroom. Some arrangements lend themselves better than others to active, meaningful, student involvement while fostering a learning environment that encourages self-regulation and organized movement. The creation of distinct areas or literacy centers (see Unit 9), designed for specific learning activities and having similar noise-level requirements, constitutes a room arrangement that furthers those behaviors. Besides the list of literacy centers in Unit 9, you may wish to consider one or more of the elements in the chart on the following page for your classroom.

There are several things to consider when planning your classroom environment. These include, but are not limited to, the following:

- Work space and storage space for each student
- Chalkboard large enough for group brainstorming, recording, and modeling reading/writing strategies
- Your personal area where teaching resources, records, and so on are stored
- Storage area for student backpacks, coats, and other belongings
- Storage area for various types of paper (lined writing paper, unlined paper, extra paper from prior lessons)
- Word bank area (large chart paper) displayed low enough for students to read and make additions
- Science observation area located away from individual work space
- Art area with organized supplies
- Featured author bulletin board with space for storage of collection of author's works
- Physical education equipment storage
- Computer area
- Speaking platform
- Separate bulletin boards for class information, student responsibilities, student of the week, and messages
- Theater area for storage of costumes and props

> *Children need to surround themselves with a print-rich environment that signals the significance of reading as a normal and natural occurrence of the school day.*

A Guide to Classroom Layout

Area	Description
Classroom Library	This area of the classroom houses books for student selection. You may wish to include a separate section for leveled books to be used in the guided reading program as well as another adjacent area for free reading books that students select on their own. It is important to include a range of genres as well as a range of levels in the free reading section of the library.
Chart Wall	This section of the classroom can be a wall or room divider that is covered with songs, chants, poems, and other word play samples. You can post materials students have read in books as well as those which they have created on their own.
Word Wall	The entire classroom is a word wall! Words should flow across each and every available wall space. Words that students learn about in the books they read as well as high-frequency words (Dolch List) should cover the walls and doors of the classroom.
Conference Area	This can be as simple as a small table and two chairs or as elaborate as a carpeted area with pillows and bean bag chairs. It is here that you will want to conference with individual children in addition to assessing their reading progress using assessment tools such as running records. This section of the room should be relatively quiet and free from any necessary distractions.
Town Meeting Area	One specific area of the room can be for "Town Meetings." During a Town Meeting, the entire class should get together to plan for an upcoming science activity, discuss the events of the week and summarize them on a Learn and Share sheet (see page 255). They can also talk about the upcoming day and its activities, sing a favorite song, or share a funny poem. This is an important area in that it helps cement important bonds and establish a true community of learners.
Author's or Reader's Chair	This is a very special chair (an overstuffed chair from the local thrift store will do) in which one student can sit and share a piece he or she has written or read aloud a favorite story or poem that he or she has mastered. This is an opportunity for one child to become the center of attention for a selected period of time each day. It is important that every child assumes this seat of importance on a regular and rotating basis.

Keep the following principles in mind when making decisions about the physical environment in your classroom:

1. The classroom should show students models of good language.

2. The classroom should offer opportunities for students to use and experiment with language.

3. The classroom should be a comfortable environment that consistently welcomes students as language learners.

4. The classroom should be learner-centered and student-owned. Students should be given responsibilities for designing the classroom and maintaining its order. This helps establish a sense of ownership that can translate into a community of learners.

The following classroom diagrams encompass many of the concepts and principles presented in this unit. These are only suggested classroom arrangements. Space considerations and room design will determine how well you will be able to incorporate these designs into your current classroom organization.

Classroom Design #1

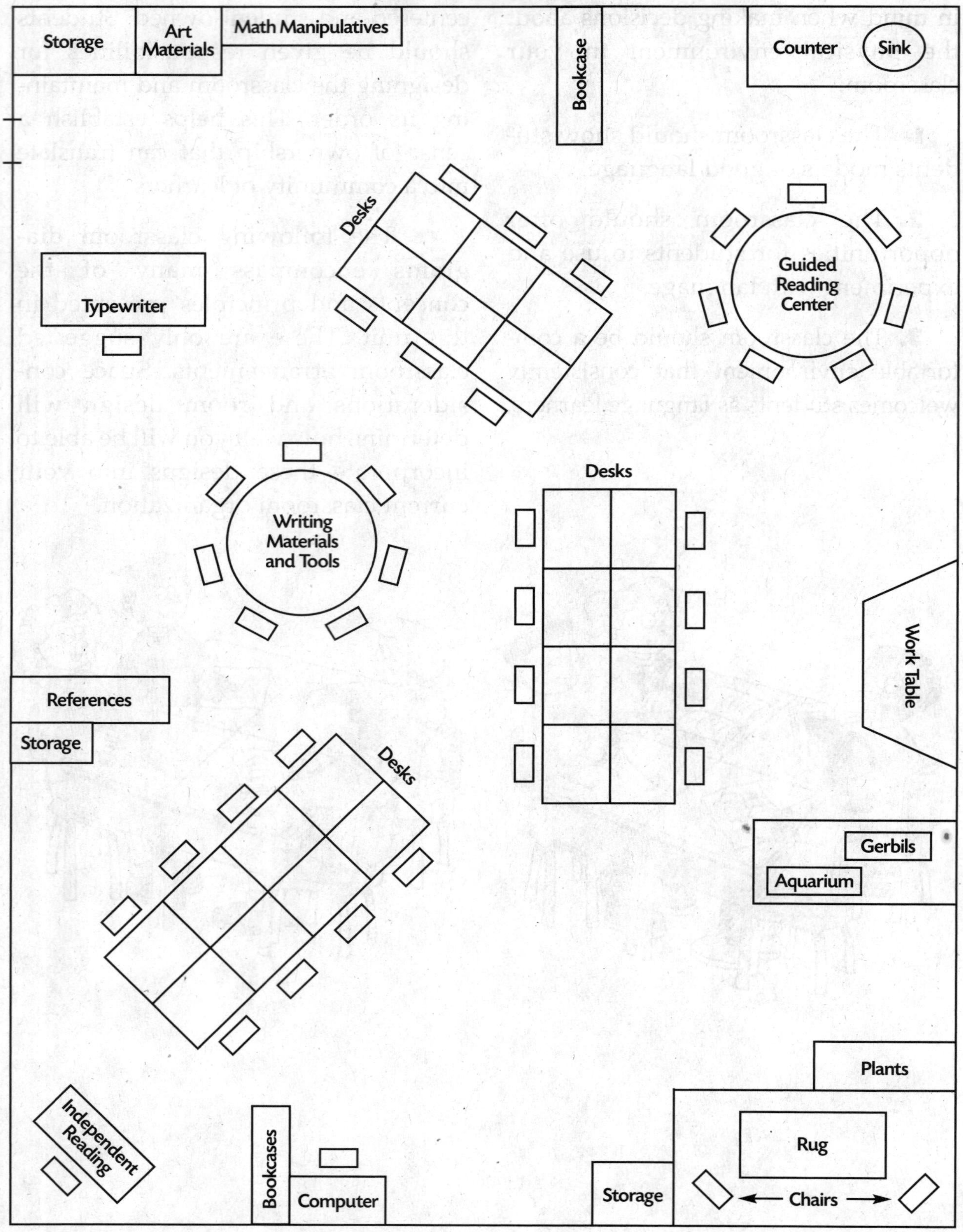

Storage | Art Materials | Math Manipulatives

Bookcase

Counter | Sink

Desks

Guided Reading Center

Typewriter

Writing Materials and Tools

Desks

References

Storage

Work Table

Desks

Gerbils

Aquarium

Independent Reading

Bookcases

Computer

Storage

Plants

Rug

← Chairs →

Classroom Design #2

Daily Schedule

Bookshelves

Chalkboard

Interest Club News

Message Boards

Playground Equipment

Social Studies Area

Conference Table

Science Area

Office for Writing

Desk

Mailboxes

Listening Center

Private Place

Desks in Clusters

Publishing Center

Supplies

Covers

Paper

Book Cart

Sofa

Bookshelves

Rug

Meeting Rug

Rocking Chair

Teacher Desk

Job List

Calendar

Special Person of the Week

Tadpole Tank and Diary

Storage Cabinets

Student Published Books

Plans and Schedules for Guided Reading

There is no ideal plan for scheduling guided reading. There are as many ways of presenting guided reading to students as there are teachers. Each classroom is unique. The needs of the children and the competencies of the teacher must be balanced against the time available for instruction and the reading objectives.

Schulman and Payne (2000) present some considerations that you may wish to keep in mind as you begin developing schedules for your guided reading program. These considerations are framed as questions simply because the answers will determine the structure of a routine that works in your particular classroom for your particular students:

• How many students do you have in your class?

• What is the range of reading abilities they possess?

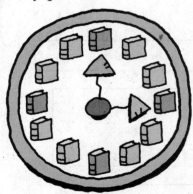

• How many separate groups can you comfortably manage?

• How many students would you like to have in each group (the ideal is four to six)?

• How long will you need to work with each group (emergent readers need about ten to fifteen minutes per session; more advanced readers about fifteen to twenty minutes per session)?

• How often do you want to meet with low-performing readers (once every day is suggested)?

• How often do you want to meet with Transitional and Fluent Readers (five meetings in a two-week period is suggested)?

• How much time do you need for assessment (running records, oral reading)?

• How much transition time between groups and activities is necessary?

The answers to these questions will help you construct a workable schedule of literacy activities that respects the needs of individuals and offers a support structure for both students and teachers.

Plans

It is important to remember that guided reading is one element in the overall reading program. A balanced reading program is one in which sufficient attention is devoted to several components (see Unit 1) on a daily basis. The individual time frames for those components will vary, depending on the philosophy of the school/district, daily time schedules, the reading curriculum, and personal preferences.

What follows are three plans for scheduling guided reading into the daily activities of your classroom. Depending on the amount of time available for reading instruction as well as for other subject areas, you may wish to modify these schedules accordingly. The three time frames are:

1. 2 hours and 45 minutes available for reading instruction each day

2. Two 45-minute blocks of time available for reading instruction each day

3. One 45-minute block of time available for reading instruction each day

Sample Schedule A
2 hours and 45 minutes for Reading Instruction
Groups

	A	**B**	**C**	**D**
9:00–9:15	Opening Daily news	→		
9:15–9:45	Shared Book Experience	→		
9:45–10:15	**Guided reading**	Individualized reading Paired reading	Language exploration Reading and writing	Individualized reading
10:15–10:30	Reading aloud	→		
10:30–11:00	Language exploration	**Guided reading**	Individualized reading Paired reading	Language exploration Reading and writing
11:00–11:30	Individualized reading	Language exploration	Reading and writing	Paired reading
11:30–11:45	Sustained silent reading	→		

Sample Schedule B
Two 45-minute Blocks of Time for Reading Instruction
Groups

	A	B	C	D
9:15–9:30	Shared book experience	→		
9:30–10:00	**Guided reading**	Individualized reading Paired reading	Language exploration Reading and writing	Individualized reading
10:00–10:45	(Content area subject)	→		
10:45–11:00	Reading aloud	→		
11:00–11:30	Language exploration	**Guided reading**	Individualized reading Paired reading	Language exploration Reading and writing

Sample Schedule C
One 45-minute Block of Time for Reading Instruction

	Monday	Tuesday	Wednesday	Thursday	Friday
Reading aloud		15 minutes		15 minutes	
Shared book experience				15 minutes	
Guided reading	30 minutes		30 minutes		30 minutes
Individualized reading		15 minutes			
Paired reading			15 minutes		
Sustained silent reading	15 minutes				15 minutes
Language exploration		15 minutes			
Reading and writing				15 minutes	

Schedules

Following are examples of daily schedules collected from several teachers who have embraced the concept of guided reading. They are examples of the wide variety of instructional schedules that support guided reading and children's developing literacy abilities. Change these schedules to suit the needs of your classroom, the needs of your students, and your own philosophy about teaching.

Daily Schedule I
Wendy Watkins, Kindergarten, Nevada

8:45–9:05	**Arrival, Opening**	Students arrive, put away their belongings, and assemble on the community rug. Share a Word of the Day. Encourage students to listen for and/or locate the word throughout the morning.
9:05–9:30	**Read aloud**	Select a book from the classroom library and read it to the students.
9:30–10:10	**Guided reading**	Students are engaged in a wide variety of guided reading activities. Typically, the teacher would work with two separate groups each day.
10:10–10:25	**Recess; Snack time**	
10:25–10:45	**D.E.A.R.**	Each student has the opportunity to select an individual book and read it silently. Monitor their reading behaviors and take notes whenever necessary.
10:45–11:10	**Math block**	Students participate in a diverse collection of manipulative activities emphasizing ordinal numbers.
11:10–11:25	**Phonemic awareness**	Using the book *The Complete Phonemic Awareness Handbook* by Anthony D. Fredericks (Rigby, 2001), you can provide students with various activities at the five stages of phonemic awareness.
11:30	**Dismissal**	

Daily Schedule 2
Carmelita Lopez, Grade 1, California

8:30–8:50	**Opening**	Students arrive and put away their book bags. They gather in small groups to "read the room" or engage in independent reading activities.
8:50–9:15	**Whole-class instruction**	A structured and planned lesson is presented to the entire class. The emphasis may be on a reading strategy or concept.
9:15–9:45	**Writing process**	Students are divided into various groups to participate in a wide variety of writing activities.
9:45–10:30	**Guided reading groups**	Students are assigned to various learning centers arranged throughout the classroom. Work with two separate guided reading groups on specific reading strategies.
10:30–11:30	**Science/Social studies**	Students participate in reading and complementary hands-on, minds-on activities that extend and expand the concepts in the text.
11:30–12:00	**Lunch**	
12:00–12:30	**Sustained silent reading**	Students and the teacher read self-selected books throughout the room.
12:30–1:15	**Math**	Students work in their math books and with manipulatives on various math concepts and principles.
1:15–1:35	**Storytelling/Read aloud**	A selection of authors, genres, and books is shared with students in the Town Center.
1:35–2:10	**Art/Music**	The art teacher or music teacher works with the students.
2:10–2:40	**Self-selected activities**	Students have the opportunity to select from a wide range of free activities, including various literacy centers.
2:40–3:00	**Responding to literature**	Students complete book-related activities and projects.
3:00–3:15	**Daily closure**	Students gather in the Town Center to discuss the day's activities and plan for the next day's lessons.
3:15	**Dismissal**	

Daily Schedule 3
Katherine McPhail, Grade 2, Michigan

8:45–9:00	**Arrival** **Prepare for the day**	
9:00–9:20	**Sustained silent reading**	Each student selects their own book, crawls under a desk, flops in a bean bag chair, or sprawls on the floor to read by themselves.
9:20–9:45	**Class meeting**	Students and teacher meet to plan the day's activities, discuss any leftover material from the day before, and outline the goals and objectives for various lessons.
9:45–10:45	**Reading**	Students are assigned to various guided reading groups. The teacher works with two separate groups on pre-selected strategies. Other students are engaged in learning center activities.
10:45–11:45	**Writing**	Stages of the writing process are taught or reinforced. Students are provided with authentic opportunities to use those stages in a variety of writing projects.
11:45–12:15	**Lunch**	
12:15–12:30	**Read aloud**	The teacher reads a book to the students that they have selected.
12:30–1:15	**Math**	Students use a variety of manipulatives to reinforce various math concepts.
1:15–1:45	**P.E.**	Students go with the P.E. teacher to the gym.
1:45–2:45	**Science**	Students work on a unit about oceans, reading ocean-related books, cleaning the classroom aquarium and designing an interactive bulletin board.
2:45–3:10	**Technology**	Students work on the classroom computers.
3:15	**Dismissal**	

Helpful Planning Forms

In addition to the right classroom layout and a good instruction schedule, it's helpful to have forms that allow you to keep track of your students' work. On the next few pages, you will find several forms that will help you.

Guided Reading Planning Grid (p. 253):

This weekly planning grid allows you to assign students to various groups for selected guided reading and independent activities.

Books I Have Read This Week (p. 254):

Invite students to complete this form as a record of the books shared in guided reading groups.

Learn and Share (p. 255):

This form can be used at the end of the week. Encourage students to record appropriate information in each of the three sections. Students may wish to take a sheet home each week to share with their parents.

Guided Reading Planning Grid

Name: _____   **Week Number:** _____

	Guided Reading Group 1 Time: _____	Guided Reading Group 2 Time: _____	Independent Work Group A	Independent Work Group B	Independent Work Group C	Independent Work Group D
Monday						
Tuesday						
Wednesday						
Thursday						
Friday						

Books I Have Read This Week

Name: _____   **Week Number:** _____

Monday _____	What I Liked:	What I Learned:
Title:		
Author:		
Tuesday _____	What I Liked:	What I Learned:
Title:		
Author:		
Wednesday _____	What I Liked:	What I Learned:
Title:		
Author:		
Thursday _____	What I Liked:	What I Learned:
Title:		
Author:		
Friday _____	What I Liked:	What I Learned:
Title:		
Author:		

Learn and Share

Name: _____   **Week Number:** _____

---

3 things I learned this week:

_____

_____

_____

---

2 things I want to share with someone:

_____

_____

---

1 thing I want to learn more about:

_____

Parent Involvement Activities

The Importance of Parent Participation

The ultimate goal of guided reading is to help children acquire the strategies and skills they need to become fluent readers. This is accomplished through a variety of processes and practices that support each child's reading progress and are part of an overall balanced literacy program.

The strength and effectiveness of a guided reading program are predicated on several factors. One of the most important factors that can lead to a successful program is the support and intervention of parents. When parents are recruited as participating members of a classroom reading program, student achievement and success follow accordingly. Parents provide children with the basic foundations on which successful reading experiences can be built. The support, encouragement, patience, and understanding of parents have a profound effect on both the academic and social development of children.

Engaging parents in the dynamics of your guided reading program can have a significant impact on the literacy growth and development of students. Not only can parents support and sustain your instructional efforts; they reinforce and re-emphasize the strategies you share with children. This is not to say that the home should be turned into a school away from school. Invite parents as active members of the literacy team—soliciting their participation and informing them about the role they can have throughout the reading curriculum.

The following sections will provide you with a selection of relevant and meaningful suggestions to share with parents. The special letters and calendars are meant to be sent home on a periodic basis to offer parents and other caregivers lively and fun activities that support positive reading experiences.

> *When parents are recruited as participating members of a classroom reading program, student achievement and success follow accordingly.*

Letters

This section provides you with several reproducible letters to send home to parents. Each of the letters focuses on direct and easy-to-implement reading activities that can be incorporated regularly into the family's daily routine. The suggestions and tips are all proven methods for developing and encouraging successful reading experiences.

You can send home these letters to the parents of your students on a regular basis, following a few simple suggestions:

1. Photocopy one letter and sign your name in the space provided at the bottom of the letter. Be sure to add the date at the top.

2. Send the letter home with your students on a selected day (every other Tuesday or every third Thursday can be "Letter Day").

3. Encourage students to ask their parents to work with them on the activities and suggestions in each letter. Emphasize that these letters are not homework assignments, but rather an opportunity for families to work and learn together.

4. Encourage students to bring in and share selected family activities with other members of the class.

The following strategies may help to facilitate two-way communication of the letters between home and school:

- Include a letter as part of a regular newsletter/newspaper sent home by the school.

- Write a brief, personalized note at the bottom of each letter commenting on something positive about the student.

- Schedule workshops at school where parents can share some of their favorite activities, books, or songs.

- Ask the principal or superintendent to prepare a special introductory letter to parents explaining the letters and their value.

- You may wish to have these letters translated for parents who don't speak English.

The next two sections have been designed to serve as resources to help you involve parents in the education of their children. Used throughout the course of your guided reading program, these letters can help ensure that everyone is working toward a common goal and that the best interests of all children are being provided for in an atmosphere of mutual trust, support, and encouragement. The letters that follow include:

General Letters

Letter of Introduction, p. 259
Sharing Reading Time, p. 260
Reading Aloud With Your Child, p. 261
Making Reading Fun, p. 262

Stage Letters

Emergent Readers
  Introductory Letter, p. 263
  Beginning Activities, p. 264
  Recommended Books, p. 265

Early Readers
  Introductory Letter, p. 266
  Word Fun, p. 267
  Recommended Books, p. 268

Transitional Readers
  Introductory Letter, p. 269
  Comprehension Letter, p. 270
  Recommended Books, p. 271

Fluent Readers
  Introductory letter, p. 272
  Comprehension Hints, p. 273
  Recommended Books, p. 274

Letter of Introduction

Dear Parents:

Our class will be learning many things in reading this year. Students will be learning how to read different types of books as well as strategies that will help them comprehend those books. These experiences are part of the reading development of every child, and are important lifelong skills.

I would like to invite you to become a partner in your child's learning experiences this year. I believe your involvement will help your child attain a higher level of reading success. This partnership between home and school can provide your child with a wealth of learning opportunities that will positively affect his or her reading performance.

In order to help reinforce the work we are doing in the classroom, I will be sending home parent letters and calendars regularly with activities for you and your child to share. They are designed to provide you with ideas that can help your child become a successful reader. Each letter and/or calendar contains several choices of activities to share that will reinforce the work we are doing in school without disrupting your family schedule. There are no special materials to buy. Your only investment is a few moments of your time each day—a few moments that can make a world of difference in your child's education.

I look forward to your participation in our learning experiences this year. If you have any question about these letters or calendars, please feel free to contact me. Let's work together this year to help your child succeed in school!

Sincerely,

Sharing Reading Time

Dear Parents:

Reading stories to your children is a valuable activity. When children listen to adults read, it helps them develop an appreciation for written material and for the ideas and thoughts that books can convey. Parents who read to their children on a regular basis are more likely to have children who are good readers. Children who have been read to will be eager to read for themselves because they know of the pleasures to be found in books. Here are some suggestions:

1. Establish a relaxed atmosphere with no radios, TV, or other distractions. Try setting aside a family reading time when everyone reads.

2. Encourage your child to stop and ask you questions while you are reading with them. This shows that your child is interested in what they are reading.

3. You may want to stop from time to time in your reading to ask questions about the characters or events in the story. Ask questions like "Why do you think he or she did that?"

4. Check with the school librarian, the children's librarian at your local public library, and bookstore personnel for suggested books. Provide opportunities for your child to select books he or she would enjoy hearing.

Together we are sending your child on the road to academic success. Thank you for your participation.

Sincerely,

Reading Aloud With Your Child

Dear Parents:

Learning to read is one of the most valuable skills your child can learn. One practice that helps children on the road to reading success is for parents to set aside a special time each day to read with their children. This sharing time is important since it demonstrates to your child that reading can be fun, exciting, and informative. Best of all, when parents and children share a book, they have a special time together. Plan to take a few moments each day to share the joy of literature with your child. Here are some ideas:

1. Give your child plenty of opportunities to choose reading materials to share together. Allow him or her to pick books based on special interests, favorite characters, or hobbies.

2. Read aloud with lots of expression. You may wish to take on the role of one of the characters in a book and adjust your voice accordingly.

3. As you read a familiar story to your child, occasionally leave out a word and ask your child to suggest the missing word or another substitute word.

4. Make reading a regular part of your family activities. Be sure to take books along on family outings or trips. Read to your child every chance you get.

Thank you for being an important part of your child's learning. Working together, we can help your child become a great reader.

Sincerely,

Making Reading Fun

Dear Parents:

In order for children to become good readers, they must be actively involved in all the fun and magic of good books. We know that children who are motivated to learn to read are those who are surrounded by the fun of reading. When children know that reading can be a fun, enjoyable, and satisfying activity, they will be actively engaged in all of the skills and activities designed to help them on the road to reading success. Children will help develop positive attitudes toward reading and learning in general when parents share some fun reading-related activities. Try these motivators:

1. Take lots of photographs of your child with books—for example, taking a book off a shelf, sharing a book with another family member, or looking at a book in a bookstore. Paste these on sheets of paper and ask your child to suggest titles for each one. Then display them.

2. After you and your child finish reading a book together, create a puppet or model of one of the characters, and put it on display at home.

3. After you have read a book to your child, ask him or her to tell you a word from the story that they especially liked. It can be a funny word, a sad word, a rhyming word, or a strange word. Write the word on an index card and place the card inside the front cover of the book. The next time you share the book with your child, talk about the word on the card and why your child selected that word after the previous reading.

4. Invite your child to draw an illustration or picture of his or her favorite character or favorite part of the story. Put it on display at home.

The time you spend with your child is important. Thank you for your contributions.

Sincerely,

Emergent Reader Introductory Letter

Dear Parents:

During our reading program this year, your child will be involved in a wide variety of reading activities, including guided reading. The purpose of guided reading is to expose students to a wide range of books, to teach comprehension strategies, and to help them read books that become increasingly more difficult as their skills improve.

Guided reading is divided into four separate stages of reading development. Your child will move up and through the stages in accordance with his or her growth and development in a variety of reading materials. Through careful testing I have placed your child in the **emergent reader** stage for our grade.

Here are some of the reading skills your child will be learning:

- *Learning that people read from left to right*
- *Using pictures to help understand the story*
- *Learning the difference between a letter and a word*
- *Learning some beginning letter sounds*
- *Learning some ending letter sounds*
- *Understanding the match between spoken words and written words*
- *Locating some known words in a story*
- *Appreciating pattern and repetition in stories*

Following is an example of the type of reading material your child will be using in this stage of his or her reading program:

The Big Bad Pig

"Look," said the cat.
"Look," said the dog.
"Look," said the rat.
It was the big bad pig.
"He is big, "said the cat.
"He is big," said the dog.
"He is big," said the rat.
"And bad," said the big bad pig.
"Oh, no," said the cat.
"Oh, no," said the dog.
"Oh, no," said the rat.
"Oh, good," said the man.

Sincerely,

Emergent Reader Beginning Activities

Dear Parents:

Learning to read is one of the most important skills your child will learn in school. In class, we are reading many books, sharing stories, and participating in many different kinds of reading-related activities. You can assist your child in this beginning stage of his or her reading growth with a few of the following activities. Plan to share these with your child over a period of several weeks.

1. As you read a book or story to your child, "track" the print with your finger. Point to each word as you say it to your child. Help your child understand that the words we see are also the words we say.

2. As you read, stop every so often and talk about pictures, illustrations, or photographs in a book. Talk about the relationship between an illustration and the words in the book.

3. After you finish reading a story to your child, go back to the book and select one or two words. Point to each letter in a word and say its name. Talk with your child about how people use several letters together to make words. For example, we can put c, a, and t together to make the word cat.

4. When you read a story to your child, point to the beginning letter of a word and make its sound. Point to the ending letter of another word and make its sound. Be sure to point to each letter while you make the sound of that letter. Help your child understand that each letter has its own unique shape and sound.

These are just a few of the activities you can do to encourage good reading habits for your child.

Sincerely,

Emergent Reader Recommended Books

Dear Parents:

Following is a list of books highly recommended for children at the emergent stage of reading development. These books have been selected on the basis of their appropriateness to children's interests and developing reading abilities. Your local public library, your child's school library, or any local bookstore should have these books available for you. Plan to visit them regularly and make these suggestions part of your child's reading adventures and explorations.

- *The Aquarium* by Carol Kloes
- *Baby Says* by John Steptoe
- *Brown Bear, Brown Bear* by Bill Martin, Jr.
- *Buzz, Said the Bee* by Wendy C. Lewison
- *Cat on the Mat* by Brian Wildsmith
- *The Cat Who Loved Red* by Lynn Salem and Josie Stewart
- *Do You Want to Be My Friend?* by Eric Carle
- *The Fox on the Box* by Barbara Gregorich
- *Hats* by Deborah Williams
- *Have You Seen My Duckling?* by Nancy Tafuri
- *I Went Walking* by Sue Williams
- *Look What I Can Do* by Jose Aruego
- *Lunch at the Zoo* by Wendy Blaxland and C. Bimage
- *Making a Memory* by Margaret Ballinger
- *Mrs. Cook's Hats* by Jan Mader
- *My Cat Muffin* by Marjory Gardner
- *Not Enough Water* by Shane Armstrong and Susan Hartley
- *Now We Can Go* by Ann Jonas
- *Rainbow of My Own* by Don Freeman
- *Scary Monster* by Kate Eifrig
- *What Has Stripes?* by Margaret Ballinger
- *What Has Wheels?* by Karen Hoenecke

Sincerely,

Early Reader Introductory Letter

Dear Parents:

During our reading program this year, your child will be involved in a wide variety of reading activities, including guided reading. The purposes of guided reading are to expose students to a wide range of books, to teach comprehension strategies, and to help them read books that become increasingly more difficult as their skills improve.

Guided reading is divided into four separate stages of reading development. Your child will move up and through the stages in accordance with his or her growth and development in a variety of reading materials. Through careful testing I have placed your child in the **early reader** stage for our grade.

Here are some of the reading skills your child will be learning:

- *Learning and building new vocabulary*
- *Matching spoken and written words*
- *Learning to self-correct*
- *Getting more information from print than from pictures*
- *Using beginning, middle, and ending sounds of words*

- *Using several reading strategies to understand written text*
- *Reading familiar books and stories*
- *Learning about different forms of punctuation*
- *Talking about what he/she learns in books*

Following is an example of the type of reading material your child will be using in this stage of his or her reading program:

The Zebra's Stripes

Once upon a time the zebra was white. It had no stripes. One day a monkey said, "Why are you white?" The zebra said, "I am white so that you can see me."

"Why do you want me to see you?" asked the monkey.

"So you will know that I am fast," said the zebra.

"But that is not smart," said the monkey.

"Why?" asked the zebra."

"Because," said the monkey, "lions can see you, too."

"Oh, no," said the zebra, "What can I do?" The monkey sat in the tree. He looked at the zebra. It was late in the day. There were shadows on the ground. Some shadows were on the zebra.

The monkey said, "I know what you can do."

"What?" said the zebra.

"Put some stripes on your back and front. Then the lion will not find you. You will look like lots of shadows." And that is what the zebra did.

Sincerely,

Early Reader Word Fun

Dear Parents:

In school we are learning about the sounds that letters make and how those sounds can be put together to form words. This is a very important skill for children because it helps them learn about the sounds in the English language and how some of those sounds can be combined to make words. Children learn that one, two, or more sounds can be put together to create words. As children learn about the sounds in words, they begin to understand that there are a wide variety of sounds.

You can help your child learn about word sounds with some of the following activities and games. As always, keep the emphasis on *fun*—be sure your child knows that making sounds and learning about them can be a playful and enjoyable way to spend a couple of minutes with you.

1. As you read a book or story with your child, look for some words that begin with the same letter—for example, two words that begin with *b*. After you've read the story, ask your child a question such as, "What sound do you hear at the beginning of these two words from the story—*boy* and *bird*?" Ask your child for the sounds at the beginning of each word, not the names of the letters.

2. Play a word pair game with your child. Locate objects in or around your house that begin with the same sound—for example, "I see a table and a tree" or "I see some green grass" or "I see a carpet and a cat." Invite your child to note the matching beginning sound for each pair of words.

3. As you read a book with your child, ask him or her to listen for words that begin with a particular sound. For example, you might say, "Today, let's listen for words that begin with the /s/ sound."

4. Introduce your child to rhythm by having him or her clap to the beat of a favorite song or tune. Demonstrate to your child how each clap of the hands stands for one beat in the music. You may want to begin with a song your child is very familiar with, for example, "Happy Birthday." Here's how you might demonstrate it: "Hap (clap) py (clap) birth (clap) day (clap) to (clap) you (clap)."

Your contributions are important to your child's future reading success. Thank you for your participation.

Sincerely,

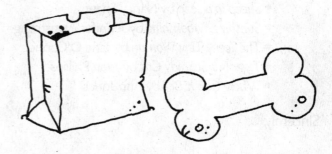

Early Reader Recommended Books

Dear Parents:

Following is a list of books highly recommended for children at the early reader stage of reading development. These books have been selected on the basis of their appropriateness to children's interests and developing reading abilities. Your local public library, your child's school library, or any local bookstore should have these books available for you. Plan to visit them regularly and make these suggestions part of your child's reading adventures and explorations.

- *All by Myself* by Mercer Mayer
- *Amy Loves the Snow* by Julia Hoban
- *Are You My Mommy?* by Carla Dijs
- *Big Friend, Little Friend* by Eloise Greenfield
- *The Blanket* by John Burningham
- *Bread, Bread, Bread* by Ann Jonas
- *Calico Cat's Rainbow* by Donald Charles
- *Cat and Dog* by Else H. Minarik
- *Dinosaurs, Dinosaurs* by Byron Barton
- *Farmer in the Dell* by Kathy Parkinson
- *Five Little Monkeys Jumping on the Bed* by Eileen Christelow
- *The Foot Book* by Dr. Suess
- *Goldilocks and the Three Bears* by Fran Hunia
- *Gum on the Drum* by Barbara Gregorich
- *Have You Seen the Crocodile?* by Colin West
- *Henry's Busy Day* by Rod Campbell
- *If I Were You* by Brian Wildsmith
- *Is This You?* by Robert Krauss
- *Just a Seed* by Wendy Blaxland
- *Just Like Daddy* by Frank Asch
- *Morris the Moose* by Bernard Wiseman
- *Our House Had a Mouse* by Denise Worthington
- *The Quarter Story* by Deborah Williams
- *Rosie's Walk* by Pat Hutchins
- *Sheep in a Jeep* by Nancy Shaw
- *Sunshine, Moonshine* by Jennifer Armstrong
- *The Teeny Tiny Woman* by Jane O'Conner
- *Tiger Is a Scaredy Cat* by Joan Phillips
- *Where Can It Be?* by Ann Jonas

Sincerely,

Transitional Reader Introductory Letter

Dear Parents:

During our reading program this year, your child will be involved in a wide variety of reading activities, including guided reading. The purpose of guided reading is to expose students to a wide range of books, to teach comprehension strategies, and to help them read books that become increasingly more difficult as their skills improve.

Guided reading is divided into four separate stages of reading development. Your child will move up and through the stages in accordance with his or her growth and development in a variety of reading materials. Through careful testing I have placed your child in the **transitional reader** stage for our grade.

Here are some of the reading skills your child will be learning:

- *Using problem-solving while reading*
- *Making predictions*
- *Monitoring his or her understanding of written material*
- *Decoding unknown words*

- *Developing a core of high-frequency words*
- *Reading written material with some fluency*
- *Reading more complex materials*
- *Understanding the ways in which stories are written*

Following is an example of the type of reading material your child will be using in this stage of his or her reading program:

To the Beach

One day we went to the beach. My mother drove the car. My brother and sister sat in the back seat with me.

We started the trip. After 15 minutes my sister asked, "Are we there yet?"

"No," said my father, "but we will be there soon."

We drove for a long time. I saw a bunch of cows in a field. I saw three barns and two tractors. I saw a lot of horses and sheep.

"Are we there yet?" my brother asked.

"No," said my mother, "but we will be there soon."

I counted the cars on the highway. I counted to 147 when I sneezed. Then, I lost count. The trip seemed to take forever.

"Are we there yet?" I asked my parents.

"Yes," they both said together. "Now we are at the beach and can swim and play."

"At last," I said.

Sincerely,

Transitional Reader Comprehension Letter

Dear Parents:

One of the major goals of reading instruction is to help children attain high levels of comprehension. Children who understand more of what they read enjoy reading more. Parents can play a vital role in helping their children attain sound comprehension skills. This can occur very naturally during your sharing time together, when you are reading a story to your child, or even when traveling in the car. Providing your child with opportunities to reflect and appreciate what he or she reads can be an important contribution to his or her reading development.

1. Before you and your child read a story together, ask him or her to formulate a question about the title or initial illustrations. This helps your child develop a purpose for reading the story.

2. Some children enjoy making up their own questions about a story after it is read. You may wish to encourage your child to develop questions like those found on school tests. Take some time to go over all the questions.

3. It is a good idea to keep a vocabulary notebook or word card box nearby when reading stories with your child. This provides an opportunity for him or her to record any new words, which can be defined and written in his or her own sentences.

4. As you and your child are reading a story together, stop every so often and ask him or her to draw a picture of a significant event. Upon completion of the story, direct your child to arrange these pictures in sequential order and/or paste them into a special scrapbook.

5. After you have finished reading a story, ask your child to summarize it in as few words as possible. Assist him or her in coming up with a statement that conveys the main idea of the entire story.

Sincerely,

Transitional Reader Recommended Books

Dear Parents:

Following is a list of books highly recommended for children at the transitional stage of reading development. These books have been selected on the basis of their appropriateness to children's interests and developing reading abilities. Your local public library, your child's school library, or any local bookstore should have these books available for you. Plan to visit them regularly and make these suggestions part of your child's reading adventures and explorations.

- *A Kiss for Little Bear* by Tana Hoban
- *Angus and the Cat* by Marjorie Flack
- *Are You My Mother?* by Philip D. Eastman
- *Buzz, Buzz, Buzz* by Byron Barton
- *The Cat in the Hat* by Dr. Suess
- *Come Out and Play, Little Mouse* by Robert Kraus
- *Danny and the Dinosaur* by Syd Hoff
- *Dogs* by Pat Hutchins
- *The Enormous Turnip* by Fran Hunia
- *Fat Cat* by Jack Kent
- *Fox All Week* by Edward Marshall
- *George Shrinks* by William Joyce
- *The Gingerbread Man* by Rita Rose
- *Goodnight, Moon* by Margaret Wise Brown
- *Goodnight, Owl!* by Pat Hutchins
- *Green Eggs and Ham* by Dr. Suess
- *Hattie and the Fox* by Mem Fox
- *Henny Penny* by Paul Galdone
- *If I Had an Alligator* by Mercer Mayer
- *Leo the Late Bloomer* by Robert Kraus
- *Let's Be Enemies* by Maurice Sendak
- *The Napping House* by Don and Audrey Wood
- *Noisy Nora* by Rosemary Wells
- *Sammy the Seal* by Syd Hoff
- *There's a Nightmare in My Closet* by Mercer Mayer
- *The Very Busy Spider* by Eric Carle
- *We Are Best Friends* by Aliki
- *Where Are You Going, Little Mouse?* by Robert Kraus

Sincerely,

Fluent Reader Introductory Letter

Dear Parents:

During our reading program this year, your child will be involved in a wide variety of reading activities, including guided reading. The purpose of guided reading is to expose students to a wide range of books, to teach comprehension strategies, and to help them read books that become increasingly more difficult as their skills improve.

Guided reading is divided into four separate stages of reading development. Your child will receive instruction in accordance with his or her growth and development in a variety of reading materials. Through careful testing I have placed your child in the **fluent reader** stage for our grade.

Here are some of the reading skills your child will be learning:

- *Detecting and correcting reading errors*
- *Decoding unfamiliar words*
- *Using more challenging vocabulary*
- *Monitoring his or her comprehension of written materials*
- *Reading with fluency*
- *Making inferences*
- *Revisiting the text to support ideas and understandings*
- *Reading a wide variety of books*
- *Summarizing what is read*

Following is an example of the type of reading material your child will be using in this stage of his or her reading program:

The African Elephant

The African elephant lives in central and southern Africa. It is the world's largest land animal. A male can weigh 15,000 pounds. That's about as heavy as a school bus. Females are smaller.

A full-grown elephant is tall. It may stand 13 feet high at the shoulder. That's taller than a basketball hoop.

African elephants have very large ears. Their ears can be 6 feet from top to bottom. Their ears are shaped like the continent of Africa. These elephants have a single bump on the top of their head. They are amazing animals!

Sincerely,

Fluent Reader Comprehension Hints

Dear Parents:

One of the most important things children learn in reading is how to comprehend written material. Parents can play a vital role in helping their children understand more of what they read, not by becoming teachers for their children, but by encouraging their children to read and think beyond the actual words in a reading selection. Here are some suggestions:

1. Cut out some photos from the newspaper or an old magazine. Ask your child to think of new titles for each picture and write them on a slip of paper. Encourage your child to combine these into a notebook or scrapbook.

2. During a commercial break in a television program you are watching together, ask your child questions such as, "Why is the character doing that?" or "What do you think will happen next?" These kinds of reasoning/anticipation questions are important in reading comprehension development.

3. As you read a story to your child, stop every so often and ask him or her to think of a word that may come next in the story. Encourage your child to be creative and think of as many words as possible for the blank.

4. Before you read a familiar story again to your child, ask him or her to give you a summary of the characters, events, or situations that occurred. Encourage your child to keep his or her review short and to the point. Compare this summation with the actual events of the story as you read.

Sincerely,

Fluent Reader Recommended Books

Dear Parents:

Following is a list of books highly recommended for children at the fluent stage of reading development. These books have been selected on the basis of their appropriateness to children's interests and developing reading abilities. Your local public library, your child's school library, or any local bookstore should have these books available for you. Plan to visit them regularly and make these suggestions part of your child's reading adventures and explorations.

- *A Bargain for Frances* by Russell Hoban
- *A Pocket for Corduroy* by Don Freeman
- *Amelia Bedelia Goes Camping* by Peggy Parish
- *Arthur's Camp Out* by Lillian Hoban
- *The Bear on Hemlock Mountain* by Alice Dalgliesh
- *Big Al* by Andrew Yoshi
- *Caps for Sale* by Esophyr Slobodkina
- *Chicken Soup with Rice* by Maurice Sendak
- *Chickens Aren't the Only Ones* by Ruth Heller
- *Clifford the Big Red Dog* by Norman Bridwell
- *Commander Toad and the Space Pirates* by Jane Yolen
- *The Day Jimmy's Boa Ate the Wash* by Trinka H. Noble
- *Deputy Dan and the Bank Robbers* by Joseph Rosenbloom
- *Frog and Toad Are Friends* by Arnold Lobel
- *George and Martha* by James Marshall
- *Goliath on Vacation* by Terrance Dicks
- *Harold and the Purple Crayon* by Crockett Johnson
- *Horrible Harry and the Ant Invasion* by Suzy Kline
- *If You Give a Mouse a Cookie* by Laura J. Numeroff
- *Magic Fish* by Freya Littledale
- *Make Way for Ducklings* by Robert McCloskey
- *Miss Nelson Is Missing* by Harry Allard
- *More Tales of Oliver Pig* by Jean Van Leeuwen
- *Nate the Great* by Marjorie Weinman Sharmat
- *Pee Wee Scouts: Piles of Pets* by Judy Delton
- *The Quilt Story* by Tony Johnston and Tomie dePaola
- *Three Billy Goats Gruff* by Janet Stevens
- *Three Little Pigs* by Paul Galdone
- *Under One Rock* by Anthony D. Fredericks

Sincerely,

Activity Calendars

The following reproducible calendars provide families with exciting and fun reading activities to do at home. The emphasis in these letters is to provide reinforcement for the guided reading strategies you are teaching children in the classroom. The difference here is that those strategies are used in a fun, easy-going, and relaxed atmosphere. Additionally, these ideas are generic in nature and can be used with a wide range of reading materials recommended to parents (see accompanying book lists).

Please note that there are some blanks for each month. This allows you to write in some of your own activities or strategies (prior to reproducing the calendars) for parents and children to share. Add activities from this book, another teacher resource book, your school/district reading curriculum, a professional publication, or your own imagination. You may want to write in "Free Time" in some of these blank spaces to allow families an opportunity to select or create their own reading-related activities.

In distributing these calendars to parents, be sure to emphasize fun and informality—not turning the home into a school-away-from-school. These activities are not meant as homework assignments. Suggest to parents that there is a wide variety of possibilities here for fostering good parent-child interactions while stimulating the development of appropriate reading strategies. Parents should have the option of choosing as many of the suggested activities as their schedules and available time allow. Obviously, the more these activities become a regular part of the daily routine of the family, the larger impact they will have on the child's reading growth and development. The calendars that follow include:

Emergent Reader Activities, p. 276

Early Reader Activities, p. 277

Transitional Reader Activities, p. 278

Fluent Reader Activities, p. 279

Emergent Reader Activities

Sunday	Monday	Tuesday	Wednesday	Thursday	Friday	Saturday
Share a favorite book with your child.		Move your finger from left to right across a page. Invite your child to copy your movements.	How many words can you and your child find that begin with *t*?	What are some words that begin with the sound of *j*?	Point to three words in a book. Invite your child to tell you the letter that ends each word.	Invite your child to talk about a picture in a book.
Share a favorite book with your child.	Point to a word. Say the word and invite your child to copy you.	Show your child two letters on a page. Then, show your child two words on a page.	Take a neighborhood walk. How many red-colored letters can you find?	Point to three words in a book. Invite your child to tell you the letter that ends each word.	Move your finger from top to bottom down a page. Invite your child to copy your movements.	
Share a favorite book with your child.	Invite your child to talk about a picture in a book.	Share some words that end with *p*.	Point to three words in a book. Invite your child to tell you the letter that begins each word.		Take your child to a store. Point to three different words on a box (of cereal, detergent, and so on.)	How many words can you and your child find that begin with *m*?
Share a favorite book with your child.		Take your child to a store. Point to three different letters on a sign.	What are some words that begin with the sound of *b*?	Show your child two letters on a page. Then, show your child two words on a page.	Take a neighborhood walk. How many blue-colored words can you find?	Point to three words in a book. Invite your child to tell you the letter that begins each word.
Share a favorite book with your child.	Move your finger from top to bottom down a page. Invite your child to copy your movements.	How many words can you and your child find that begin with *c*?	Point to a word. Say the word and invite your child to copy you.	Move your finger from left to right across a page. Invite your child to copy your movements.		Share some words that end with *s*.

Early Reader Activities

Sunday	Monday	Tuesday	Wednesday	Thursday	Friday	Saturday
Share a favorite book together.	Open a book and invite your child to point to six words he or she can read on his/her own.		Invite your child to locate a question mark and a period in a book.	Read a book with your child and talk about why the pictures are important.	Read a book with your child. Invite him or her to ask you three questions about the book.	Begin reading a sentence in a book. Stop in the middle of the sentence and ask your child to finish the sentence.
Share a favorite book together.	Invite your child to locate the beginning, middle, and end of a story.	Point to five words. Invite your child to tell you the beginning letter for each word.	Look on a tube of toothpaste and find a word with two sounds.	Read a book with your child. Invite him or her to ask you three questions about the book.	Invite your child to locate a quotation mark and an exclamation mark in a book.	
Share a favorite book together.	Begin reading a sentence in a book. Stop in the middle of the sentence and invite your child to finish the sentence.	Invite your child to locate a question mark and a period in a book.	Invite your child to locate the beginning, middle, and end of a story.	Point to five words. Invite your child to tell you the ending letter for each word.		Open a book and invite your child to point to six words he or she can read on his or her own.
Share a favorite book together.	Begin reading a sentence in a book. Stop in the middle of the sentence and invite your child to finish the sentence.	Read a book with your child. Invite him or her to ask you three questions about the book.	Open a book and invite your child to point to six words he or she can read on his or her own.		Point to five words. Invite your child to tell you the beginning letter for each word.	Read a book with your child and talk about why the pictures are important.
Share a favorite book together.		Point to five words. Invite your child to tell you the ending letter for each word.	Read a book with your child. Invite him or her to ask you three questions about the book.	Begin reading a sentence in a book. Stop in the middle of the sentence and invite your child to finish the sentence.	Invite your child to locate a quotation mark and an exclamation mark in a book.	Open a book and invite your child to point to six words he or she can read on his or her own.

Transitional Reader Activities

Sunday	Monday	Tuesday	Wednesday	Thursday	Friday	Saturday
Share a favorite book with your child.	Invite your child to locate four words that he or she can read without help.	Invite your child to ask you four questions about a book or story you have shared together.		Invite your child to locate four separate punctuation marks in a story.	Invite your child to read the beginning of a sentence but to stop halfway. You can then read the rest of the sentence. Do this four or five times during a book.	Show your child the front of a book. Invite him or her to make a prediction about the topic of the book.
Share a favorite book with your child.	Begin reading a story. You can read the first paragraph, your child can read the second, and so on.	Take your child to the public library. Invite him or her to locate two informa- tional books.	Invite your child to read the beginning of a sentence but to stop halfway. You can then read the rest of the sentence. Do this four or five times during a book.	Invite your child to locate ten words in a book that he or she knows without thinking about them (high-frequency words).		Invite your child to ask you four questions about a book or story you have shared together.
Share a favorite book with your child.		Invite your child to locate four words that he or she can read without help.	Invite your child to read a story silently. Ask him or her to point to any words he or she doesn't know. Ask your child to tell you what he or she does with those unknown words.	Show your child the front of a book. Invite him or her to make a prediction about the topic of the book.	Begin reading a story. You can read the first paragraph, your child can read the second, and so on.	Invite your child to locate ten words in a book that he or she knows without thinking about them (high-frequency words).
Share a favorite book with your child.	Invite your child to locate four separate punctuation marks in a story.	Invite your child to read a story silently. Ask him or her to point to any words he or she doesn't know. Ask your child to tell you what he or she does with those unknown words.	Invite your child to ask you four questions about a book or story you have shared together.	Take your child to the public library. Invite him or her to locate two informational books.	Invite your child to locate four words that he or she can read without help.	
Share a favorite book with your child.	Invite your child to read the beginning of a sentence but to stop halfway. You can then read the rest of the sentence. Do this four or five times during a book.	Show your child the front of a book. Invite him or her to make a prediction about the topic of the book.		Invite your child to locate ten words in a book that he or she knows without thinking about them (high-frequency words).	Invite your child to locate four separate punctuation marks in a story.	Begin reading a story. You can read the first paragraph, your child can read the second, and so on.

Fluent Reader Activities

Sunday	Monday	Tuesday	Wednesday	Thursday	Friday	Saturday
Share a favorite book together.	Work with your child to create a list of the most interesting words in a book or story.	Take your child to a bookstore or library. Invite your child to select two books—one fiction and one nonfiction.	Begin reading a book with your child. After one paragraph, ask your child a question. After the second paragraph, have your child ask you a question, and so on.	Invite your child to tell you how he or she uses other words in a sentence to figure out unknown words.		Show your child the covers of several books. Ask him or her to make a prediction about the theme or plot of each book before reading.
Share a favorite book together.		As your child reads a book silently, invite him or her to point to any unknown words.	Ask your child to create four questions about a book—all beginning with the word *why*.	Work with your child to create a list of the most interesting words in a book or story.	Invite your child to make a random list of eight words. Ask him or her to find five of those words in a story or book.	Begin reading a story. You can read the first paragraph, your child can read the second, and so on.
Share a favorite book together.	Invite your child to tell you how he or she uses other words in a sentence to figure out unknown words.	Invite your child to make a random list of eight words. Ask him or her to find five of those words in a story or book.		Begin reading a book with your child. After one paragraph, ask your child a question. After the second paragraph, have your child ask you a question, and so on.	As your child reads a book silently, invite him or her to point to any unknown words.	Ask your child to create four questions about a book—all beginning with the word *who*.
Share a favorite book together.	Begin reading a story. You can read the first paragraph, your child can read the second, you read the third, and so on.	Show your child the covers of several books. Invite your child to make a prediction about the theme or plot of each book before reading.	Take your child to a bookstore or library. Invite your child to select two books—one fiction and one nonfiction.	Ask your child to create four questions about a book—all beginning with the word *where*.	Invite your child to tell you how he or she uses other words in a sentence to figure out unknown words.	
Share a favorite book together.	Begin reading a book with your child. After one paragraph, ask your child a question. After the second paragraph, have your child ask you a question, and so on.	As your child reads a book silently, invite him or her to point to any unknown words.		Work with your child to create a list of the most interesting words in a book or story.	Invite your child to make a random list of eight words. Ask him or her to find five of those words in a story or book.	Take your child to a bookstore or library. Invite your child to select two books—one fiction and one nonfiction.

Appendix

100 Must-Have Books for Guided Reading

Alligator Shoes by Arthur Dorros (Dutton)

Amber Brown Is Not a Crayon by Paula Danzinger (Scholastic)

Angus and the Cat by Marjorie Flack (Viking)

The Awful Mess by Anne Rockwell (Four Winds)

Baby Says by John Steptoe (Morrow)

The Baby by John Burningham (Crowell)

Bear Shadow by Frank Asch (Simon & Schuster)

Bears on Wheels by Stan and Jan Berenstain (Random House)

The Boxcar Children by Gertrude Warner (Scholastic)

Bringing the Rain to Kapiti Plain by Verna Aardema (Puffin)

Brown Bear, Brown Bear, What Do You See? by Bill Martin, Jr. (Holt)

Buzz Said the Bee by Wendy Lewison (Scholastic)

The Carrot Seed by Ruth Krauss (Harper & Row)

Cars by Anne Rockwell (Dutton)

The Cat in the Hat by Dr. Seuss (Random House)

Cat on the Mat by Brian Wildsmith (Oxford)

A Chair for My Mother by Vera B. Williams (Scholastic)

Charlie Needs a Cloak by Tomie dePaola (Prentice-Hall)

The Chick and the Duckling by Mirra Ginsburg (Macmillan)

Come Out and Play, Little Mouse by Robert Kraus (Morrow)

Commander Toad in Space by Jane Yolen (Putnam)

Cookie's Week by Cindy Ward (Putnam)

Corn Is Maize by Aliki (HarperCollins)

Count and See by Tana Hoban (Macmillan)

Danny and the Dinosaur by Syd Hoff (Scholastic)

Dinosaurs, Dinosaurs by Byron Barton (HarperCollins)

The Doorbell Rang by Pat Hutchins (Greenwillow)

Drummer Hoff by Ed Emberley (Prentice-Hall)

Fat Cat by Jack Kent (Scholastic)

Father Bear Comes Home by Else H. Minarik (HarperCollins)

Fish Face by Patricia Reilly Giff (Dell)

Five Little Monkeys Jumping on the Bed by Eileen Christelow (Houghton Mifflin)

Five True Dog Stories by Margaret Davidson (Scholastic)

Fox and His Friends by Edward and James Marshall (Puffin)

Frog and Toad Are Friends by Arnold Lobel (HarperCollins)

George Shrinks by William Joyce (HarperCollins)

Green Eggs and Ham by Dr. Seuss (Random House)

Gregory the Terrible Eater by Marjorie Weinman Sharmat (Scholastic)

Harry Takes a Bath by Harriet Ziefert (Penguin)

Hattie and the Fox by Mem Fox (Bradbury)

Have You Seen My Duckling? by Nancy Tafuri (Greenwillow)

Henny Penny by Paul Galdone (Scholastic)

Henry and Mudge: The First Book by Cynthia Rylant (Aladdin)

How Many Bugs in a Box? by David Carter (Simon & Schuster)

I Can Build a House by Shigeo Watanabe (Viking)

I Like Books by Anthony Browne (Random House)

I Went Walking by Sue Williams (Harcourt Brace)

If You Lived in Colonial Times by Ann McGovern (Scholastic)

In One Tidepool by Anthony D. Fredericks (Dawn)

It Looked Like Spilt Milk by Charles Shaw (Harper & Row)

Jamberry by Bruce Degan (Harper & Row)

Leo the Late Bloomer by Robert Kraus (Simon & Schuster)

Let's Be Enemies by Maurice Sendak (Harper & Row)

Lionel and Louise by Stephen Krensky (Puffin)

Little Bear by Else H. Minarik (Harper & Row)

The Little Red Hen by Paul Galdone (Viking)

Look What I Can Do by Jose Aruego (Macmillan)

M & M and the Halloween Monster by Pat Ross (Penguin)

Make Way for Ducklings by Robert McCloskey (Puffin)

Making a Memory by Margaret Ballinger (Scholastic)

The Missing Tooth by Joanna Cole (Random House)

Monster Can't Sleep by Virginia Mueller (Puffin)

Mouse Soup by Arnold Lobel (HarperCollins)

Mr. Noisy by Wendy Lewiston (Random House)

Nate the Great by Marjorie Weinman Sharmat (Bantam Doubleday)

Noisy Nora by Rosemary Wells (Scholastic)

Norma Jean, Jumping Bean by Joanna Cole (Random House)

Now We Can Go by Ann Jonas (Greenwillow)

Pee Wee Scouts: Eggs with Legs by Judy Delton (Bantam)

Peter's Chair by Ezra Jack Keats (Harper Trophy)

The Quilt by Ann Jonas (Morrow)

Rosie's Walk by Pat Hutchins (Macmillan)

School Bus by Donald Crews (Morrow)

The School by John Burningham (Crowell)

Seven Little Monsters by Maurice Sendak (HarperCollins)

Sheep in a Jeep by Nancy Shaw (Houghton Mifflin)

Skyfire by Frank Asch (Scholastic)

Small Pig by Arnold Lobel (Harper Trophy)

Small Wolf by Nathaniel Benchley (Harper Trophy)

Snail Saves the Day by John Sadler (HarperCollins)

The Snowy Day by Ezra Jack Keats (Scholastic)

Spots, Feathers and Curly Tails by Nancy Tafuri (Morrow)

Stone Soup by Ann McGovern (Scholastic)

The Stories Julian Tells by Ann Cameron (Knopf)

Surprise Party by Pat Hutchins (Macmillan)

The Teeny Tiny Woman by Barbara Seuling (Scholastic)

Ten Sleepy Sheep by Holly Keller (Morrow)

There's a Nightmare in My Closet by Mercer Mayer (Penguin)

The Three Bears by Paul Galdone (Scholastic)

The Three Billy Goats Gruff by Marcia Brown (Harcourt Brace)

Too Many Rabbits by Peggy Parish (Bantam)

Under One Rock by Anthony D. Fredericks (Dawn)

The Very Busy Spider by Eric Carle (Philomel)

The Very Hungry Caterpillar by Eric Carle (Putnam)

We Are Best Friends by Aliki (Morrow)

What Has Stripes? by Margaret Ballinger (Scholastic)

Wheels on the Bus by Harriet Ziefert (Random House)

Where the Wild Things Are by Maurice Sendak (Harper & Row)

Where's Al? by Byron Barton (Houghton Mifflin)

Where's Spot? by Eric Hill (Putnam)

Concepts of Print Checklist

Name: _____ **Date:** _____

Teacher: _____

✓ If competency is demonstrated

	October	January	May
Understands Book Handling Conventions:			
1. Front of book			
2. Left page is read before right page			
3. Print carries message			
4. Knows where to start within a text			
5. Direction (left to right)			
6. Controls return sweep			
Knowledge of Concepts About Print:			
7. Matches words 1:1 as teacher reads			
8. Word concept (frames word)			
9. Letter concept (frames letter)			
10. Capital letter concept			
11. First and last letter concept			
Total Score (out of 11):			

Websites

The following websites can provide you with background information, resources, lessons, and numerous tools for expanding your guided reading program. They are appropriate for all teachers in grades K–2.

Note: These websites were current and accurate as of the writing of this book. Please be aware that some may change, others may be eliminated, and new ones will be added to the various search engines that you use at home or at school.

http://www.era-publications.com.au/paper_Guided.html

This article discusses the purposes and benefits of guided reading and offers a structure for guided reading sessions.

http://www.mcps.k12.md.us/curriculum/english/guided_rdg.html

This article offers teachers a quick and easy guide to the dynamics of guided reading. Included are sections on What Is Guided Reading?, How Are Guided Reading Groups Determined?, Principles of Guided Reading, Materials for Guided Reading, Conducting Guided Reading Groups, and Evaluating Guided Reading.

http://www.readinga-z.com/

This site provides downloadable materials for teaching guided reading.

Included are 200 leveled reading books, 173 guided reading lesson plans, and 346 guided reading worksheets (at this writing).

http://208.183.128.8/read/guidedr.html

This site provides ideas created by teachers for teachers on a wide variety of topics related to guided reading. Full of great ideas and lots of practical advice, this site can become an important part of your inservice training in guided reading practices.

http://www.geocities.com/teachingwithheart/guidedreading.html

This site offers a variety of teacher resources that can help you in developing a guided reading program and in making it an integral part of your overall reading program. This is another teacher-created site that has a host of links and resources.

http://www.mefnj.com/wood/cas/gr.html

This site provides an overview of guided reading. Here you will find a clear definition, outlined plans for a primary classroom, and a description of the strategies and practices that should be part of an emergent or early reader's reading repertoire.

Additional Resources

The following resources will assist you in keeping up to date on the latest in children's literature, methods and materials for the teaching of reading, and specific ideas on the successful implementation of a guided reading program.

Reading Instruction

International Reading Association
P.O. Box 8139
800 Barksdale Road
Newark, DE 19714
http://www.reading.org

IRA publishes the professional journal *The Reading Teacher*, which has the latest information and research on the effective teaching of reading. Their website offers valuable information for elementary teachers at all grade levels.

Professional Seminars

Bureau of Education and Research
915 118th Avenue SE
P.O. Box 96068
Bellevue, WA 98009
http://www.ber.org

Check out the various seminars on guided reading and literacy centers. They are filled with practical ideas and resources for any classroom teacher in grades K–2. Also, look for the seminars by Peggy Sharp. Peggy offers detailed information on the latest in children's books and how they can be used in any classroom.

Children's Literature

Book Links
American Library Association
50 E. Huron Street
Chicago, IL 60611
http://www.ala.org/BookLinks

An excellent periodical on the best in children's books. Books are organized thematically and the articles are packed with annotations and classroom applications.

Teacher Magazine

Teaching K–8
40 Richards Ave.
Norwalk, CT 06854
http://www.TeachingK-8.com

Check out Carol Hurst's column in each issue. Carol provides the best in children's literature along with annotations and recommendations for classroom use.

Teacher Resources

Anthony D. Fredericks
http://www.afredericks.com

Here you will find an array of creative and exciting teacher resource books in a variety of subject areas. Additionally, Tony is an award-winning children's author who visits schools around the country sharing the magic of literature with young readers.

References

Baumann, J., Hoffman, J., Duffy-Hester, A., & Ro, J. (2000). The first R yesterday and today: U.S. elementary reading instruction practices reported by teachers and administrators. *Reading Research Quarterly*, 35, 338–377.

Clay, M. (1993). *An observation survey.* Portsmouth, NH: Heinemann.

Cunningham, P., & Allington, R. (1999). *Classrooms that work: They can all read and write.* New York: Longman.

Duffy, G., & Hoffman, J. (1999). In pursuit of an illusion: The flawed search for a perfect method. *The Reading Teacher*, 53, 10–16.

Fawson, P. C., and Reutzel, D. R. (2000). But I only have a basal: Implementing guided reading in the early grades. *The Reading Teacher*, 54(1), 84–97.

Ford, M. P., and Opitz, M. F. (2002). Using centers to engage children during guided reading time: Intensifying learning experiences away from the teacher. *The Reading Teacher*, 55(2), 710–717.

Fountas, I. C., and Pinnell, G. S. (1996). *Guided reading: Good first teaching for all children.* Portsmouth, NH: Heinemann.

Fowler, G. L. (1982). Developing comprehension skills in primary grades through the use of story frames. *The Reading Teacher*, 36(2), 176–179.

Fredericks, A. D. (1997). *Tadpole tales and other totally terrific treats for readers theatre.* Englewood, CO: Teacher Ideas Press.

Fredericks, A. D. (2002). *In one tidepool: Crabs, snails and salty tails.* Nevada City, CA: Dawn.

Fredericks, A. D., Blake-Kline, B., and Kristo, J. (1997). *Teaching the integrated language arts: Process and practice.* New York: Addison Wesley Longman.

Freppon, P., & Dahl, K. (1998). Theory and research into practice: Balanced instruction: Insights and considerations. *Reading Research Quarterly*, 33, 240–251.

Garison, J. (1997). *Dewey and Eros: Wisdom and desire in the art of teaching.* New York: Teachers College Press.

Haack, P. (1999). Using guided reading to help your students become better readers (Grades 3–6). Bellevue, WA: Bureau of Education and Research.

Kane, K. (1995). *Keeping your balance: Teacher's guide for guided reading in the early grades.* Danbury, CT: Grolier.

Mooney, M. (1990). *Reading to, with, and by children.* Kanotah, NY: Richard C. Owen.

Moore, D. W., and Moore, S. A. (1986). Possible sentences. In E. K. Dishner, T. W. Bean, J. E. Readance, and D. W. Moore (Eds.), *Reading in the content areas: Improving classroom instruction* (2nd ed., pp. 174–179). Dubuque, IA: Kendall/Hunt.

Ogle, D. (1986). K-W-L: A teaching model that develops active reading of expository text. *The Reading Teacher*, 39, 564–570.

Opitz, M. F. (1994). *Learning centers: Getting them started, keeping them going.* New York: Scholastic.

Pincus, M. (1986). Unpublished manuscript. Philadelphia, PA.

Rosenblatt, L. (1978). *The reader, the text, the poem.* Carbondale, IL: Southern Illinois University Press.

Routman, R. (1991). *Invitations: Changing as teachers and learners, K–12.* Portsmouth, NH: Heinemann.

Schulman, M. B., and Payne, C. D. (2000). *Guided reading: Making it work.* New York: Scholastic.

Stauffer, R. (1969). *Directing reading maturity as a cognitive process.* New York: Harper & Row.

Strickland, D. (1995). Reinventing our literacy programs. *The Reading Teacher*, 48, 294–302.

Vacca, R., and Vacca, J. (1989). *Content area reading.* New York: HarperCollins.

Weaver, C. (Ed.). (1998). *Reconsidering a balanced approach to reading.* Urbana, IL: National Council of Teachers of English.

About the Author

Tony is a nationally recognized reading expert well known for his practical, down-to-earth, and stimulating resources. His teacher books in language arts and science have captivated thousands of educators from coast to coast and border to border—all with rave reviews! His background includes extensive experience as a classroom teacher, curriculum coordinator, staff developer, author, professional storyteller, and university specialist in children's literature.

Tony has written more than 60 teacher resource books in a variety of areas, including several best-selling books for Rigby's Best Teachers Press. These include the hugely praised *Guided Reading in Grades 3–6: 300+ Guided Reading Strategies, Activities, and Lesson Plans for Reading Success* (ISBN: 0-7635-7750-2); the incredibly successful *The Complete Phonemic Awareness Handbook: More Than 300 Playful Activities for Early Reading Success* (ISBN: 0-7635-7347-7), and the wildly applauded *Redefining the Three R's: Relax, Refocus, Recharge* (ISBN: 0-7398-7598-1) which has quickly become a valued resource on teachers' desks in thousands of schools.

Tony is also an award-winning children's author of more than 25 highly acclaimed books. These include the 2003 Teacher's Choice Award-winning *Under One Rock: Bugs, Slugs and Other Ughs* (Dawn Publications); *Bloodsucking Creatures* (Watts); the 2001 Outstanding Science Trade Book, *Slugs* (Lerner); *In One Tidepool: Crabs, Snails and Salty Tails* (Dawn Publications); and *Elephants for Kids* (NorthWord Press), among many others. Tony is currently a professor of education at York College in York, Pennsylvania. There, he teaches elementary methods courses in children's literature, reading, and science. Additionally, each year he is a visiting author at numerous elementary schools around the country where he conducts humor-packed assemblies and shares the writing life with the next generation of young authors. He has a children's author website (www.afredericks.com) designed specifically for elementary teachers.